THE NEW GROVE
RUSSIAN MASTERS 2

THE NEW GROVE
DICTIONARY OF MUSIC AND MUSICIANS

Editor: Stanley Sadie

The Composer Biography Series

THE NEW GROVE®

Russian Masters 2

RIMSKY-KORSAKOV   SKRYABIN
RAKHMANINOV
PROKOFIEV   SHOSTAKOVICH

Gerald Abraham
Hugh Macdonald
Geoffrey Norris
Rita McAllister
Boris Schwarz

W. W. NORTON & COMPANY
NEW YORK   LONDON

First published in
The New Grove Dictionary of Music and Musicians®,
edited by Stanley Sadie, 1980

The New Grove and *The New Grove Dictionary of Music and Musicians*
are registered trademarks of Macmillan Publishers Limited, London

First published in UK in paperback with additions 1986 by
PAPERMAC
a division of Macmillan Publishers Limited
London and Basingstoke

First published in UK in hardback with additions 1986 by
MACMILLAN LONDON LIMITED
4 Little Essex Street London WC2R 3LF
and Basingstoke

British Library Cataloguing in Publication Data

Russian Masters 2: Rimsky-Korsakov, Skryabin, Rakhmaninov,
Prokofiev, Shostakovich.—(The Composer biography series)
1. Composers—Soviet Union—Biography
I. Abraham, Gerald,   II. The new Grove dictionary
of music and musicians   III. Series
780′.92′2   ML390

ISBN 0-333-40237-5 (hardback)
ISBN 0-333-40238-3 (paperback)

First American edition in book form with additions 1986 by
W. W. NORTON & COMPANY
500 Fifth Avenue, New York NY 10110

ISBN 0-393-02283-8 (hardback)
ISBN 0-393-30103-6 (paperback)

Printed in Great Britain by
Redwood Burn Limited, Trowbridge, Wiltshire,
and bound by Pegasus Bookbinding, Melksham, Wiltshire.

Contents

List of illustrations

Illustration acknowledgments

We are grateful to the following for permission to reproduce illustrative material: Editions d'Art Lucien Mazenod, Paris: from J. Lacroix: *Les musiciens célèbres* (1948) (fig.1); M.E.Saltïkov-Schchedrin State Public Library, Leningrad (fig.3); Novosti Press Agency, London (figs.4, 6, 12, 15, cover); M. I. Glinka State Central Museum of Musical Culture, Moscow (figs.5, 11, 14); Royal College of Music, London (fig.8); RCA Ltd, London (fig.9); H. Roger-Viollet, Paris (fig.10); Boosey & Hawkes Ltd, London (fig.11); from D. Rabinovich: *Dmitri Shostakovich, Composer* (1959) (fig.13); Society for Cultural Relations with the USSR (fig.16)

General abbreviations

A	alto, contralto [voice]	ob	oboe
acc.	accompaniment, accompanied by	orch	orchestra, orchestral
		orchd	orchestrated (by)
		ov.	overture
B	bass [voice]		
b	born	perc	percussion
Bar	baritone [voice]	perf.	performance, performed by
bn	bassoon	PO	Philharmonic Orchestra
c	circa [about]	prol	prologue
cl	clarinet	pubd	published
collab.	in collaboration with		
conc.	concerto	qt	quartet
cond.	conductor, conducted by	R	photographic reprint
		RAPM	Russian Association of Proletarian Musicians
D	Deutsch catalogue [Schubert]	repr.	reprinted
db	double bass	rev.	revision, revised (by/for)
ded.	dedication, dedicated to	Russ.	Russian
fl	flute	S	soprano [voice]
frag.	fragment	SO	Symphony Orchestra
		str	string(s)
hn	horn	sym.	symphony, symphonic
inc.	incomplete	T	tenor [voice]
		tpt	trumpet
Jg.	Jahrgang [year of publication/volume]	transcr.	transcription, transcribed by/for
		trbn	trombone
lib	libretto	U.	University
Mez	mezzo-soprano	v, vv	voice, voices
movt	movement	va	viola
		vc	cello
NBC	National Broadcasting Company (USA)	vn	violin
n.d.	no date of publication	ww	woodwind

Bibliographical abbreviations

Preface

This volume is one of a series of short biographies derived from *The New Grove Dictionary of Music and Musicians* (London, 1980). In their original form, the texts were written in the mid-1970s, and finalized at the end of that decade. For this reprint, they have been re-read and modified mostly by their original authors; corrections and changes have been made and bibliographies have been brought up to date. The texts on Skryabin and Prokofiev have been substantially expanded. The original author of the Shostakovich entry, Boris Schwarz, died at the end of 1983 and for this reprint some minor modifications have been made to his text by Laurel E. Fay, who has provided a new work-list and bibliography.

The fact that the texts of the books in the series originated as dictionary articles inevitably gives them a character somewhat different from that of books conceived as such. They are designed, first of all, to accommodate a very great deal of information in a manner that makes reference quick and easy. Their first concern is with fact rather than opinion, and this leads to a larger than usual proportion of the texts being devoted to biography than to critical discussion. The nature of a reference work gives it a particular obligation to convey received knowledge and to treat of composers' lives and works in an encyclopedic fashion, with proper acknowledgment of sources and due care to reflect different standpoints, rather than to embody imaginative or speculative writing about a composer's character or his music. It is hoped that the comprehensive work-lists and extended bibliographies, indicative of the origins of the

books in a reference work, will be valuable to the reader who is eager for full and accurate reference information and who may not have ready access to *The New Grove Dictionary* or who may prefer to have it in this more compact form.

S.S.

NIKOLAY RIMSKY-KORSAKOV

Gerald Abraham

CHAPTER ONE

Life

I 1844–71

Nikolay Andreyevich Rimsky-Korsakov was born at Tikhvin in the Novgorod government (district) on 18 March 1844. He came of a distinguished naval and military family, and his father had been civil governor of the Volïn government; but both his grandmothers were of humble origin, a priest's daughter and a peasant, and from them he claimed he had inherited his love of folksong and his love of religious ceremonies. In his *Chronicle of my Musical Life* he wrote:

The first signs of musical ability showed themselves in me very early. . . . Before I was two I could distinguish all the melodies my mother sang to me; at three or four I was an expert at beating time on a drum to my father's piano playing . . . I soon began to sing very accurately everything he played, and often sang with him; then I began to pick out the pieces with the harmonies for myself on the piano; and, having learned the names of the notes, would stand in another room and call them out when they were struck.

From the age of six he had piano lessons from various local teachers, learning for the most part easy fantasias on contemporary opera melodies, but his deepest musical impressions came from some numbers of Glinka's *Life for the Tsar*, which he found at home, and the music of Bortnyansky which he heard at the nearby monastery. Before long he was tempted to compose, one of his earliest essays being a piano 'overture' in progressively quicker tempos. But his heart was set not on

1

music but on a career in the navy in emulation of his brother, 22 years older than himself. Accordingly at the end of July 1856 his father took him to St Petersburg to enter the College of Naval Cadets; he took the passing-out examination on 20 April 1862, a few months after his brother's appointment to the directorship.

While at the Cadet School, Rimsky-Korsakov continued to take piano lessons, but he was not interested in the instrument except as a means of recapturing the delights of opera. Family friends took him to the theatre to see and hear Rossini and Weber, Meyerbeer and (still his favourite) Glinka. His first opera, early in 1857, was Flotow's *Indra* but it was the orchestra that excited him most:

Dearest uncle, Imagine my joy, today I'm going to the theatre! I shall see *Lucia*! I shall hear the enormous orchestra and tam-tam! and I shall see how the conductor waves his little stick! In the orchestra 12 violins, 8 violas, 6 cellos, 6 double basses, 3 flutes, 8 clarinets, 6 horns, and all that sort of thing.

His real introduction to symphonic music came during the 1859–60 season, when he heard two of Beethoven's symphonies and Mendelssohn's *Midsummer Night's Dream* overture, though none of these 'dazzled' him as Glinka's *Jota aragonesa* did. At the same time (autumn 1859) he found a more inspiring piano teacher, Théodore Canille, who did much to form his taste, weaning him from the Italians, encouraging him to study Beethoven, Schumann, Mendelssohn, Chopin, and Bach's fugues, and sharing his love of Glinka. Canille helped the boy to harmonize chorales, to compose variations and even a sonata movement; his instruction was very unsystematic but even when the piano lessons stopped, as they did after a year, Canille invited his

pupil to visit him weekly to play duets and talk about music. More important still, in December 1861 he introduced him to Balakirev, Cui and Musorgsky, all three in their early 20s but already known as composers.

Rimsky-Korsakov fell completely under the spell of Balakirev, who in turn detected the youth's talent. Shown 'a sort of beginning of a symphony in E♭ minor', he insisted that Rimsky-Korsakov should finish it; the first movement was completed in a month and the orchestration begun under Balakirev's guidance; the scherzo and finale were written during the early months of 1862. But a crisis came in April when Rimsky-Korsakov graduated as a midshipman and his brother reasonably refused to allow him to abandon his career in the service, as he now wished to do. Balakirev went to the Caucasus for the summer; the symphony came to a standstill; and on 2 November its composer sailed in the clipper *Almaz* for a cruise of two and a half years which took him to Gravesend (where he finished the slow movement of the symphony), the Baltic, New York, Rio de Janeiro and the Mediterranean. When he returned to Russia at the beginning of May 1865 he had become, in his own words, 'an officer-dilettante who sometimes enjoyed playing or listening to music'. He was rescued for music by renewed contact with Balakirev, who made him finish the symphony; the missing trio for the scherzo was composed in October. The entire symphony was reorchestrated under the supervision of Balakirev, who gave the first performance on 31 December at one of the concerts of the Free School of Music at St Petersburg which he had founded during Rimsky-Korsakov's absence. A second performance,

3

under Konstantin Lyadov, father of the composer, followed in March 1866.

Rimsky-Korsakov's naval duties now occupied only two or three hours a day, and he had leisure for composition and for social life in a circle which now included Borodin, Dargomïzhsky, and an amateur singer, Sofiya Zotova, for whom he composed some of his earliest songs (op.2, published by Bernard in the summer of 1866). More songs (opp.3 and 4) followed and then another orchestral work, the Overture on Three Russian Themes modelled on Balakirev's folksong overtures (performed at a Free School concert, 23 December 1866). In lighter vein, he was also writing quadrilles on themes from *Martha* and *La belle Hélène*, which he played for dancing on Sunday evenings at his brother's, where he was considered a 'beautiful pianist'; by professional standards he was not, and he never dared to play before his musical friends.

The compositions of 1867 included the beginning of a symphony in B minor (too obviously influenced by the opening of Beethoven's Ninth), an orchestral Fantasia on Serbian Themes written in a great hurry for Balakirev's concert of pan-Slavonic music on 24 May, and a 'musical picture' based on the legend of the Novgorod merchant Sadko, completed on 12 October, in which the main influence was that of Liszt's *Mephisto Waltz*. Berlioz paid his last visit to Russia from November 1867 to February 1868; he was a sick man and, despite Stravinsky's story (*Conversations with Igor Stravinsky*; New York and London, 1959, p.29), Rimsky-Korsakov never met him; but the *Symphonie fantastique*, played on 7 December, and *Harold en Italie*, with which Berlioz ended his last concert on 8

February, were directly reflected in a programmatic symphony which Rimsky-Korsakov began on 21 January, *Antar*, based on an oriental tale by Osip Senkovsky (Baron Brambeus). All these orchestral works were scored for natural horns and trumpets, as described in Berlioz's *Traité de l'instrumentation*, and all were reorchestrated and sometimes drastically revised at least once in later years. Yet he was already recognized by Balakirev and his circle as a particularly gifted orchestrator, with the result that Balakirev asked him to score a Schubert march (D885) for a concert in May, Cui asked him to orchestrate the opening chorus of *William Ratcliff*, and the ailing Dargomïzhsky (who died in January 1869) bequeathed him the task of scoring *The Stone Guest*. At the same time he was giving a great deal of thought to an opera project of his own, based on Lev Mey's historical drama *Pskovityanka* ('The Maid of Pskov'); he had no sooner finished *Antar* (5 September 1868) than he began *The Maid of Pskov*, a month or two before his friend Musorgsky was to begin *Boris Godunov*. During the winter of 1871–2 the two composers shared a single room and worked on their operas at the same table and piano, Musorgsky in the morning, Rimsky-Korsakov in the afternoon.

II   1871–81

Before he completed the full score of *The Maid of Pskov* with the overture, in January 1872, Rimsky-Korsakov had taken two important steps. In July 1871, despite his astonishing ignorance of elementary technicalities, he had accepted an invitation from Mikhail Azanchevsky, the newly appointed director of the St Petersburg Conservatory, to become professor of prac-

5

tical composition and instrumentation and to direct the orchestral class with an annual salary of 1000 rubles; and in December he had become betrothed to Nadezhda Purgold, an excellent pianist and far better-trained musician than himself (they married on 12 July 1872 and enjoyed an extensive honeymoon in Switzerland and Italy). Nadezhda was beautiful, capable, and strong-minded; she was responsible for the published piano arrangements not only of her husband's works but of some of those of his friends, and her influence on him was no less than Clara Schumann's on Robert.

In February 1872 *The Stone Guest* was produced, with Rimsky-Korsakov's orchestration, and (perhaps as a consequence) the director of the imperial theatres commissioned him to collaborate with Cui, Borodin and Musorgsky in the composition of an 'opera-ballet', *Mlada*, though this came to nothing and the collaborators used most of their music in other works. *The Maid of Pskov* was published by Bessel in vocal score and successfully produced at the Mariinsky Theatre on 13 January 1873. Four months later the composer was allowed to resign his commission; instead, his friend Krabbe, the Minister of Marine, created for him the special civil post of Inspector of Naval Bands, which carried a handsome salary. During the summer he wrote most of his Third Symphony, in C (*Antar* was reckoned as the second, only in 1897- being restyled 'symphonic suite'). But this marked the end of serious composition for several years. Rimsky-Korsakov embarked with zeal on the inspection of naval bands and on practical study of the various instruments, their mechanism and technique; he planned a great treatise on instrumentation, a project which he abandoned and returned to at various

times in later life but left unfinished at his death; he taught himself harmony from Tchaikovsky's textbook and counterpoint from Cherubini and Bellermann with the success demonstrated in the six piano fugues of 1875 (published by Bessel as op.17) and the many fugal passages in a string quartet from the same year (op.12); and he began his not very successful career as a conductor on 2 March 1874 with a charity concert, the programme including his C major Symphony. In the following year he succeeded Balakirev as conductor of the Free School concerts, giving the first performance in Russia of arias from Bach's *St Matthew Passion* and, in 1876, excerpts from the B minor Mass and Handel's *Samson* (orchestrated by himself and some of his conservatory pupils). He made his first revisions of *Antar* and *The Maid of Pskov* (in the latter case a complete rewriting), compiled two collections of Russian folksongs, supplying them with piano accompaniments, and participated with Balakirev and Lyadov in the preparation of a new edition of Glinka's opera scores.

This intensive occupation with folk music and with Glinka's transparent orchestration had a cathartic effect: in February 1878 he began the composition of an opera in a folkish melodic idiom, harmonically and orchestrally modelled on Glinka's style, and very different from the 'grand opera' of *The Maid of Pskov*. This was *Mayskaya noch'* ('May Night'), based on one of Gogol's short stories of peasant life in the Ukraine, *Vecheri na khutore bliz Dikan'ki* ('Evenings on a Farm at Dikanka'), on which Tchaikovsky had already drawn for his *Vakula the Smith* (*Cherevichki*) and Musorgsky for *Sorochintsy Fair*. It was Rimsky-Korsakov's first essay in that blend of the fantastic with the comic in

7

1. Nikolay Rimsky-Korsakov

which he was to score most of his greatest successes. It was written directly in full score, completed (apart from the overture) in eight months, and produced at the Mariinsky Theatre on 21 January 1880, with Nápravník conducting and the part of the village headman sung by Fyodor Stravinsky.

Meanwhile, during the summer of 1879, Rimsky-Korsakov had composed a string quartet entirely based on Russian folktunes and begun what he described as 'an orchestral piece of fantastic character on Pushkin's prologue to *Ruslan and Lyudmila*' (in which the poet described all the characteristic figures of Russian folklore, such as the witch Baba-Yaga, whose name was at first given to the orchestral piece). The quartet was scrapped as such although the first three movements were later revised and orchestrated as the Sinfonietta on Russian Themes; the orchestral piece was completed in 1880 with the title *Skazka* ('Legend'). Immediately after the production of *May Night* Rimsky-Korsakov chanced to re-read Ostrovsky's fantastic play *Snegurochka* ('Snow Maiden') for which in 1873 Tchaikovsky had supplied incidental music. Previously Rimsky-Korsakov had not been attracted by it; now he 'fell deeply in love with it':

My mild interest in the ancient Russian customs and heathen pantheism flamed up. There seemed no better subject than this, no more poetic figures than Snegurochka, Lel or the Spring Fairy, no better realm than the kingdom of the Berendeys with their marvellous tsar, no better religion and philosophy of life than the worship of the Sun God, Yarilo.

Ostrovsky gave him permission to adapt the libretto and he spent the summer of 1880 in the depths of the Russian countryside, composing his opera in a state of extra-

ordinary excitement, actually (as he confessed long afterwards)

praying to nature – to a crooked old tree-stump, to some willow or century-old oak, to the forest stream, to the lake . . . or at the cockcrow scattering the sorcery of the night. . . . It sometimes seemed to me that animals, birds, and even trees and flowers, know more of the magic and fantastic than human beings do; that they understand the language of nature far better. . . . I warmly believed in all this, as a child would . . . and in those minutes the world seemed to me nearer, more understandable, and I was somehow merged with it!

The whole of *Snow Maiden* was composed in short score in three months and, after the completion of the *Legend*, the full score of the opera (in which he at last abandoned natural brass) was finished in April 1881; it was produced on 10 February 1882.

III 1881–93
After the completion of *Snow Maiden* in April 1881, Rimsky-Korsakov was characteristically deflected from composition for nearly two years. Musorgsky died in March 1881 and his old friend took upon himself the colossal labour of setting in order his manuscripts and preparing them for publication, which in his view entailed the 'correction' of Musorgsky's innumerable harmonic 'solecisms' and 'improvement' of his melodies and part-writing. The worst part of the task was the chaotic score of the opera *Khovanshchina*, which occupied Rimsky-Korsakov mainly from December 1881 to July 1882, but there were also a number of songs (including the *Songs and Dances of Death*), choral pieces, orchestral pieces and piano pieces. The *Night on the Bare Mountain*, which Musorgsky had left in more than one version, temporarily baffled him and he compiled his well-known score only in 1886. Another

distraction from composition had been the direction of the Free School of Music, which in September 1881 he persuaded Balakirev to resume. But the Musorgsky labours had not long been completed before he was more or less obliged to take another official post: in February 1883 Balakirev was appointed musical director of the imperial chapel, with Rimsky-Korsakov as his assistant (on the other hand, the Inspectorship of Naval Bands was abolished by a new minister in 1884). At nearly the same time he was beginning to be drawn into another circle soon involving other activities. This revolved about an extremely wealthy timber merchant, Mitrofan Petrovich Belyayev, an amateur viola player and passionate lover of chamber music at whose house young musicians (mostly Rimsky-Korsakov's ex-pupils, Lyadov, Glazunov and others) gathered on Friday evenings to play and hear string quartets, including their own compositions. Having printed their works at his own expense and hired orchestras and halls for their performance, Belyayev found himself becoming a music publisher and, in 1886, the backer of a regular series of 'Russian Symphony Concerts'; in both these undertakings Rimsky-Korsakov was his chief musical adviser. From then on, most of Rimsky-Korsakov's works were published by his firm. A further blow was the death of Borodin (February 1887), which presented Rimsky-Korsakov with what he conceived to be the duty of completing and orchestrating *Prince Igor*; this he proceeded to do with the help of Glazunov.

The mid-1880s were thus almost a complete blank creatively. From the beginning of 1883 came a one-movement piano concerto on a Russian theme, then nothing of any consequence for nearly four years. The

First Symphony was revised, transposed to E minor and reorchestrated in 1884; the Third Symphony was also revised and reorchestrated (1886), but a fourth was no sooner begun than abandoned. Eight songs (opp.26 and 27, 1882–3), a very little church music (1883–4), a harmony textbook for the students of the imperial chapel (1884) and a movement for string quartet (1886) constituted his total original output. The Fantasia on Two Russian Themes for violin and orchestra at the end of 1886 was a more substantial though not a very important work, but it had important consequences, for a proposed companion piece on Spanish themes became in the summer of 1887 the popular *Kaprichchio na ispanskiye temï* ('Spanish Capriccio') for orchestra only. This was a study in virtuoso orchestration in which, as the composer insisted, the brilliant instrumental colouring is 'the very essence of the composition, not its mere dressing-up'. Work on *Prince Igor* precluded original composition for the time being, but during summer 1888 Rimsky-Korsakov produced two more major works in the same style as the *Spanish Capriccio*: the symphonic suite *Sheherazade* and *Svetlïy prazdnik* ('Russian Easter Festival'), an 'overture on liturgical themes'. In his autobiography, which he had already begun to write in a desultory way, he observed that the *Capriccio*, *Sheherazade* and the *Easter Festival* overture 'close a period of my work, at the end of which my orchestration had attained a considerable degree of virtuosity and warm sonority without Wagnerian influence, limiting myself to the normally constituted orchestra used by Glinka'. They were in fact his last important purely orchestral compositions; during the last 20 years of his life he wrote only a few occasional pieces

for orchestra and suites or other concert arrangements from his operas.

The climacteric of Rimsky-Korsakov's creative life, after which he became almost exclusively an opera composer, was the visit to St Petersburg of Angelo Neumann's travelling 'Richard Wagner Theatre' which gave four cycles of the *Ring* under Karl Muck during March 1889. Rimsky-Korsakov attended all the rehearsals with Glazunov, following with the score and 'astonished by Wagner's handling of the orchestra' which soon began to influence his own. Just before the *Ring* experience, on the second anniversary of Borodin's death, the playing over of his contribution to the collective *Mlada* of 1872 had suggested to Rimsky-Korsakov not only that he should orchestrate it (which he did the following year) but that he should compose a complete *Mlada* of his own, revising and extending the original libretto himself. The composition of *Mlada* was interrupted by a visit to Paris to conduct the Colonne orchestra in two concerts of Russian music, including *Antar*, the Piano Concerto and *Spanish Capriccio*, at the Trocadéro on 22 and 29 June as part of the Universal Exhibition of 1889; yet the composition sketch of the opera was finished by the end of August. The orchestration, also interrupted by a visit to the west, to conduct in Brussels in April 1890, as well as by family troubles, took another year. *Mlada* was produced on 1 November 1892, but had no lasting success; the composer himself described it as 'cold – like ice' and prophesied that it would probably be his last composition, 'at any rate, the last important one'. Fearing that the end of his creative life was approaching, he set about winding up his affairs. He made yet a third version

(published as the second) of his orchestral piece *Sadko* and, between April 1891 and April 1892, a third version of *The Maid of Pskov*, based in substance on the first and ignoring the second (1877). 'I closed my account with the past', he wrote. 'Not one of my major works of the period before *May Night* remained in its original form.'

Indeed in his current state of mind he found little satisfaction in anything he had written except *Snow Maiden*, in the music of his old friends or his new, younger ones, or for that matter in hardly any other music. He wrote to his wife in August 1891:

No music that I hear now pleases me. Beautiful harmony, texture, melodious phrases don't touch me, it all seems to me dry and cold. . . . A Beethoven quartet or symphony is another matter. There technique and working out are only the form; it is all pervaded with life and soul; of course it's the same with Chopin and Glinka and (just imagine) – the Italians with the sextet from *Lucia*, the quartet from *Rigoletto*, and all their melodies. That is where real life is. 'La donna è mobile' is music, but Glazunov is only technique and conventional acceptance of contemporary fashion and taste as beauty. I fancy that a great part of the Russian school is not music, but cold and brain-spun stuff.

The depression, perhaps brought on in the first place in 1890 by the dangerous illnesses of his wife and one of his sons, the deaths of his mother and youngest child, and the beginning of the prolonged and ultimately fatal illness of his second youngest child, deepened during 1891–3, a period in which one physical and intellectual crisis succeeded another. Having almost completely abandoned music – he hardly touched a piano for a whole year – he turned to vast programmes of reading aesthetics and philosophy and to writing on musical aesthetics; but these projects were continually interrupted by alarming physical symptoms: rushes of blood

to the head and complete confusion of thoughts, frequent loss of memory and unpleasant obsessive ideas. The medical diagnosis was cerebro-spinal neurasthenia. He gave up the conducting of Belyayev's Russian Symphony Concerts and his post in the imperial chapel (though his resignation did not become official until January 1894).

IV 1893–1908

The turning-point for Rimsky-Korskov came in December 1893 when Tchaikovsky's death stimulated him to conduct a programme of his friend's works at one of the Russian Symphony Concerts (12 December); he went on to conduct the remaining concerts of the season. The death also removed a hindrance to the composition of an opera on a subject which had long attracted him: another of Gogol's stories, *Noch's pered Rozhdestvom* ('Christmas Eve'), on which Tchaikovsky had based *Vakula the Smith* (*Cherevichki*). For summer 1894 the Rimsky-Korsakovs found a new country home in most beautiful surroundings at Vechasha in the Luga district, to which they frequently returned, and in a letter of 4 July to Stasov announcing that he had embarked on an opera he gave two pieces of information; first he had

taken it into [his] head to connect Gogol's story with Kolyada and Ovsen. ... I've long felt an obligation to them, since I dealt with 'Rusalka week' in *May Night*, Maslyanitsa and Yarilo in *Snow Maiden* and Kupala in *Mlada*. Now I shall have completed the whole solar cycle.

These pagan ritual figures connected with the winter solstice, the spring equinox, and midsummer are discussed at length in the preface to the opera. He added that the composition-sketch was already more than half finished. His second piece of news was that, as a result

2. *Title-page of the first edition (1908) of the vocal score of Rimsky-Korsakov's 'The Golden Cockerel'*

16

of a letter from the musical historian Findeyzen, he was contemplating an opera on the subject of Sadko, 'in which I shall make use, among other things, of the music of my symphonic picture'; with the help of a house-guest, Nikolay Shtrup, he had already worked out a detailed scenario which Shtrup would take to Stasov for his advice. Musical ideas for *Sadko* were already pouring into his head. But first of all *Christmas Eve* had to be finished, as indeed it was in sketch by the end of August despite the composer's paralysing consciousness that much of it was 'cold and brain-spun' and fears that he had lost his creative power for ever. *Sadko* restored his self-confidence; the greater part of the composition-sketch was completed during the summer of 1895, though additions to the plan suggested by a new friend Vladimir Bel'sky, who supplied the libretto for them, were not composed until the following year. In the meantime Rimsky-Korsakov pressed ahead with the orchestration. He was so full of ideas that in October 1895 he wrote part of a libretto and sketched some of the music for the one-act *Bagdadskiy borodobrey* ('Barber of Baghdad'), from which the music of Nureddin's first aria was resuscitated as the Hymn to the Sun in *Zolotoy petushok* ('The Golden Cockerel').

The Barber of Baghdad was probably set aside in favour of preparations for the first performance of *Christmas Eve* on 10 December, from which Rimsky-Korsakov stayed away in protest at the absurd changes enforced by the imperial family. But still *Sadko* had to remain unfinished, for the composer was occupied from December until May 1896 with a task for which he has been bitterly censured, the rewriting and reorchestration of Musorgsky's *Boris Godunov*, some of which had been

17

done desultorily during 1892–4. The full score of *Sadko* was completed in September 1896. But the play-through to Vsevolozhsky, the director of the imperial theatres, and his colleagues went badly; the production would obviously be complicated and difficult. Finally Nicholas II himself, on being told that the music was in the vein of *Mlada* and *Christmas Eve*, personally crossed *Sadko* from the list and instructed Vsevolozhsky to 'find something gayer' in its place. The consequent break with the imperial theatres, which lasted until Vsevolozhsky's supercession in 1899, would have had very serious consequences if private enterprise had not come to the rescue. The railway magnate Savva Mamontov, patron of music, painting and the theatre, financed what was called the Private Russian Opera in Moscow, with such singers as Shalyapin and Nadezhda Zabela-Vrubel (a remarkable lyric-coloratura soprano whom Rimsky-Korsakov regarded as the ideal type of opera singer); he had already put on the new version of *The Maid of Pskov* in the Solodovnikov Theatre with Shalyapin as Ivan the Terrible (24 December 1896). In June 1897 Mamontov's adviser, the critic Semyon Kruglikov, invited Rimsky-Korsakov to send him the score of *Sadko*, with the result that it was produced on 7 January 1898: a poor performance was redeemed by a very fine one two months later when the company gave a short season in the great hall of the St Petersburg Conservatory.

The period between the rejection of *Sadko* and its production by Mamontov, particularly summer 1897, was extraordinarily productive. Rimsky-Korsakov was now obsessed with vocal writing; he wrote no fewer than 40 songs, and also a miniature opera, a setting of

18

Pushkin's 'little tragedy' *Mozart and Salieri*, in all of which the voice part was conceived first, and that of piano or orchestra afterwards, a complete reversal of his usual procedure before then. A cantata, *Switezianka*, dates from the same period and purely instrumental composition was not neglected; he composed a second string quartet in G and a piano trio in C minor, both of which he regarded as failures, and made yet another and much more drastic revision of *Antar*, which was now styled 'symphonic suite' instead of 'symphony'. This version was not published until 1913; the 'Nouvelle ré-daction (1897)' of the miniature scores is nothing of the kind, but a minor revision (1903) of the 1875 version.

The compositions of 1898 included the Prologue to *The Maid of Pskov* omitted from the first and third versions and now completely reconstructed as a one-act opera, *Boyarïnya Vera Sheloga*, and a full-length opera also on a subject by Mey, *Tsarskaya nevesta* ('The Tsar's Bride'), in which the heroine's part was written specifically for Zabela-Vrubel. This was completely carried out, from first sketches to complete full score, between February and 6 October. Mamontov produced *Mozart and Salieri*, with Shalyapin as Salieri, on 7 December and *Vera Sheloga* on 27 December. *The Tsar's Bride* had to wait until 3 November 1899.

By that time Rimsky-Korsakov had nearly completed another opera, *Skazka o Tsare Saltane* (in its full title 'The Tale of Tsar Saltan, of his son the famous and mighty hero Prince Gvidon Saltanovich, and of the beautiful Swan Princess'), again with Zabela-Vrubel in mind as the heroine. Musically it was in some respects a return to the style of *Snow Maiden*. But its production (3 November 1900) almost marked the end of Rimsky-

19

Korsakov's connection with the Moscow Private Opera. Shalyapin had deserted to the imperial theatres; Mamontov himself had disappeared from the scene after a railway financial scandal, leaving an artists' cooperative to carry on, while in St Petersburg a new director of imperial theatres opened the Mariinsky to Rimsky-Korsakov once more. Even Vsevolozhsky had made a conciliatory gesture by reviving *Snow Maiden* in December 1898; his successor put on *Sadko* with great success (8 February 1901) before the tsar and most of the imperial family.

But Rimsky-Korsakov's first new work on the Mariinsky stage, *Serviliya* (14 October 1902), a deliberate attempt to get away from Russian subjects, was a failure. Even before its production, he was contemplating, even beginning, other operatic experiments. One, on the Nausicaa episode from the *Odyssey*, had been in his mind since 1894; he wrote a 'prelude-cantata' *Iz Gomera* ('From Homer') and then abandoned the idea. He was also thinking of combining the legend of the invisible city of Kitezh with the story of St Fevroniya, though that too was laid aside for a while. But he finished the one-act *Kashchey bessmertnïy* ('Kaschchey the Immortal', produced by the former Mamontov company in Moscow, 25 December 1902), a Russian subject treated with unusual harmonic sophistication and little national colouring. By contrast, the full-length, melodramatic *Pan Voyevoda* (completed in 1903, and produced in St Petersburg, 16 October 1904, by another private company) is an extended (and unsuccessful) essay in a different national idiom, that of Poland; it was intended as a tribute to Chopin, to whose memory it is dedicated.

With *Kitezh*, taken up again in March 1903, Rimsky-Korsakov reverted to a profoundly Russian subject, underlaid by a pantheism much deeper than that of *Snow Maiden*, which stimulated his creative imagination to its highest level. But before he finished the full score, on 11 February 1905, he had become involved in distracting events. The long-simmering political discontents, naturally involving the students of the conservatory, had come to their first major crisis on 'Bloody Sunday' (22 January); Rimsky-Korsakov tried to calm the students but firmly supported their cause; on 18 February he publicly endorsed a letter to the press demanding political reforms which had been signed by Grechaninov, Taneyev, Rakhmaninov, Shalyapin and 25 other leading musicians; on 1 April, 'the conservatory being surrounded by foot and mounted police', he published an open letter to the director, his former pupil Bernhard, supporting the student strikers and making a stinging attack on the 'circle of dilettanti' of the Russian Musical Society who really controlled the institution. The 'cowardly and tactless' Bernhard resigned, but on 5 April Rimsky-Korsakov was dismissed. Still more extraordinary events followed. On 9 April a student performance of *Kashchey*, conducted by Glazunov, was followed not by a short concert, as intended, but by a wild political demonstration of homage to the composer. As a result, the performance of his music was temporarily forbidden by the police.

Rimsky-Korsakov went to Vechasha for the summer, continued his autobiography (which he had resumed in 1904 after an 11-year break), began a thematic analysis of *Snow Maiden* and wrote a considerable part of his book on orchestration. He also pondered two opera

21

subjects, an old one, Byron's *Heaven and Earth*, which came to nothing, and a new one, the 17th-century rebel Stenka Razin, in which he proposed to introduce tunes popular with the rebels of his own day. One of these, *Dubinushka* ('The little oak stick'), he orchestrated in October but *Sten'ka Razin* was abandoned in December. With Ziloti and others he had contemplated setting up a private school of music in St Petersburg, but in the end the conservatory was reopened with a freer constitution, the professors who had been dismissed or who had resigned in sympathy were invited to return and in December Glazunov was elected director.

Rimsky-Korsakov was partly occupied in 1906 with a new version of *Boris Godunov* in which he restored the cuts of 1896 (the next year he composed two additional passages for the Coronation Scene, for the Paris production). On 4 September, at Riva on Lake Garda, he completed his autobiography and not long after his return to Russia he noted down on 28 October the opening theme of *Zolotoy petushok* ('The Golden Cockerel'), an opera based on Pushkin's fairy-tale satire on stupid autocracy. Bel'sky, the librettist of *Sadko*, *Tsar Saltan* and *Kitezh*, skilfully augmented Pushkin's verses. Composition of the *Cockerel* went smoothly, although it was interrupted by the Mariinsky rehearsals of *Kitezh* (produced on 20 February 1907) and by a visit to Paris in May to conduct part of the Cinq Concerts Historiques Russes arranged by Dyagilev. The score of the *Cockerel* was finished on 11 September. But the libretto caused endless troubles with the censorship, which clouded the last three or four months of Rimsky-Korsakov's life. These difficulties probably worsened the heart trouble (attacks of angina) of which he died

22

on 21 June 1908 in Lyubensk. *The Cockerel* was first performed by the Zimin opera company at the Solodovnikov Theatre, Moscow, on 7 October 1909.

Works

Rimsky-Korsakov's operas are of far greater importance than his compositions in other fields. The purely orchestral works by which he is best known – *Sheherazade*, the *Spanish Capriccio* and the *Easter Festival* overture – are essentially brightly coloured mosaics; although the thematic ideas lack organic cohesion, they are often striking and piquant. The composer set them off by scoring which frequently involves the juxtaposition of 'pure' orchestral groups, as in the opening of the third movement of *Antar* where the melody is played by all the woodwind in octaves (with two horns which omit the ornamental notes) against a background of pure brass chords, with cymbals. Another example is the final tutti of *Sheherazade* where the theme on unison trombones is accompanied simultaneously by a combination of string patterns, another set of patterns, alternating with chromatic scales, on woodwind, and a third pattern of rhythms on percussion, with harp glissandos. But such passages can easily be matched in the operas; the procession of princes in *Mlada*, the harbour scene of *Sadko*, the wedding procession in *The Golden Cockerel*, are no less brilliant. And the operas give scope for a far wider variety of orchestral effect – fantastic, sensuous, grotesque or humorous.

Again, Rimsky-Korsakov's finest vocal writing is to

be found in the operas, not in the solo songs with piano. He was a copious but not a great songwriter. His early songs tend to be declamatory, with the voice over-shadowed by the piano part, while (conversely) the much more numerous later ones are more melodiously vocal but weakened by conventional piano figuration. (The solo piano compositions, which include some well-made fugues, are – like the handful of chamber works – negligible in value.) Even the best of the songs, beautiful as they are, never reach the level of Marfa's great aria in *The Tsar's Bride* or Fevroniya's music in *Kitezh*.

Yet as an opera composer Rimsky-Korsakov suffered from what might seem to be a crippling disability: lack of dramatic power, in particular the capacity to create characters in sound. In all his 15 operas there are no more than three or four solid characters realized in terms of music: Ivan the Terrible in *The Maid of Pskov*, the spiritually tormented drunken scoundrel Grishka Kuterma (his psychological masterpiece) in *Kitezh*, the saintly virgin Fevroniya in the same opera. He could provide a librettist's characters – the tenor lovers and the simple Russian heroines – with suitable, often lyrically beautiful music, but the music hardly ever seems to have grown out of the character's inner being. Rimsky-Korsakov's operas paradoxically succeed by being, in most cases, deliberately non-dramatic. As he repeatedly affirmed in the prefaces to the scores, he 'regarded an opera as first and foremost a *musical* work'. Instead of dramas, he created musico-scenic fairy tales; instead of characters, delightful fantastic puppets. In this field he is supreme, indeed unique. He even devised a type of short-breathed, rhythmically precise music suggesting the movements of puppets,

3. Autograph score from Act 3 of Rimsky-Korsakov's 'The Golden Cockerel', composed 1906–7

which he associated, for instance, with the Tsar in *Snow Maiden* and with Tsar Saltan. And he employed a dual musical language: on the one hand diatonic and lyrical, shot through with the idioms of Russian folk music, sometimes actually quoting or closely imitating actual folk melodies, for the 'real' human characters; on the other, chromatic and highly artificial, often based on the whole-tone scale, a scale of alternate tones and semitones, even a scale invented by his librettist Bel'sky, or making play with harmonic ingenuities, e.g. alternating chords hinged on the two notes common to two dominant 7ths an augmented 4th apart, for the 'unreal' magical beings. These puppets inhabit a world – the world of *May Night*, *Christmas Eve*, *Sadko*, *Tsar Saltan*, *The Golden Cockerel* – 'in which the common-place and matter-of-fact are inextricably confused with the fantastic, naïveté with sophistication, the romantic with the humorous, and beauty with absurdity'. Even *Kitezh*, despite its mystical heights and psychological depths, belongs in some degree to the same world.

This duality in Rimsky-Korsakov's musical style is matched by strange contradictions in his personality: although cool and objective to an unusual degree, a religious sceptic, he not only delighted in depicting religious ceremonies but was capable of total surrender to the nature-mysticism which possessed him during the composition of *Snow Maiden*. He recognized this self-contradiction very clearly, as he recognized all his faults and weaknesses and limitations. Nothing annoyed him more than to be hailed as a 'genius' and he carried pitiless self-criticism to a point dangerously near creative annihilation. In his writings and in conversation with friends he not only drew attention to, but exagger-

ated, his unconscious echoes of other composers' ideas and his adoption of their techniques. Neither his employment of leitmotifs nor his orchestration was deeply affected by Wagner after hearing the *Ring*. He had already devised a subtle and personal scheme of miniature motifs in *Snow Maiden* and his orchestral technique was only enriched, not deeply modified, by Wagner's.

His own style, pellucid and based on the bold use of primary instrumental colours over a framework of very clearly defined part-writing and harmony, was based on Glinka and Balakirev, Berlioz and Liszt. He transmitted it directly to two generations of Russian composers, from Lyadov (*b* 1855) and Glazunov (*b* 1865) to Myaskovsky (*b* 1881), Stravinsky (*b* 1882) and Prokofiev (*b* 1891), all of whom were his pupils, and his general influence is evident, if less pronounced, in the orchestral music of Ravel, Debussy, Dukas and Respighi.

WORKS

Edition: N. *Rimsky-Korsakov: Polnoye sobraniye sochineniy* [Complete edition of compositions], ed. A. Rimsky-Korsakov and others (Moscow, 1946–70) [RK]

Numbers in the right-hand column denote references in the text.

STAGE

Moscow first performances at Solodovnikov Theatre, St Petersburg first performances at Mariinsky Theatre unless otherwise stated; * – full score; † – vocal score with pf acc.

op.	Title	Translation	Description	Libretto	Composed	Published	First performance	RK	
—	Pskovityanka	The Maid of Pskov	opera, 4	Rimsky-Korsakov, after L. A. Mey					24–8, 81
									19, 25
	1st version				1868–72	†St Petersburg, 1872	St Petersburg, 13 Jan 1873	*1a, b †29a	5, 6, 14
	2nd version				1876–7	—			7, 14
	3rd version				1891–2	St Petersburg, 1892	St Petersburg, Panayevsky, 18 April 1895	*1v, g †29b	14
	new Aria, act 3				1898				
—	Mlada, collab. Borodin, Cui, Musorgsky and Minkus; unfinished		opera-ballet, 4	V. A. Krilov	1872			—	6, 13
—	Mayiskaya noch'	May Night	opera, 3	Rimsky-Korsakov, after Gogol	1878–9	Leipzig 1893	St Petersburg, 21 Jan 1880	*2a, b †30	7, 9, 14, 15, 27
—	Pskovityanka	The Maid of Pskov	incidental music to Mey's play	—					
	1st version				1877	—		—	
	2nd version				1882	Moscow, 1951		*19b	14, 15, 19, 20, 21, 27, 28
—	Snegurochka	Snow Maiden	opera, prol, 4	Rimsky-Korsakov, after A. N. Ostrovsky					
	1st version				1880–81	St Petersburg, 1881	St Petersburg, 10 Feb 1882	—	9–10
	2nd version				c1895	St Petersburg, 1895	—	*3a, b †31a, b	

op.	Title	Translation	Description	Libretto	Composed	Published	First performance	RK	
—	Mlada		opera-ballet, 4	Rimsky-Korsakov, after Krïlov	1889–90	Leipzig, 1891	St Petersburg, 1 Nov 1892	*4a, b †32	13, 15, 18, 24
—	Noch' pered Rozhdestvom	Christmas Eve	opera, 4	Rimsky-Korsakov, after Gogol	1894–5	Leipzig, 1895	St Petersburg, 10 Dec 1895	*5a, b †33	15, 17, 18, 27
—	Sadko		opera, 7 scenes	Rimsky-Korsakov, V. I. Bel'sky	1894–6	Leipzig, 1897	Moscow, 7 Jan 1898	*6a, b, v †34	17, 18, 20, 22, 24, 27
—	Bagdadskiy borodobrey	The Barber of Baghdad	opera, 1, sketches	Rimsky-Korsakov	1895	—	—	—	17
48	Motsart i Sal'yeri	Mozart and Salieri	opera, 1	Pushkin	1897	Leipzig, 1898	Moscow, 7 Dec 1898	*7 †35	18–19
54	Boyarïnya Vera Sheloga [orig. prol to 2nd version of opera Pskovityanka, 1876-7]		opera, 1	Rimsky-Korsakov, after Mey	1898	St Petersburg, 1898	Moscow, 27 Dec 1898	*8 †36	19
—	Tsarskaya nevesta new Aria, act 3	The Tsar's Bride	opera, 4	after Mey; 1 scene, I. F. Tyumenev	1898 1899	Leipzig, 1899	Moscow, 3 Nov 1899	*9a, b †37	19, 25
—	Skazka o Tsare Saltane, o sïne evo slavnom i moguchem bogatïre knyaze Gvidone Saltanoviche i o prekrasnoy tsarevne lebedi	The Tale of Tsar Saltane, of his son the famous and mighty hero Prince Gvidon Saltanovich and of the beautiful Swan Princess	opera, prol, 4	Bel'sky, after Pushkin	1899–1900	St Petersburg, 1901	Moscow, 3 Nov 1900	*10a, b †38	19, 22, 27
—	Serviliya		opera, 5	Rimsky-Korsakov, after Mey	1900–01	St Petersburg, 1902	St Petersburg, 14 Oct 1902	*11a, b †39	20
—	Kashchey bessmertnïy [conclusion rewritten 1906]	Kashchey the Immortal	opera, 1	Rimsky-Korsakov, after E. M. Petrovsky	1901–2	St Petersburg, 1902	Moscow, 25 Dec 1902	*12 †40	20, 21
—	Pan Voyevoda		opera, 4	Tyumenev	1902–3	St Petersburg, 1904	St Petersburg Conservatory, 16 Oct 1904	*13a, b †41	20, 83

Skazaniye o nevidimom grade Kitezhe i deve Fevronii	Legend of the Invisible City of Kitezh and the Maiden Fevroniya	opera, 4	Bel'sky	1903–5	Leipzig, 1906	St Petersburg, 20 Feb 1907	*14a, b, suppl. †42	20, 21, 22, 25, 27
Zolotoy petushok	The Golden Cockerel	opera, 3	Bel'sky, after Pushkin	1906–7	Moscow, 1908	Moscow, 7 Oct 1909	*15a, b, v †43	16, 17, 22, 23, 24, 26, 27
Sten'ka Razin	—	opera, sketches	Bel'sky	1906	—	—	—	22
Zemlya i nebo	Heaven and Earth	opera, sketches	Byron	1906	—	—	—	22

CHORAL WORKS
(* full score; † vocal score with pf acc.)

op.	Title	Translation	Text	Forces	Composed	Published	RK
13	2 choruses:		Lermontov	3 female vv	1875	Leipzig, 1875	—
	1 Tuchki nebesnïya	Clouds in the sky					
	2 Nochevala tuchka zolotaya	The golden cloud had slept					
14	4 variations and fughetta on a Russian folksong, Nadoyeli nochi			4 female vv, pf/harmonium ad lib	1875	Leipzig, 1875	—
16	6 choruses:					St Petersburg, 1876	—
	1 Na severe dikom	In the wild north		SATB	1875		
	2 Bakkhicheskaya pesn'	Bacchic song		TTBB	1875		
	3 Staraya pesnya: Iz lesov dremuchikh severnïkh	Old song: From the dense northern forests		SATB	1876		
	4 Mesyats plïvet i tikh i spokoyen	The moon floats peacefully		SATB	1876		
	5 Poslednyaya tucha razseyannoy buri	The last cloud of the storm		SSAA	1876		
	6 Molitva: Vladïko dney moikh	Prayer: Rule my days		SATB	1875		

31

op.	Title	Translation	Text	Forces	Composed	Published	RK
18	2 choruses:			SATB	1876	St Petersburg, 1876	—
	1 Pred raspyat'yem	Before the Cross					
	2 Tatarskiy polon	The Tatar captivity					
23	4 choruses:			3 male vv, pf ad lib	1876	Leipzig, 1876	—
	1 Krest'yanskaya pirushka	The peasant feast					
	2 Voron k voron letit	Raven flies to raven					
	3 Plenivshis' rozoy solovey	Enslaved by the rose the nightingale					
	4 Dayte bokali	Give me the goblet					
20	Stikh ob Alexeye Bozh'yem cheloveke	Poem about Alexey, the man of God		ATB, orch	1878	Leipzig, c1880	*24, 44
19	15 Russian folksongs:			mixed vv	1879	Moscow, 1879	—
	1 Iz za lesu, lesu temnovo	From the forest, the dark forest					
	2 Kak pri vechere	As at evening					
	3 A i gusto na beryoze list'ye	The leaves are thick on the birch tree					
	4 Zelyona grusha vo sadu	The green pear tree in the garden					
	5 Kak za rechoyu	As across the river					
	6 Vo luzyakh	In the meadows					
	7 Chto vilis'-to moi rus'i kudri	When you waved my light brown curls					
	8 Poduy, poduy nepogodushka	Begone, begone bad weather					
	9 Akh, talan-li moy	Oh, my good fortune					
	10 Ti vzoydi solntse krasnoye	Rise, red sun					
	11 Vzoydi ti, solntse, ni nizko, v'isoko	Rise, O sun, not low but high					
	12 Ay, vo pole lipen'ka	In the field there is a lime-tree					
	13 Zapletisya pleten'	Plait the wattle fencing					
	14 Posmotrite-ka dobriye lyudi	Just see, good people					
	15 So v'yunom ya khozhu	With a youth I walk					

op.	Title	Translation	Text	Forces	Composed	Published	RK	
21	Slava	Be praised		SATB, orch	1879–90	—	*24 —	12
—	Tebe Boga khvalim	We praise thee O God	Greek chant	SATB	1883	St Petersburg, 1883	—	12
22	8 settings from the Liturgiya sv. Ioanna Zlatausta [Liturgy of St John Chrysostom]			SATB	1883	St Petersburg, 1884	—	12
22b	Traditional chants:			SATB	1884	St Petersburg, 1885–6	—	12

22b Traditional chants:
1. Kheravimskaya pesnya — Song of the cherubim
2. Da molchit vsyakaya plot' chelovecha — Let all mortal flesh keep silent
3. Voskresnovo prichastnovo stikha — From the verses concerned with the Resurrection
4. Se zhenikh gryadet — See the bridegroom comes
5. Chertog tvoy vizhdu, Spase Moy — I enter thy hall, my Saviour
6. Psalm: Na rekakh Vavilonskikh — By the waters of Babylon

op.	Title	Text	Forces	Composed	Published	RK	
44	Switezianka, cantata	L. A. Mey, after Mickiewicz	S, T, SATB, orch	1897	Leipzig, 1898	*24 †44	19
58	Pesn' o veshchem Olege [Song of Oleg the Wise]	A. K. Tolstoy	T, B, TB, orch	1899	St Petersburg, 1901	*24 †44	
60	Iz Gomera, prelude-cantata [From Homer]	from the Odyssey	S, Mez, A, SA, orch	1901	Leipzig, 1905	*24 †44	20

ORCHESTRAL

12–13

(* – full score; † – composer's arr. pf 4 hands; ‡ – pf reduction of orch pt.)

op.	Title	Composed	Published	Remarks	RK	
1	Symphony no.1					
	1st version	1861–5	Moscow, 1953		*16	3–4
	2nd version	1884	St Petersburg, 1885		*16	12
28	Overture on Three Russian Themes					4
	1st version	1866	Moscow, 1954		*20	
	2nd version	1879–80	Leipzig, 1886		*20, †49b	

op.	Title	Composed	Published	Remarks	RK	
6	**Fantasia on Serbian Themes**					
	1st version	1867	Moscow, 1870		*19b, †49b	4
	2nd version	1886–7	Moscow, 1895		*19b	
5	**Sadko**					
	1st version	1867	Moscow, 1951	entitled Epizod iz bīlīnī o Sadko [Episode from the legend of Sadko]	*19a	17
	2nd version	1869	Moscow, 1870	entitled Muzikal'naya kartina – Sadko [Musical picture – Sadko] in 2nd and 3rd versions	*19a	4
	3rd version	1892	Moscow, 1892		*19a	13–14
—	Symphony, b	1866–9	Moscow, 1970	sketches only; pt. of 2nd subject used in Mizgir's aria O lyubi menya, lyubi, in Snegurochka	*50	4
9	**Symphony no.2 'Antar'**					
	1st version	1868	—		*17	13, 24
	2nd version	1875	St Petersburg, 1880	rev. 1903 (St Petersburg, 1903)		5, 6
	3rd version	1897	St Petersburg, 1913	described as Symphonic Suite		7
32	**Symphony no.3, C**					
	1st version	1866–73	Moscow, 1959	scherzo composed 1866, trio 1870, other movts 1873	*18	6, 19
	2nd version	1886	Leipzig, 1888		*18	6, 7
—	Concerto, trbn, military band, B♭	1877	Moscow, 1950		*25	11
—	Variations, ob, military band, g	1878	Moscow, 1950	on Glinka's song Chto krasotka molodaya	*25	
—	Concertstück, cl, military band, E♭	1878	Moscow, 1950		*25	
29	Skazka [Legend]	1879–80	Leipzig, 1886	orig. title Baba-Yaga	*20, †49b	9, 10
31	Sinfonietta on Russian Themes, a	1880–84	Leipzig, 1887	based on first 3 movts of str qt, 1878–9	*20	9
30	Pf concerto, c♯–D♭	1882–3	Leipzig, 1886		*26, ‡48	11, 13
—	Symphony no.4	1884	Moscow, 1970		50	11
33	Fantasia on Two Russian Themes, vn	1886–7	Leipzig, 1887	pf sketches for scherzo, d	*26, ‡48	12
34	Kaprichchio na ispanskiye temī [Spanish capriccio]	1887	Leipzig, 1888	based on projected Fantasia on Spanish themes, vn, orch	*21, †49b	12, 13, 24
—	Malorossiyskaya fantaziya [Little Russian fantasia]	1887	Moscow, 1970	pf sketches only	50	
35	Sheherazade, symphonic suite	1888	Leipzig, 1889		*22, †49b	12, 24
—	Souvenir de trois chants polonais, vn	1888	‡Moscow, 1949	Polish themes used later in Pan Voyevoda; arr. pf, vn 1893	*26, ‡48	

op.	Title	Composed	Published	Remarks	RK
	Festival], ov.				
—	Variation no.4, A	1901	Leipzig, 1903	for Variations on a Russian theme, Uzh ti pole moye, collab. Artsïbushev, Vitols, Lyadov, Sokolov and Glazunov	*23
—	Noch' na gore Triglave [Night on mount Triglav]	1899–1901	—	orch arr. of act 3 of opera Mlada	*4 suppl.
37	Serenade, vc	1903	—	orch arr. of Serenade, vc, pf, 1893	*26
57	Skazka o tsare Saltane [Tale of Tsar Saltan], musical pictures	1903	Leipzig, 1904	suite from the opera	—
59	Pan Voyevoda	1903	Leipzig, 1904	suite from the opera	—
—	Mlada	1903	Leipzig, 1904	suite from the opera	—
—	Noch' pered rozhdestvom [Christmas Eve], chorus ad lib	1903	Leipzig, 1904	suite from the opera	—
61	Nad mogiloy [On the tomb]	1904	Leipzig, 1905	in memory of M. P. Belyayev	*23, †49b
62	Dubinushka [The little oak stick] 1st version	1905	Moscow, 1966		*23
	2nd version, chorus ad lib	1906	Leipzig, 1907		*23, †49b
—	Zdravitsa [Greeting]	1906	Moscow, 1966	for Glazunov's jubilee, 1907	*23
63	Neapolitanskaya pesenka [Neapolitan song]	1907	Moscow, 1966	arr. of Denza: Funiculì, funiculà	*23, †49b
—	Zolotoy petushok [The Golden Cockerel]	1907	—	concert arr. of introduction and wedding march to the opera	—
—	Skazka o rïbake i o rïbke [Tale of the fisherman and the fish], sym. poem	1907	—	after Pushkin; sketches only	—

CHAMBER MUSIC

op.	Title	Composed	Published	Remarks	RK
12	String Quartet, F	1875	Moscow, c1875		27
—	String Sextet, A, 2 vn, 2 va, 2 vc	1876	Moscow, 1912		27
—	Quintet, B♭, fl, cl, hn, bn, pf	1876	Leipzig, 1911		28a
—	String Quartet on Russian themes:	1878–9	—	first 3 movts used later in Sinfonietta, op.31; last movt arr. of 4 hands as V tserkvi	—
	1 V pole [In the field]				—
	2 Na devichnike [At the wedding-eve party]				—
	3 V Khorovode [At Khorovod]		—		—
	4 U monastirya [At the monastery]		Moscow, 1955		27

op.	Title	Composed	Published	Remarks	RK
—	4 variations on a chorale, g, str qt	1885	Moscow, 1955		27
—	String Quartet 'B la F'	1886	Leipzig, 1887	1st movt only, remainder by Lyadov, Glazunov and Borodin; arr. pf 4 hands	27, 12
—	String Quartet 'Jour de fête'	1887	Leipzig, 1889	finale only, remainder by Glazunov and Lyadov	27
—	Nocturne, F, 4 hn	c1888	Moscow, 1955		27
—	2 Duets, F, 2 hn	?1883–94	Moscow, 1955		27
—	Canzonetta and Tarantella, 2 cl	?1883–94	Moscow, 1955		27
—	Serenade, vc, pf	1893	Leipzig, 1895		48
—	String Quartet, G	1897	Moscow, 1955		27, 19
—	Trio, c, vn, vc, pf	1897	Moscow, 1970	orchd 1903 as op.37	28b, 19
—	Theme and variation no.4, G, str qt	1898	Leipzig, 1899	for Variations on a Russian theme, Nadoyeli nochi nadoskuchili, collab. Artsibushev, Skryabin, Glazunov, Lyadov, Vitols, Blumenfeld, Ewald, Winkler and Sokolov	27
—	Allegro, B♭, str qt	1899	Leipzig, 1899	for collective qt 'Les vendredis'; collab. Glazunov, Artsibushev, Sokolov, Lyadov, Vitols, Osten-Sacken, Blumenfeld, Borodin and Kopilov	27

PIANO
(all for solo pf unless otherwise stated)

4, 6, 25

op.	Title	Composed	Published	Remarks	RK
—	Overture	1855	—	unfinished	—
—	Allegro, d	1859–60	—		—
—	Variations on a Russian theme	1859–60	—		—
—	Nocturne, d	1860	—		—
—	Funeral march, d	1860	—		—
17	Scherzo, c, pf 4 hands	1875	St Petersburg, c1875		7
—	6 fugues, d, F, C, E, A, e	1875	Moscow, 1951		—
—	4-pt. fugue, C	1875	Moscow, 1951	arr. pf 4 hands 1875	49a
—	3 4-pt. fugues, C, e, g	1875	Moscow, 1951	nos.2 and 3 are double fugues; no.3 on B-A-C-H	49a
—	6 3-pt. fugues, G, F, E, A, d, D	1875	Moscow, 1951		49a
—	3 fughettas on Russian themes: 4-pt., g; 4-pt., d; 3-pt., g	1875	Moscow, 1951		49a
15	? …ige, Romance, Fugue	1875–6	St Petersburg, c1880		49a

18, 25

op.	Title	English version	Composed	Published	Remarks	
11	4 pieces: Impromptu, Novellette, Scherzino, Etude		1876–7	St Petersburg, 1878		49a
10	6 variations on B–A–C–H: Valse, Intermezzo, Scherzo, Nocturne, Prelude, Fugue		1878	St Petersburg, 1878		49a
—	Chopsticks paraphrases		1878	St Petersburg, 1880	Variations nos.1, 2, 6, 11–13, 16, 19 and Berceuse, Fughetta on B–A–C–H, Tarantella, Minuet, Carillon and Grotesque March; remainder by Borodin, Cui, Lyadov, Liszt and Shcherbachev	49a
—	V tserkvi [In church], pf 4 hands		1879	Moscow, 1966	arr. of last movt of str qt, 1878–9	49b
—	Variations on a theme by Misha, pf 4 hands		?1878–9	Moscow, 1959	theme by Rimsky-Korsakov's eldest son, Mikhail	49a
—	Shutka kadril' [Joke quadrille]		1885	Leipzig, 1891	figure 6 (finale) only; remainder by Artsibushev, Vitols, Lyadov, Sokolov and Glazunov	49a
—	String quartet 'B-la-F', arr. pf 4 hands		1886	Moscow, 1966	1st movt only	49b
38	Prelude-impromptu, Mazurka		1894	St Petersburg, 1896	for Bessel's 25th jubilee album, collab. Artsibushev, Cui, Glazunov, Lyadov and Sokolov	49a
—	Allegretto, C		1895	Moscow, 1959		49a
—	Prelude, G		1896	Moscow, 1959		49a
—	Fugal intermezzo, pf 4 hands		1897	—	intended for Motsart i Sal'yeri	—
—	Variation no.1, A		1899	Leipzig, 1900	for Variations on a Russian theme, collab. Winkler, Blumenfeld, Sokolov, Vitols, Lyadov, Glazunov	49a
—	Pesenka [Song]		1901	St Petersburg, 1903	in the Dorian mode: melody later included as no.3 in Armenian collection Artsunker [Tears] (St Petersburg, 1907)	49a

SONGS

(unless otherwise stated, for 1v, pf acc. and in RK 45)

op.	Title	English version	Text	Composed	Published	Remarks
—	Babochka, duet	The butterfly	anon.	1855	—	not in RK
—	Vikhodi ko mne, signora	Come out to me, signora	anon.	1861	—	not in RK
—	V krovi gorit	My blood burns	Pushkin	1865	—	not in RK

37

op.	Title	English version	Text	Composed	Published	Remarks	
2	4 songs:				St Petersburg, 1866		4
	1 Shchekoyu k shcheke ti moyey prilozhis'	Lean thy cheek to mine	Heine, trans. M. Mikhaylov	1865			
	2 Plenivshis' rozoy, solovey	Enslaved by the rose, the nightingale	A. Kol'tsov	1866			
	3 Bayu, bayushki, bayu	Lullaby	L. Mey	1866		later used in 2nd version of Pskovityanka and in Boyarïnya Vera Sheloga	
	4 Iz slyoz moikh	From my tears	Heine, trans. Mikhaylov	1866			
3	4 songs:				St Petersburg, 1866		4
	1 El' i pal'ma	The pine and the palm	Heine, trans. Mikhaylov	1866		orchd 1888 (Leipzig, 1891), RK 23	
	2 Yuzhnaya noch'	Southern night	N. Shcherbina				
	3 Nochevala tuchka zolotaya	The golden cloud had slept	Lermontov				
	4 Na kholmakh Gruzii	On the hills of Georgia	Pushkin	1866			
4	4 songs:				St Petersburg, 1866		4
	1 Chto v imeni tebe moyem?	What is my name to thee?	Pushkin				
	2 Gonets	The messenger	Heine, trans. Mikhaylov				
	3 V temnoy roshche zamolk solovey	In the dark grove the nightingale is silent	I. Nikitin			nos.3 and 4 orchd 1891 (Moscow, 1922), RK 23	
	4 Tikho vecher dogorayet	Quietly evening falls	A. Fet	1867	St Petersburg, 1867		
7	4 songs:						
	1 Moy golos dlya tebya i laskovïy, i tomnïy	My voice for thee is sweet and languid	Pushkin			orig. op.5	
	2 Evreyskaya pesnya	Hebrew song	Mey				
	3 Switezianka	Switezianka	Mickiewicz, trans. Mey			later used in the choral setting, op.44	

op.	Title	English version	Text	Composed	Published	Remarks
	3 Na nivï zheltïye niskhodit tishina	Silence descends on the golden cornfields				
	4 Usni, pechal'nïy drug	Sleep, my poor friend				
40	4 songs:			1897	Leipzig, 1897	
	1 Kogda volnuyetsya zhelteyushchaya niva	When the golden cornfield waves	Lermontov			
	2 Po nebu polunochi	Across the midnight sky	Lermontov			
	3 O chem v tishi nochey	Of what I dream in the quiet night	A. Maykov			
	4 Ya v grote zhdal tebya v urochnïy chas	I waited for thee in the grotto at the appointed hour	Maykov			
41	4 songs:			1897	Leipzig, 1897	
	1 Nespyashchikh solntse	Sun of the sleepless	A. K. Tolstoy, after Byron			
	2 Mne grustno	I am unhappy	Lermontov			
	3 Lyublyu tebya, mesyats	I love thee, moon	Maykov			
	4 Posmotri v svoy vertograd	Look in thy garden	Maykov			
42	4 songs:			1897	Leipzig, ?1897	
	1 Shopot, robkoye dïkhan'ye	A whisper, a gentle breath	Fet			
	2 Ya prishol k tebe s privetom	I have come to greet thee	Fet			
	3 Redeyet oblakov letuchaya gryada	The clouds begin to scatter	Pushkin			
	4 Moya balovnitsa	My spoiled darling	Mickiewicz, trans. Mey			
43	Vesnoy [In spring]:			1897	Leipzig, 1898	
	1 Zvonche zhavoronka pen'ye	The lark sings louder	A. K. Tolstoy			
	2 Ne veter, veya s vïsotï	Not the wind, blowing from the heights	A. K. Tolstoy			
	3 Svezh i dushist tvoy roskoshnïy venok	Cool and fragrant is thy garland	Fet			
	4 Ta kto razosu	Early spring	A. K. Tolstoy			

45	Poetu [To the poet]:				Leipzig, 1898 [1899]	
	1 Ekho	The echo	Pushkin	1897		
	2 Iskusstvo	Art	Maykov	1897		
	3 Oktava	The octave	Maykov	1897		
	4 Somneniye	Doubt	Maykov	1897		
	5 Poet	The poet	Pushkin	1899		
46	U morya [By the sea]:				Leipzig, 1898	
	1 Drobitsya, i pleshchet, i brizzhet volna	The wave breaks into spray	A. K. Tolstoy	1897		
	2 Ne penitsya more	Not a sound from the sea				
	3 Kolishetrya more	The sea is tossing				
	4 Ne ver' mne, drug	Do not believe me, friend				
	5 Vzdimayutsya volni	The waves rise up like mountains				
47	2 duets, Mez, Bar, or S, T:			1897	Leipzig, 1898	in RK 46a; orchd 1905 (Leipzig, 1906), RK 46a
	1 Pan	Pan	Maykov			
	2 Pesnya pesen	The song of songs	Mey			
49	2 songs, B:		Pushkin		Leipzig, 1898	
	1 Anchar	The upas tree		1882		rev. 1897; orchd 1906 (Leipzig, 1907), RK 23
	2 Prorok	The prophet		1897		orchd, with male vv ad lib, 1899 (Leipzig, 1899), RK 23
50	4 songs:		Maykov, after modern Greek poems		Leipzig, 1898	
	1 Deva i solntse	The maiden and the sun		1897		
	2 Pevets	The singer		1897		
	3 Tikho more goluboye	Quiet is the blue sea		1897		
	4 Eschcho ya poln, o drug moy miliy	I am still filled, dear friend		1898		
51	5 songs:		Pushkin		Leipzig, 1898	
	1 Meditel'no vlekutsya dni moi	Slowly drag my days		1897		

op.	Title	English version	Text	Composed	Published	Remarks
	2 Ne poy, krasavitsa, pri mne	Do not sing to me, o lovely one				
	3 Tsvetok zasokhshiy	Withered flower				
	4 Krasavitsa	The beauty				
	5 Nenastniy den' potukh	The rainy day has waned				
52	2 duets:		Maykov	1897	Leipzig, 1898	in RK 46a
	1 Gorniy kluch, S, Mez, or T, Bar	The mountain spring				orchd as trio. S, Mez, A, op.52b, 1905 (Leipzig, 1906), RK 46a
	2 Angel i demon, S, Bar, or T, Mez	Angel and demon		1898		
53	Strekozï, 2 S, Mez	Dragonflies	A. K. Tolstoy	1897	Leipzig, 1898	in RK 46a; orchd, with female vv ad lib, 1897 (Leipzig, 1897 (Leipzig, 1898), RK 46a
55	4 songs, T:				Leipzig, 1898	
	1 Probuzhden'ye	Awakening	Pushkin	1897		
	2 Grechanke	To a Grecian girl	Pushkin	1898		
	3 Snovideniye	The dream	Pushkin	1898		
	4 Ya umer ot schast'ya	I died from happiness	L. Uhland, trans. ?Zhukovsky	1898		
56	2 songs, S:		Maykov	1898	Leipzig, 1899	
	1 Nimfa	The nymph				orchd 1905 (Leipzig, 1908), RK 23
	2 Son v letnyuyu noch'	Summer night's dream				orchd 1906, ?unpubd, lost

FOLKSONG COLLECTIONS

op.	Title	Translation	Compiled	Published	Remarks	RK
	40 narodnïkh pesen	40 folksongs	1875	Moscow, 1882	collab. T. I. Filippov	47
24	Sbornik 100 russkikh narodnïkh pesen	Collection of 100 Russian folksongs	1875-6	St Petersburg, 1877	—	47

WORK ON COMPOSITIONS BY OTHERS

Schubert: March for the Coronation of Nicholas I, orchd 1868 — 10
Cui: 1st number of William Ratcliff, orchd 1868 — 5
Dargomïzhsky: The Stone Guest, orchd 1869; 1st scene reorchd c1900, remainder reorchd and some passages rewritten 1902 — 5, 6
Dargomïzhsky: Chorus of Maidens from Rogdana, orchd ?1873
Musorgsky: 2nd version of trio of Destruction of Sennacherib, orchd 1874; complete work orchd later
Handel: seven numbers from Samson, orchd 1875-6 — 7
Glinka: music for stage band in Ruslan and Lyudmila, 1878
Borodin: final chorus of Prince Igor, orchd 1879; prol and Act 1 scene i, rev. 1885; whole opera completed and orchd with Glazunov, 1887-8 — 11, 12
Musorgsky: Persian dances from Khovanshchina, ed. and orchd 1879; whole opera rewritten, completed and orchd 1881-3 — 10
Musorgsky: miscellaneous orch and choral works, songs etc, ed. and orchd, 1881-3 — 10
Musorgsky: Dream Intermezzo from Sorochintsy Fair, rewritten and rescored for orch only as Night on the Bare Mountain, 1886 — 10
Glinka: excerpts from operas, arr. str qt 1884
Borodin: Nocturne from String Quartet no.2, arr. vn, orch 1887
Musorgsky: Polonaise from Boris Godunov, reorchd 1888; Coronation Scene, reorchd 1892; whole opera cut, rewritten and reorchd 1892-6; — 17, 18, 22
  rewritten and reorchd with cuts restored 1906; two passages composed for the Coronation Scenes from Dyagilev's Paris production, 1907
Borodin: finale to Act 4 of collective Mlada, orchd 1890 — 13
Borodin: song The Sleeping Princess, orchd 1397
Borodin: song The Sea, orchd 1906
Musorgsky: The Marriage, rev. and partly orchd 1906
Musorgsky: songs Hopak, Gathering Mushrooms and Peasant Lullaby, orchd 1906
Musorgsky: song With Nurse, 'free musical rendering' 1908
Musorgsky: songs Night and The Field Marshal and pt. of Serenade, orchd 1908

TRANSCRIPTIONS FOR MILITARY BAND (1873-83)

Meyerbeer: Coronation March from Le prophète
Meyerbeer: Isabella's aria from Robert le diable, cl, military band
Meyerbeer: Conspiracy Scene from Les Huguenots
L. de Meyer: Berlioz's version of Marche marocaine
Schubert: March, b
Wagner: Prelude to Lohengrin
Mendelssohn: Nocturne and Wedding March from Midsummer Night's Dream
Beethoven: Overture Egmont

43

WRITINGS

Edition: *Polnoye sobraniye sochineniy: literaturnïye proizvedeniya i perepiska* [Complete edition of compositions: literary works and correspondence] (Moscow, 1955–) [RKL] — 14, 27

Uchebnik garmonii [Textbook of harmony] (St Petersburg, 1884–5, 2/1886 as *Prakticheskiy uchebnik garmonii*, 19/1949; Ger. trans., 1895; Fr. trans., 1910), RKL, iv, ed. V. V. Protopopov (Moscow, 1960), 7–387 — 12

Letopis' moyey muzïkal'noy zhizni [Chronicle of my musical life] (St Petersburg, 1909; Fr. trans., 1914; Eng. trans., 1924; enlarged 3/1926; Eng. trans., 1942/R1974), RKL, i, ed. A. V. Ossovsky and V. N. Rimskaya-Korsakov (Moscow, 1955), 3–236 — 1, 12, 21, 22

ed. N. Rimsky-Korsakov: *Muzïkal'nïye stat'i i zametki 1869–1907* [Articles and notes on music 1869–1907] (St Petersburg, 1911)

ed. M. O. Shteynberg: *Osnovï orkestrovki* [Principles of orchestration] (St Petersburg, 1913, 2/1946; Fr. trans., 1914; Ger. trans., 1922; Eng. trans., 1922, 2/1964), RKL, iii, ed. A. N. Dmitriyev (Moscow, 1959) — 6–7, 21

ed. A. V. Ossovsky and V. N. Rimsky-Korsakov: *Dnevnik 1904–7* [Diary 1904–7; fragments only], RKL, i (Moscow, 1955), 237ff

ed. V. V. Protopopov: *Razbor Snegurochka* [An analysis of *Snow Maiden*], RKL, iv (Moscow, 1960), 381–426

ed. N. V. Shelkov: *Muzïkal'no-kriticheskiye stat'i* [Critical articles on music], RKL, ii (Moscow, 1963), 11–44

—: *Stat'i i materialï po voprosam istorii muzïki i estetiki* [Articles and materials on the history of music and aesthetics], RKL, ii (Moscow, 1963), 45ff

—: *Vïstupleniya v pechati* [Miscellaneous articles and letters], RKL, ii (Moscow, 1963), 235ff

BIBLIOGRAPHY

(*RKL – see edn. of writings*)

N. Findeyzen: *Nikolay Andreyevich Rimsky-Korsakov: ocherk evo muzïkal'noy deyatel'nosti* [Outline of his musical career] (St Petersburg, 1908)

V. V. Yastrebtsev: *Nikolay Andreyevich Rimsky-Korsakov: ocherk evo zhizni i deyatel'nosti* [Outline of his life and career] (Moscow, 1908)

N. Sokolov: *Vospominaniya o N. A. Rimskom-Korsakove* [Memories of Rimsky-Korsakov] (St Petersburg, 1909)

I. I. Lapshin: *Filosofskiye motivï v tvorchestve N. A. Rimskovo-Korsakova* [Philosophical motives in Rimsky-Korsakov's works] (St Petersburg, 1911)

V. V. Yastrebtsev: *Moi vospominaniya o Nikolaye Andreyeviche Rimskom-Korsakove* [My reminiscences of Rimsky-Korsakov] (Moscow, 1917) [incomplete; see Yastrebtsev (1959–60)]

N. van Gilse Van der Pals: *N. A. Rimsky-Korssakow: Opernschaffen nebst Skizzen über Leben und Wirken* (Paris and Leipzig, 1929)

A. N. Rimsky-Korsakov: *N. A. Rimsky-Korsakov: zhizn' i tvorchestvo* [Life and works] (Moscow, 1933–46)

I. Markévitch: *Rimsky-Korsakov* (Paris, 1934)

G. Abraham: 'Rimsky-Korsakov's First Opera', 'Rimsky-Korsakov's Gogol Operas', 'Snow Maiden', 'Sadko', 'The Tsar's Bride', 'Kitezh', 'The Golden Cockerel', *Studies in Russian Music* (London, 1935), 142–310

——: 'Rimsky-Korsakov's *Mlada* and *Tsar Saltan*', *On Russian Music* (London, 1939), 113

B. V. Asaf'yev: *Nikolay Andreyevich Rimsky-Korsakov (1844–1944)* (Moscow and Leningrad, 1944)

G. Abraham: *Rimsky-Korsakov: a Short Biography* (London, 1945)

M. O. Yankovsky: *Rimsky-Korsakov i revolyutsiya 1905 goda* [Rimsky-Korsakov and the 1905 revolution] (Moscow and Leningrad, 1950)

V. A. Kiselyov, ed.: *N. A. Rimsky-Korsakov: sbornik dokumentov* [Collection of documents] (Moscow and Leningrad, 1951)

V. V. Stasov: *Stat'i o Rimskom-Korsakove* [Articles on Rimsky-Korsakov], ed. V. A. Kiselyov (Moscow, 1953)

I. F. Belza: *Motsart i Sal'yeri, tragediya Pushkina: dramaticheskiye stsenï Rimskovo-Korsakova* [Mozart and Salieri, Pushkin's tragedy: Rimsky-Korsakov's dramatic scenes] (Moscow, 1953)

A. A. Solovtsov: *Simfonicheskiye proizvedeniya Rimskovo-Korsakova* [Rimsky-Korsakov's symphonic works] (Moscow, 1953)

M. O. Yankovsky and others, eds.: *Rimsky-Korsakov: issledovaniya, materialï, pis'ma* [Research, materials, letters] (Moscow, 1953–4)

M. F. Gnesin: *Mislï i vospominaniya o N. A. Rimskom-Korsakove* [Thoughts and reminiscences about Rimsky-Korsakov] (Moscow, 1956)

A. A. Gozenpud: *N. A. Rimsky-Korsakov: temï i idei evo opernovo tvorchestva* [The themes and ideas in his operas] (Moscow, 1957)

V. A. Kiselyov, ed.: *Avtografï N. A. Rimskovo-Korsakova v fondakh gosudarstvennovo tsentral'novo muzeya muzïkal'noy kul'turï imeni M. I. Glinki: katalogspravochnik* [Rimsky-Korsakov's autographs in the collection of the State Central Glinka Museum of Musical Culture: a reference catalogue] (Moscow, 1958)

S. L. Ginzburg, ed.: *N. A. Rimsky-Korsakov i muzïkal'noye obrazovaniye* [Rimsky-Korsakov and musical education] (Leningrad, 1959)

V. V. Yastrebtsev: *Nikolay Andreyevich Rimsky-Korsakov: vospominaniya* [Reminiscences], ed. A. V. Ossovsky (Leningrad, 1959–60)

L. Danilevich: *Posledniye operï N. A. Rimskovo-Korsakova* [Rimsky-Korsakov's last operas] (Moscow, 1961)

Yu. A. Kremlyov: *Estetika prirodï v tvorchestve N. A. Rimskovo-Korsakova* [The aesthetics of nature in the works of Rimsky-Korsakov] (Moscow, 1962)

A. S. Lyapunova, ed.: *Perepiska N. A. Rimskovo-Korsakova* [Rimsky-Korsakov's correspondence, with Balakirev (1862–98), Borodin (1871–86), Cui (1862–1908), Musorgsky (1867–80), V. V. Stasov (1869–1906), D. V. Stasov (1866–1907), V. V. Vasil'yev (1870–72) and L. I. Shestakova (1878–89)], RKL, v (Moscow, 1963)

N. V. Shelkov, ed.: *Dokumentï i materialï, svyazannïye s deyatel'nost'yu v orkestrakh voyenno-morskovo flota* [Documents and materials in connection with Rimsky-Korsakov's activities in the naval military bands], RKL, ii (Moscow, 1963), 73–127

——: *Materialï, svyazannïye s deyatel'nost'yu v pridvornoy pevcheskoy kapelle* [Materials in connection with Rimsky-Korsakov's activities in the imperial chapel choir], RKL, ii (Moscow, 1963), 129–68

——: *Materialï, svyazannïye s deyatel'nost'yu v Peterburgskoy konservatorii* [Materials in connection with Rimsky-Korsakov's activities at the St Petersburg Conservatory], RKL, ii (Moscow, 1963), 169–222

——: *Materialï, svyazannïye s deyatel'nost'yu v Russkom muzïkal'nom obshchestve i v kachestve uchreditelya vïsshikh muzïkal'nïkh kursov* [Materials in connection with Rimsky-Korsakov's activities in the Russian Musical Society and in his role as the founder of higher education courses in music], RKL, ii (Moscow, 1963), 223ff

A. Solovtsov: *Zhizn' i tvorchestvo N. A. Rimskovo-Korsakova* [Life and works] (Moscow, 1964)

E. E. Yazovitskaya, ed.: *Perepiska N. A. Rimskovo-Korsakova* [Rimsky-Korsakov's correspondence, with Lyadov (1878–1908) and Glazunov (1882–1908)], RKL, vi (Moscow, 1965)

G. Abraham: '*Pskovityanka*: the Original Version of Rimsky-Korsakov's First Opera', *MQ*, liv (1968), 58; repr. in *Essays on Russian and East European Music* (Oxford, 1984)

Bibliography

——: 'Rimsky-Korsakov as Self-critic', 'Rimsky-Korsakov's Songs', *Slavonic and Romantic Music* (London, 1968), 195

S. Feinberg: 'Rimsky-Korsakov's Suite from *Le coq d'or*', *MR*, xxx (1969), 47

E. Garden: 'Classic and Romantic in Russian Music', *ML*, 1 (1969), 153

A. Orlova and V. Rimsky-Korsakov, eds.: *Stranitsï zhizni Rimskovo-Korsakova* [Pages from Rimsky-Korsakov's life] (Leningrad, 1969)

S. Slonimsky: 'Die lebendige, moderne Kunst Rimski-Korsakovs', *Kunst und Literatur*, xvii (1969), 1307

S. Evseyev: *Rimsky-Korsakov i russkaya narodnaya pesnya* [Rimsky-Korsakov and Russian folksong] (Moscow, 1970)

G. Abraham: 'Satire and Symbolism in *The Golden Cockerel*', *ML*, lii (1971), 46; repr. in *Essays on Russian and East European Music* (Oxford, 1984)

M. Smirnov: *Fortepiannïye proizvedeniya kompozitorov moguchey kuchki* [The piano works of the composers of the Mighty Handful] (Moscow, 1971)

G. Abraham: 'Arab Melodies in Rimsky-Korsakov and Borodin', *ML*, lvi (1975), 313; repr. in *Essays on Russian and East European Music* (Oxford, 1984)

E. Garden: 'Three Russian Piano Concertos', *ML*, lx (1979), 166

I. F. Kunin: *Nikolay Andreevich Rimskiy-Korsakov* (Moscow, 1979)

R. C. Ridenour: *Nationalism, Modernism and Personal Rivalry in Nineteenth-century Russian Music* (Ann Arbor, 1981)

G. Norris: 'An Opera Restored: Rimsky-Korsakov, Shostakovich and the Khovansky Business', *MT*, cxxiii (1982), 672

ALEXANDER SKRYABIN

Hugh Macdonald

CHAPTER ONE

Life

Alexander Nikolayevich Skryabin was born in Moscow
on 6 January 1872. He came from an aristocratic
family with military and patriarchal leanings. His father
Nikolay Alexandrovich had broken somewhat with
family tradition by entering the legal profession, and his
mother, Lyubov Petrovna (née Shchetinina), was a
gifted pianist, a pupil of Leschetizky at the St Petersburg
Conservatory and a favourite of Anton Rubinstein.
Skryabin was the first and only child of an early marriage, and a little over a year after his birth (he later set
much store by the significance of being born on
Christmas Day, old style), his mother died of consump-
tion. His father spent the rest of his life abroad in the
Russian consular service, mostly in Turkey, and died in
1914, so Skryabin was brought up by his aunt Lyubov,
his grandmother and his great-aunt, all of whom doted
passionately on the boy, pampered him endlessly and set
his mind towards the fastidiousness and egocentricity of
his later years as well as giving him a certain effeminacy
in his manners. Skryabin never grew to more than
diminutive height and, though he soon showed an
aptitude for the piano and eventually became a member
of the great generation of Russian pianists that included
Rakhmaninov, Lhévinne and Metner, his hand could
never comfortably stretch more than an octave.

His early fondness for music and for the mechanics of

the piano was nourished by his aunt, and in 1882 he joined the Moscow cadet corps where he remained until 1887. When he was 11 he had lessons with Georgy Konyus, himself only 21, and in 1884, on the recommendation of Taneyev, he joined Zverev's class, where Rakhmaninov was a fellow pupil. The two men remained friends despite later attempts in the Russian press to fan a rivalry between them. From 1885 Skryabin studied theory with Taneyev himself, then director of the Moscow Conservatory, and began to compose. He compiled a list of orchestral and piano works from these years (very few of the pieces have survived) and he also wrote poetry. In 1888, still attended hand and mouth by his devoted aunt, he entered the Moscow Conservatory, where he continued theory lessons with Taneyev and later Arensky, and studied the piano with Safonov, who succeeded Taneyev as director in 1889. Safonov and Taneyev became champions of Skryabin as pianist and composer, though Arensky clearly took a more doubtful view. In 1892 Skryabin left the conservatory with the second gold medal (Rakhmaninov won the first) and embarked on a career as concert pianist. The previous year he had damaged his right hand practising Balakirev's *Islamey* and Liszt's *Réminiscences de Don Juan* (which he nevertheless performed the following year) and devoted more attention to cultivating his left-hand technique, one fruit of which may be seen in the left-hand pieces op.9. While his concert programmes included works by Bach, Mendelssohn, Schumann and Liszt, his strongest leaning at this time was to the music of Chopin, the predominant influence over his earlier music both in style and in the titles of works.

Life

In 1893 five works, opp.1, 2, 3, 5 and 7, were published by Jürgenson in Moscow, but a year later Skryabin was introduced by Safonov to the St Petersburg patron and publisher Belyayev, who thenceforth took complete control of Skryabin's musical affairs until his death in 1903; the firm remained Skryabin's publisher until 1908. Belyayev started by issuing the First Sonata and the *Douze études* op.8, organized Skryabin's tours, paid him generously for his compositions, gave him presents, lent him money and seemingly took over the role of doting parent previously enacted by his aunt. In 1895 Belyayev sent Skryabin on a tour of Germany, Switzerland, Italy and Belgium, and a second tour, this time of Paris, Brussels, Berlin, Amsterdam, The Hague and Rome, followed soon after in 1896. During both tours Skryabin was composing intently. The Preludes opp.11, 13, 15, 16 and 17 date mainly from this period as do the Second Sonata, the Symphonic Poem and other works; on his return to Moscow in the autumn of 1896 he composed the Piano Concerto op.20. He became engaged to a young pianist, Vera Ivanovna Isaakovich, a conservatory gold medallist and a devoted admirer of Skryabin and his music, and despite aunt Lyubov's not unexpected resistance they were married in August 1897. They left for Odessa, where Skryabin gave the first performance of the Piano Concerto, and then moved to Paris for five months, where he worked principally on the Third Sonata. In 1898, at Safonov's invitation, Skryabin joined the staff of the Moscow Conservatory and, although he found the duties gradually more burdensome, he continued to compose. He turned more to orchestral music with the brief *Rêverie* in 1898 and the

4. Alexander Skryabin in about 1914

First Symphony in 1899, laid out in six movements with a choral finale, a setting of his own words in praise of art.

1901 was devoted to the Second Symphony, and from 1902 an increasing preoccupation with philosophical and mystical ideas precipitated a radical change in his thinking, his life and his music. The works from op.30 to *Le divin poème* op.43 (his Third Symphony) represented an intensive flowering of a more individual manner, and the high productivity of 1903 sprang from this discovery of a more personal idiom, the need for money to free himself from the conservatory (which he left in 1903) and his study of philosophy, especially that of Nietzsche. He planned a 'philosophical opera', probably the seed of the long-meditated but never written *Mysterium*. The new direction was shown too in his personal life: he left Russia for what was to be six years spent in Italy, Switzerland and Brussels, and abandoned Vera and their four children for a young admirer, Tatyana Schloezer, niece of Paul Schloezer, who as piano professor at the Moscow Conservatory had encouraged Skryabin's studies and presided over Vera's. Tatyana's devotion to Skryabin stimulated his music and served to narrow his outlook ever more consumingly into an egocentric world where his own creativity and genius became his exclusive concern. In 1905 he encountered the theosophical teaching of Madame Blavatsky and this quickly superseded Nietzschean philosophy as his primary reading. He filled notebooks with philosophical, mostly disjointed, jottings, and a lengthier poem, *Poema extaza* ('The poem of ecstasy'), became the basis of his next orchestral work as well as of the Fifth Sonata. In the piano pieces op.44 to op.57

he advanced into a new style, most powerfully represented in the single-movement *Le poème de l'extase* for orchestra, completed in 1908 and first performed that year in New York; Skryabin had appeared there himself two years previously in a series of recitals.

In 1908 Skryabin met Koussevitzky, who took charge of his affairs in a manner similar to that of Belyayev previously, acting as concert manager and publisher. He induced Skryabin to return to Russia, where performances of *Le poème de l'extase* in both Moscow and St Petersburg generated extraordinary fervour and put him firmly in the forefront of contemporary composers. Returning to Brussels he began work on *Prométhée*, his last orchestral work, which embraced the play of coloured light in the score as a preliminary step towards the fusion of the arts and senses which was to have been realized in the *Mysterium*. After *Prométhée* was completed, in 1910 (it was first played in 1911, in Moscow, but without the colour part), Skryabin concentrated once more on piano music. The works of the remaining years, from op.58 onwards, embody a refining and perfecting of his mature idiom, seen most clearly in the last five piano sonatas, each in one movement; the very last works press even further into the van of modernism, leaving tonality well behind and preparing the ground for the still unwritten *Mysterium*. (For its preliminary part, the *Acte préalable*, he had written the text and a considerable body of musical sketches at his death.) In these last years he continued to travel widely, giving recitals and tasting with satisfaction the universal success of his orchestral works in the years before World War I. He visited London in 1914 and there first suffered from a boil on his upper lip which eventually

turned into a septic carbuncle. Early in 1915 he gave three recitals in Petrograd, but he had to undergo a series of operations, which nonetheless failed to stem the septicaemia from which he died, in Moscow, on 27 April 1915.

CHAPTER TWO

Works

There is clearly a close relationship between the ego-
mania of Skryabin's personality and the singularly
direct development of his music from the derivative,
charming style of his youth to the powerfully progressive works of his last years; but the weaknesses of his
character – his capacity for self-delusion, his overbear-
ing demands on others and his undisguised conceit – are
not to be imputed as weaknesses of his music too. The
characteristics of a spoilt child were the result of his
unusual upbringing, and his compulsive interest in
theosophy and mysticism was shared by many at that
time, especially in Russia (it was peculiarly Russian to
embrace this interest with uncompromising zeal). Skryabin believed in the coming regeneration of the world
through a cataclysmic event; the new Nirvana would
spring from his own Promethean creativity and combine
all the arts and appeal to all the senses in a grand
synthesis. To this end he spent 12 years planning and
discussing the *Mysterium* and its ultimate performance
in an Indian temple. He even welcomed the outbreak of
war in 1914 as an initial step towards cosmic regeneration.

His interest in the synaesthesia of colour and music
sprang from discussions with Rimsky-Korsakov in
1907, when they found they both experienced (different)
associations of notes and colours; Skryabin's linking of

notes and colours was subjective rather than scientific. He also worked closely with Alexander Mozer, who devised a colour organ – such ideas were widely cultivated at the time. The languorous, harmonic feeling of Skryabin's music is strongly suggestive of slowly shifting colours. Music so patently sensuous and yet daringly modern suffered the inevitable reverse of fortune in the 1920s, when later Romantic styles were discredited, and more bracing, rhythmic mannerisms won favour. Stravinsky, who scorned Skryabin and his music, personified the new spirit, and the extraordinary decline of Skryabin's reputation between the wars cast works that were once the height of fashion and favour into the shade. Latterly a more unbiassed study of Skryabin has made possible a fairer appreciation of his achievement, assisted by the contemporary delight in all visual media in association with music.

The achievement of Skryabin in forging a powerful personal style out of his musical background is not to be belittled, and the rapidity of his development was exceptional. He cannot be linked directly to composers of the Russian school, although he admired their music and learnt much from them. Apart from the strong influence of Chopin, which confined him almost exclusively to piano music, the clearest characteristics of his early music are the compound metres, triple units and remote key signatures. These are already evident in the E♭ minor piano sonata of 1887–9, the first movement of which was published as the *Allegro appassionato* op.4. Chopin's example lies behind the series of preludes, impromptus, mazurkas and etudes from his early years. Skryabin's 24 Preludes op.11 reproduce the key sequence of Chopin's 24 Preludes op.28 exactly, and the

subsequent groups (opp.13, 15, 16 and 17) show signs of being planned as a second set of the same design. The character of his early music ranges from the abrupt violence of some of the minor-key Preludes to the lyrical and harmonic warmth of the third movement of the Third Sonata. He also contributed to the repertory of leonine piano music with the First Sonata, the Concert Allegro op.18, the Polonaise op.21 and the Fantaisie op.28, all demanding a massive concert technique. In his early music there are echoes also of Liszt, Wagner and Franck, more easily observed in his orchestral works, particularly the first two symphonies.

The years 1902 to 1904, dominated by the composition of the Third Symphony ('Le divin poème'), show a marked development in style, reflecting the change in his public and private life. His new preoccupation with the philosophical and mystical significance of his music is revealed in his titles (often 'poème') and in the fanciful directions (mostly in Italian, later in French) scattered throughout the music. He also began to exploit more advanced harmonies and worked out a style in which the sense of pulse is yet further weakened, the harmonic rhythm is slowed and the fundamental ambiguity of the tritone begins to dominate his harmonic vocabulary. There are traces of 4th-based and whole-tone harmony in his early works (even in op.1 the germ of the later direction can be detected), but the Fourth Sonata shows a new inclination towards 4th-based harmony and an unease about traditional tonal forces. Full cadences begin to sound out of place as chromaticism becomes more prevalent, but it was not until 1906 (the *Enigme* op.52 no.2) that he concluded a piece on any chord other than the tonic. His most thorough-going advance

in harmony played on the ambivalence of the dominant 7th with its 5th flattened (or its 11th sharpened). His music became reluctant to make firm tonal progressions; his bass notes tended to move through a tritone leaving the upper harmony unaltered, or through a 5th without resolving the upper dominant harmony. Final cadences became more infrequent and delayed, and the tonal sense, though not abandoned until *Prométhée*, became blurred. The effect is to suspend the listener's sense of time, for the harmony loses its conventional progressive tonal function and becomes an entity in its own right, independent of what precedes or follows it; the dissolving rhythms, for all the fluttering and agitation that enliven the music, also suspend the music in time.

The *Poème satanique* op.36 (for piano) and the *Divin poème* (the Third Symphony, for orchestra) display a wealth of intricate detail as well as some sharply modern features. The symphony is uninhibitedly romantic in expression but subject to tight thematic organization, and in all his later music he sought to reduce its external dimensions in pursuit of concentration of thought and argument. The Fifth Sonata thus runs in a single movement and *Le poème de l'extase* is also in a single movement, more symphonic poem than symphony, heightening its intense emotional expression. The poem of the same name to which it is loosely related recounts the spirit's search for ecstasy, with themes symbolizing longing, aspiration, victory and so forth; the music alternates between erotic languor and triumphant clamour.

Skryabin's last works, from 1910 to 1915, are constructed from harmonic elements rather than themes,

5. *Autograph score from Skryabin's 'Prométhée', composed 1908–10*

usually variants of the so-called 'mystic' chord, which has the basic form shown in ex.1, though it is rarely presented in this elemental state. The dissolution of a

Ex.1

sense of time inevitably led to condensed forms. The early sonatas and symphonies use sonata form and cyclic procedures in conventional fashion, but the last six sonatas, *Le poème de l'extase* and *Prométhée*, being each conceived as single movements, rely less on thematic structure than on patterns of mood and harmonic and textural intensity. At a time when most composers were writing on ever larger canvases, Skryabin composed entirely in single movements, often in aphorisms such as the intensely concentrated final Preludes op.74. But he had always been a miniaturist, producing his best effects in the briefest span (see, for example, many of the Preludes op.11), and one of the most endearing features of the 1896 Piano Concerto is its lack of bombast. The First Symphony, with its tendency to inflation, is correspondingly the weakest of his major works.

The last five piano sonatas belong together as a group; the last three of them were composed and completed all at once, in the summer of 1913. All are in one movement and use advanced tritonal harmony, and all explore the three-note shape of minor and major 3rds (usually a falling minor 3rd followed by a rising major 3rd) which had already played an important part in

Prométhée. The Sixth, Seventh and Eighth have fundamental chords as building blocks. The Ninth has the character of extreme desolation and concentration, and the Tenth shows, in among much fluttering and brilliance, elements of chromaticism explored still further in some of the last works: the Prelude op.67 no.1, the *Poème* op.71 no.1, *Guirlandes* op.73 no.1 and especially the five Preludes op.74. These point towards an advanced atonal language which Skryabin did not live to explore.

In one sphere, that of orchestration, he was unrestrained, calling for immense forces for both *Le poème de l'extase* and *Prométhée* (though he rarely used any percussion). His consummate skill as an orchestrator is generally undervalued, for he brought to life the fluttering, volatile figures that permeate his piano textures, as well as catching the sensuous flavour of lush, complex harmony. His piano playing was noted for its freedom and unpredictability and also for a refined pedalling; despite the hand injury and his small stretch, he clearly possessed an impressive Lisztian technique.

Skryabin had few pupils and never contemplated the continuance of his own musical language without himself. Some composers, like Prokofiev, Szymanowski and Bridge, came briefly under his spell, and some cranks, like Obukhov, inherited his Messianic follies. The composer closest to Skryabin's blend of the sensuous and the mystic is undoubtedly Messiaen, which perhaps serves to emphasize the strong French element in Skryabin's make-up. On the broad canvas, Skryabin can be seen as a truly visionary composer who initiated a new musical language, as Schoenberg and Debussy were doing at much the same time, no less radical and

advanced than theirs, and like them breaking decisively with tonality. His sketches for the *Acte préalable* (1914–15) reveal him experimenting with 12-note chords, which is just one reason for supposing that, but for his early death, his standing as a major figure in 20th-century music would be all the more conspicuous.

WORKS

Numbers in right-hand margins denote references in the text.

ORCHESTRAL

op.		
20	Piano Concerto, f♯, 1896	52, 56
—	Symphonic Poem, d, 1896–7	53, 63
24	Rêverie, 1898	53
—	Andante, str, 1899, unpubd	53
26	Symphony no.1, E, with chorus in finale, 1899–1900	55, 50, 63
29	Symphony no.2, c, 1901	55, 60
43	Symphony no.3 'Le divin poème', 1902–4	55, 60, 61
54	Le poème de l'extase, 1905–8	55, 56, 61
60	Prométhée, le poème du feu, 1908–10	56, 61, 62, 63, 64

PIANO

op.		
—	Canon, 1883	52, 59
—	Nocturne, A♭, 1884	
1	Valse, f, 1885	
—	Sonate-fantaisie, 1886	53, 60
—	Valse, g♯, 1886	
—	Valse, D♭, 1886	
—	Variations on a Theme by Mlle Egorova, 1887	
2	Sonata, e♭, 1887–9	59
2	Three Pieces, 1887–9	53
—	Feuillet d'album, A♭, 1889	
3	Ten Mazurkas, 1889	53
—	Mazurka, F, ?1889	
—	Mazurka, b, ?1889	
—	Fantasy, 2 pf, ?1889	
4	Allegro appassionato [after Sonata, c♯: movt 1], 1892	59
5	Two Nocturnes, 1890	53
6	Sonata no.1, 1892	53, 60
7	Deux impromptus à la Mazur, 1892	53
8	Douze études, 1894	53
9	Two Pieces, left hand, 1894	52
10	Two Impromptus, 1894	
11	Twenty-four Preludes, 1888–96	53, 59, 60, 63
12	Two Impromptus, 1895	53, 60
13	Six Preludes, 1895	
14	Two Impromptus, 1895	53, 60
15	Five Preludes, 1895–6	53, 60
16	Five Preludes, 1894–5	53, 60
17	Seven Preludes, 1895–6	60
18	Allegro de concert, 1896	60
19	Sonata no.2 (Sonata-fantasy), 1892–7	53
21	Polonaise, 1897	60
22	Four Preludes, 1897	
23	Sonata no.3, 1897–8	53, 60
25	Nine Mazurkas, 1899	
27	Two Preludes, 1900	
28	Fantaisie, 1900	60
30	Sonata no.4, 1903	55, 60
31	Four Preludes, 1903	
32	Deux poèmes, 1903	
33	Four Preludes, 1903	
34	Poème tragique, 1903	
35	Three Preludes, 1903	
36	Poème satanique, 1903	61
37	Four Preludes, 1903	
38	Valse, 1903	
39	Four Preludes, 1903	
40	Two Mazurkas, 1902–3	
41	Poème, 1903	
42	Huit études, 1903	
44	Deux poèmes, 1905	
45	Three Pieces, 1904–5: Feuillet d'album, Poème fantasque, Prélude	55
46	Scherzo, 1905	55
47	Quasi-valse, 1905	55
48	Four Preludes, 1905	55
49	Three Pieces, 1905: Etude, Prélude, Rêverie	55
—	Feuille d'album, 1905	
51	Four Pieces, 1906: Fragilité, Prélude, Poème ailé, Danse languide	55

OTHER WORKS

Vocal: Aria, 1891, fragment of opera Keistut i Birut; Romance (Skryabin), 1894

Chamber: Romance, hn, pf, 1890; Variation II in Variations on a Russian Theme, str qt, 1899, collab. Artsibushev, Glazunov, Rimsky-Korsakov, Lyadov, Vitols, Blumenfeld, Ewald, Winkler and Sokolov

Principal publisher: Belyayev

WRITINGS   52, 55

'Autobiograficheskaya zapiska A. N. Skryabina', *RMG* (1915), nos.17–18

'Zapiski A. N. Skryabina', *Russkiye propilei*, vi (1919), 95–247

ed. V. M. Belyayev: *Perepiska A. N. Skryabina i M. P. Belyayeva 1894–1903* (Petrograd, 1922)

ed. L. Sabaneyev: *Pis'ma A. N. Skryabina* (Moscow, 1923)

Prometheische Phantasier, trans. O. Riesemann (Stuttgart, 1924, 2/1968)

ed. A. Kashperov: *Pis'ma* (Moscow, 1965)

BIBLIOGRAPHY

N. A. Rimsky-Korsakov: *Letopis' moyey muzïkal'noy zhizni* [Chronicles of my musical life] (St Petersburg, 1909; Eng. trans., 1924, enlarged 3/1926)

L. Sabaneyev: 'Prometheus von Skrjabin', *Der blaue Reiter* (Munich, 1912, 2/1965; Eng. trans., 1974)

G. H. Clutsam: 'The Harmonies of Scriabine', *MT*, liv (1913), 156, 441, 512

I. Lipayev: *A. N. Skryabin* (Moscow, 1913)

R. Newmarch: 'Scriabin and Contemporary Russian Music', *Russian Review*, ii (1913), 153

C. S. Myers: 'Two Cases of Synaesthesia', *British Journal of Psychology*, vii (1914), 112

R. Newmarch: 'Prometheus: the Poem of Fire', *MT*, lv (1914), 227

E. Gunst: *Skryabin i evo tvorchestvo* [Skryabin and his work] (Moscow, 1915)

V. G. Karatïgin: *Skryabin* (Petrograd, 1915)

R. Newmarch: 'Alexander Scriabin', *MT*, lvi (1915), 329

J. F. Runciman: 'Noises, Smells and Colours', *MQ*, i (1915), 149

MS, iv (1915); v (1916) [Skryabin nos.]

N. Cherkass: *Skryabin kak pianist i fortepiannïy kompozitor* (Petrograd, 1916)

A. E. Hull: *A Great Russian Tone-poet: Scriabin* (London, 1916, 2/1927/*R*1970)

———: 'The Pianoforte Works of Scriabin', *MT*, lvii (1916) 492, 539

———: 'Scriabin's Scientific Derivation of Harmony versus Empirical Methods', *PMA*, xliii (1916–17), 17

———: 'A Survey of the Pianoforte Works of Scriabin', *MQ*, ii (1916), 601

A. P. Koptyayev: *A. N. Skryabin* (Petrograd, 1916)

M. Montagu-Nathan: *Handbook to the Piano Works of A. Scriabin* (London, 1917, 2/1922)

B. de Schloezer: 'Scriabine', *ReM*, ii (1921), 28

I. I. Lapshin: *Zevetnïye dumï Skryabina* [Skryabin's intimate thoughts] (Petrograd, 1922)

O. Riesemann: 'Alexander Skrjabin im Lichte einer Jugendbriefe', *Die Musik*, xv (1922–3), 841

L. Sabaneyev: *A. N. Skryabin* (Moscow, 1922, 2/1923)

B. V. Asaf'yev: *Skryabin 1871–1915* (Petrograd, 1923)

B. de Schloezer: *A. Skrjabin lichnost mysteriya* [A. Skryabin, character of mystery] (Berlin, 1923)

A. J. Swan: *Scriabin* (London, 1923/*R*1969)

H. Antcliffe: 'The Significance of Scriabin', *MQ*, x (1924), 333

C. Gray: *A Survey of Contemporary Music* (London, 1924), 151ff

A. V. Lunacharsky: 'Taneyev i Skryabin', *Novïy mir* (1925), 113

Bibliography

L. Sabaneyev: *Vospominaniya o Skryabina* [Memories of Skryabin] (Moscow, 1925)

V. V. Yakovlev: *A. N. Skryabin* (Moscow, 1925)

A. Brent-Smith: 'Some Reflections on the Work of Scriabin', *MT*, lxvii (1926), 593, 692

E. von Tideböhl: 'Memories of Scriabin's Volga Tour (1910)', *MMR*, lvi (1926), 137, 168

K. Westphal: 'Die Harmonik Skrjabins', *Anbruch*, xi (1929), 64

L. Sabaneyev: 'Scriabin and the Idea of a Religious Art', *MT*, lxxii (1931), 789

M. Glinski: *Alexander Skrjabin* (Warsaw, 1934)

M. Cooper: 'Scriabin's Mystical Beliefs', *ML*, xvi (1935), 110

P. Dickenmann: *Die Entwicklung der Harmonik bei A. Skrjabin* (Berne and Leipzig, 1935)

M. Metshik: *A. Skryabin* (Moscow, 1935)

G. Abraham: *Masters of Russian Music* (London, 1936), 450–98

A. A. Al'shvang and others: *A. N. Skryabin: k 25-letiyu so dnya smerti* [On the 25th anniversary of his death] (Moscow, 1940, 2/1945)

A. Nikolayev: *Alexander Skryabin* (Moscow, 1940)

N. N. Rimskaya-Korsakova: 'Rimsky-Korsakov i Skryabin', *SovM* (1950), no.5, p.67

L. Danilevich: *A. N. Skryabin* (Moscow, 1953)

B. de Schloezer: 'A. Scriabine', *Musique russe*, ii (Paris, 1953), 229

H. Boegner: *Die Harmonik der späten Klavierwerke Skrjabins* (diss., U. of Munich, 1955)

R. H. Wood: 'Skryabin and his Critics', *MMR*, lxxxvi (1956), 222

R. H. Myers: 'Scriabin: a Reassessment', *MT*, xcviii (1957), 17

B. Pasternak: *I Remember* (New York, 1959)

Z. Lissa: 'Über die Verbindungen zwischen der Harmonik von A. N. Skriabin und der Harmonik von F. Chopin', *Chopin Congress: Warszawa 1960*, 335

D. D. Blagoy: *Etyudï Skryabina* (Moscow, 1963)

C. C. von Gleich: *Die sinfonischen Werke von Alexander Skrjabin* (Bilthoven, 1963) [incl. full bibliography]

Z. Lissa: 'Chopin i Skryabin', *Russko-polskiye muzïkalne svyazi* (Moscow, 1963), 293–374

A. A. Al'shvang: 'Die Stellung Skrjabins in der Geschichte', *BMw*, vi (1964), 143

H. Förster: *Die Form in den symphonischen Werken von Alexander N. Skrjabin* (diss., U. of Leipzig, 1964)

P. Dickinson: 'Skryabin's Later Music', *MR*, xxvi (1965), 19

M. C. Hughes: *Tonal Orientation in Skriabin's Preludes: an Analysis on the Basis of Information Theory* (diss., U. of Texas, 1965)

O. Sakhaltuyeva: *O garmoniya Skryabina* [Skryabin's harmony] (Moscow, 1965)

M. Mikhailov: *A. N. Skryabin* (Moscow, 1966)
S. Randlett: *The Nature and Development of Scriabin's Pianistic Vocabulary* (diss., Northwestern U., 1966)
B. Pasternak: 'O Skryabine i Shopen', *SovM* (1967), no.1, p.95
V. Dernova: *Garmoniya Skryabina* [Skryabin's harmony] (Leningrad, 1968)
B. Galeyev: 'Skryabin and the Evolution of the Notion of Visible Music', *Muzïka i sovremennost'*, vi (1968)
F. Bowers: *Scriabin* (Tokyo, 1969, 2/1970)
R. Dikmann: 'Alexander Skrjabin, Beschluss und Vollendung', *SMz*, cix (1969), 266
S. Pavchinsky: *Proizvedeniya Skryabin pozdnevo perioda* [The works of Skryabin's last period], (Moscow, 1969)
Ye. Nazaykinsky: 'O khudozhestvennïkh vosmozhnostyakh sinteza muzïki i tsveta' [The artistic possibilities of the synthesis of music and colour], *Muzïkalnoye iskusstvo i nauka* (Moscow, 1970)
J. Coller: *Scriabin's Progressive Attenuation of Tonal Definition* (diss., Cornell U., 1971)
V. Delson: *Skryabin* (Moscow, 1971)
M. Kelkel: 'Les esquisses musicales de l'Acte préalable de Scriabine', *RdM*, lvii (1971), 40
C. Rüger: *Ethische Konstanz und stilistische Kontinuität im Schaffen Alexander Nikolaevič Skrjabins* (diss., U. of Leipzig, 1971)
V. Belyayev: *Musorgsky, Skryabin, Stravinsky* (Moscow, 1972)
V. Bobrovsky: 'O dramaturgii Skryabinskikh sochineniy' [The dramaturgy of Skryabin's works], *SovM* (1972), no.1, pp.114–92
E. Carpenter: *Thematic Development and Continuity in the Ten Piano Sonatas of Alexander Scriabin* (diss., Kent State U., 1972)
L. Danilevich: 'Velikiy romantik' [A great romantic], *SovM* (1972), no.1, p.102
W. Evrard: *Scriabine* (Paris, 1972)
A. Forschert: 'Bemerkungen zum Schaffen Alexander Skrjabins', *Festschrift Ernst Pepping zu seinem 70. Geburtstag* (Berlin, 1972), 298
H.-L. de la Grange: 'Prometheus Unbound', *Music and Musicians*, xx/5 (1972), 34
E. Kaufman: *The Evolution of Form and Technique in the Late Works of Scriabin* (diss., Yale U., 1972)
H. Macdonald: 'Words and Music by A. Skryabin', *MT*, cxiii (1972), 22
C. Palmer: 'A Note on Skryabin and Pasternak', *MT*, cxiii (1972), 28
A. Pasternak: 'Skryabin: Summer 1903 and After', *MT*, cxiii (1972), 1169
F. Prieberg: 'Skriabin und die Sowjetmusik', *HiFi-Stereophonie*, xi (1972), 14

Bibliography

C. Rüger: 'Alexander Skrjabin: Humanitas oder Mystik?', *Musik und Gesellschaft*, xxii (1972), 536

H. H. Steger: *Der Weg der Klaviersonaten bei Alexander Skrjabin* (Munich, 1972)

I. Vanechkina: 'O svetomuzïkal'nikh zamïslakh Skryabina' [Skryabin's ideas on music and light], *Voprosï istorii, teorii, muzïki i muzïkal'-novo vospitaniya* (Kazan, 1972)

F. Bowers: *The New Scriabin: Enigma and Answers* (New York, 1973)

M. Kelkel: 'Alexandre Scriabine et "le charme des impossibilités" ', *Revue musicale de Suisse romande*, xxvii (1974), 26, 45

J. Samson: 'Scriabin: the Evolution of a Method', *Soundings*, iv (1974), 64

D. W. Shitomirsky: 'Die Harmonik Skrjabins', *Convivium musicorum: Festschrift Wolfgang Boetticher* (Berlin, 1974), 344

D. Pecaud: 'Le temps d'un espace', *Musique en jeu*, xxvi (1977), 109

H. H. Steger: *Materialstrukturen in den fünf späten Klaviersonaten Alexander Skrjabins* (Regensburg, 1977)

I. Vanechkina: 'Partiya "Luce" kak klyuch k pozdney garmonii Skryabina' [The 'Luce' part as the key to Skyrabin's late harmony], *SovM* (1977), no.4, p.100

T. D. Woolsey: *Organizational Principles in Piano Sonatas of Alexander Scriabin* (diss., U. of Texas at Austin, 1977)

G. Eberle: *Zwischen Tonalität und Atonalität: Studien zur Harmonik Alexander Skrjabins* (Munich, 1978)

M. Kelkel: *Alexandre Scriabine, sa vie, l'ésotérisme et le langage musical dans son oeuvre* (Paris, 1978)

H. Macdonald: *Skryabin* (London, 1978)

G. Neuwirth: 'Zur Alexander-Skrjabin-Renaissance', *ÖMz*, xxxiii (1978), 421

W. Szmolyan: 'Ein Skrjabin-Symposion in Graz', *ÖMz*, xxxiii (1978), 675

H. Connor: 'Varfoer inte Skrjabin?' [Why not Skyrabin?], *Musikrevy*, xxxiv (1979), 240

J. A. Gorman: *An Analysis of Performance Problems in Selected Pianoforte Sonatas of Alexander Scriabin* (diss., New York U., 1979)

R. J. Guenther: *Varvara Dernova's 'Garmoniia Skriabina': a Translation and Critical Commentary* (diss., Catholic U. of America, 1979)

E. N. Rudakova and A. I. Kandinsky: *Aleksandr Nikolayevich Skryabin* (Moscow, 1979)

M. Brown: 'Skryabin and Russian "Mystic" Symbolism', *19th Century Music*, iii (1979–80), 42

O. Kolleritsch, ed.: *Alexander Skrjabin*, Studien zur Wertungsfor-

schung, xiii (Graz, 1980) [articles by M. Scriabine, M. Kelkel, H. Weber, H. Macdonald, R. Brinkmann, L. Hoffmann-Erbrecht, S. Gut, G. Eberle, J.-H. Lederer, V. P. Dernova, M. Pinter and A. Voigt]

D. Mast: 'Skrjabin – verlorene Originalität um die Jahrhundertwende?', *NZM*, Jg.141 (1980), 431

M. Nyffeler: 'Florenz: Skrjabins *Prometheus* mit Farbenklavier', *SMz*, cxx (1980), 164

——: 'Neues Licht für eine Lichtmusik: Skrjabins *Prometheus* in Turin aufgeführt', *Neue Musikzeitung*, iii (1980), 26

H. Macdonald: 'Skryabin's Conquest of Time', *Hudba Slovanských Narodů* (Brno, 1981), 305

J. Samson: 'Skryabin and Szymanowski', *Hudba Slovanských Narodů* (Brno, 1981), 309

S. Schibli: 'Skrjabin spricht – sieben Stichworte zu einem Problem', *NZM*, Jg.143 (1982), 22

J. W. Clark: 'Divine Mysteries: on Some Skriabin Recordings', *19th Century Music*, vi (1982–3), 264

J. Reise: 'Late Skriabin: Some Principles Behind the Style', *19th Century Music*, vi (1982–3), 220

J. Rodgers: 'Four Preludes Ascribed to Yulian Skriabin', *19th Century Music*, vi (1982–3), 213

I. Belza: *Aleksandr Nikolayevich Skryabin* (Moscow, 1983)

H. Macdonald: 'Lighting the Fire: Skryabin and Colour', *MT*, cxxiv (1983), 600

H. K. Metzger and R. Riehn, eds.: *Aleksandr Skrjabin und die Skrjabinisten*, i, *Musik-Konzepte*, nos.32–3 (Munich, 1983) [incl. M. Scriabine: 'Überlegungen zum "Acte préalable"', 11; A. Lunačarskij: 'Taneev und Skrjabin', 26; G. Eberle: '"Ich erschaffe dich als vielfältige Einheit"', 42 [on the symphonic works]; S. Schibli: 'Skrjabins Flug', 69; M. Goldstein: 'Skrjabins und die Skrjabinisten', 178]; ii, *Musik-Konzepte*, nos.37–8 (Munich, 1984) [incl. H. R. Zeller: 'Monodynamik und Form in den Klavierzyklen Skrjabins', 4; M. Schmidt: 'Komposition als Symbol', 44 [mainly on op.53]; S. Mauser: 'Harmonik im Aufbruch', 53 [on op.74 no. 1]]

A. Pople: 'Skryabin's Prelude, Op.67, No.1: Sets and Structure', *Music Analysis*, ii (1983), 151

S. Schibli: 'Alexander Skrjabin: *Le Poème de l'Extase* op.54', *NZM*, Jg.144 (1983), 28

——: *Alexander Skrjabin und seine Musik: Grenzüberschreitungen eines prometheischen Geistes* (Munich, 1983)

G. Perle: 'Scriabin's Self-Analyses', *Music Analysis*, iii (1984), 101

M. Cooper: 'Alexander Skriabin and the Russian Renaissance', *Slavonic and Western Music: Essays for Gerald Abraham* (Ann Arbor and Oxford, 1985), 219

SERGEY RAKHMANINOV

Geoffrey Norris

Life

Rakhmaninov was one of the finest pianists of his day and, as a composer, the last great representative of Russian late Romanticism. The influences of Rimsky-Korsakov, Tchaikovsky and other Russian composers in his early works soon gave way to a highly individual, lyrical idiom which, if it has not had any important lasting effect on the development of Russian music, nevertheless is characterized by sincere expression and skilful technique.

I 1873–92

Sergey Vasil'yevich Rakhmaninov was born in Semyonovo on 1 April 1873. His improvident father soon squandered the family fortune, and they were rapidly reduced to a single estate, Oneg, near Novgorod. It was here that Rakhmaninov had his earliest piano lessons, first from his mother, then from Anna Ornatskaya, a graduate of the St Petersburg Conservatory. In 1882 even Oneg had to be sold to settle debts, and the family moved to St Petersburg, where Rakhmaninov attended the conservatory, receiving a general education and studying the piano with Vladimir Demyansky and harmony with Alexander Rubets. But soon the family was again in turmoil: during an epidemic of diphtheria Rakhmaninov's sister Sofiya died, and, to make matters worse, relations between his parents became so strained that they

decided to separate. This emotional upheaval had a decisive effect on Rakhmaninov's future career. With her increased domestic responsibilities, his mother was unable adequately to supervise his homework, and as a result he failed all his general subjects at the end-of-term examinations in 1885. The conservatory hinted that his scholarship might be withdrawn and so, on the recommendation of his cousin Alexander Ziloti, Rakhmaninov was sent to the Moscow Conservatory to study with the strict disciplinarian Nikolay Zverev. Living at Zverev's flat together with two other young pupils, Maximov and Presman, he was subjected to rigorous tuition, beginning practice at 6 a.m., acquiring a basic knowledge of music from four-hand arrangements of symphonies, and attending concerts in the city. It was also at Zverev's, during his Sunday afternoon gatherings, that Rakhmaninov first encountered many of the prominent musicians of the day: Anton Rubinstein, Taneyev, Arensky, Safonov and Tchaikovsky, the most influential figure of his formative years.

In spring 1888 Rakhmaninov transferred to the senior department of the conservatory to study the piano with Ziloti, while still living with Zverev; in the autumn he began to study counterpoint with Taneyev and harmony with Arensky. Zverev, who was concerned solely with the development of Rakhmaninov's piano technique, had never encouraged him to compose, though it was at Zverev's that Rakhmaninov wrote his earliest works, a Mendelssohnian orchestral scherzo (1887), some piano pieces (1887–8) and sketches for an opera *Esmeralda* (1888). But his creative instincts finally led to a breach with Zverev in 1889. In the single workroom at the flat Rakhmaninov found it impossible to

concentrate on composition while the others were practising; but Zverev met his request for more privacy with peremptory dismissal from the household, refusing even to speak to him for three years.

Rejecting his mother's idea that he should return to St Petersburg to study with Rimsky-Korsakov, Rakhmaninov remained in Moscow, living for a while with a conservatory colleague, Mikhail Slonov, then with his relatives, the Satins. Here he sketched some ideas for a piano concerto (which came to nothing) and completed two movements of a string quartet (dedicated to Ziloti); and in spring 1890 he composed the six-part motet *Deus meus* and his earliest songs. During the summer he stayed at Ivanovka, the Satins' country estate, where he met the three Skalon sisters, distant cousins by marriage, conceiving a calf-love for the youngest, Vera, and dedicating to her his new cello Romance. It was also for the Skalon sisters that he composed a six-hand piano Waltz (1890) and Romance (1891). Returning to Moscow, he taught for a while in a class for choir trainers, and sketched at least two movements of an orchestral piece, *Manfred*, possibly inspired by the Tchaikovsky symphony, which he had transcribed for piano duet in 1886.

In spring 1891 Ziloti resigned from the conservatory because of constant disagreements with the director, Safonov. Rather than transfer to another teacher for the remaining year of his course, Rakhmaninov was allowed to take his piano finals a year early, and he graduated with honours on 5 June. During the summer, again at Ivanovka, he completed his First Piano Concerto (begun in 1890), and back in Moscow in December he set to work on his first symphonic poem, *Knyaz' Rostislav*

('Prince Rostislav'), which he dedicated to Arensky. Early in 1892 he gave the première of his first *Trio élégiaque* with Anatoly Brandukov and David Kreyn, and also played the first movement of his concerto at a conservatory concert on 29 March. Shortly afterwards he began to prepare for his finals in composition, which, like his piano examinations, he was taking a year early. The main exercise was to be a one-act opera *Aleko*, based on Pushkin's poem *Tsïganï* ('The gypsies'). For his work Rakhmaninov was awarded the highest possible mark, and he graduated from the conservatory with the Great Gold Medal, previously awarded only to Koreshchenko and Taneyev.

II 1892–1901

After his graduation in 1892 Rakhmaninov signed a publishing contract with Gutheil, and in the autumn of that year composed what was quickly to become his best-known composition, the piano prelude in C♯ minor, a work to which Rakhmaninov owed much of his early popularity but which became for him a tiresome encore at most of his concerts. In the following spring *Aleko* was given its première at the Bol'shoy. Tchaikovsky, who attended the rehearsals and the performance, was enthusiastic about it, and Kashkin, in his perceptive, not uncritical review in the *Moskovskiye vedomosti* (29 April/11 May 1893), commented that 'of course there are faults, but they are far outweighed by merits, which lead one to expect much from this young composer in the future'.

Spurred by his success, Rakhmaninov composed with ease during the summer and autumn: he completed his op.4 and op.8 songs, the two-piano *Fantaisie-tableaux*

6. *Sergey Rakhmaninov (second left) with his teacher Zverev and fellow pupils Presman and Maximov*

op.5, a sacred choral piece *V molitvakh neusïpayush-chuyu bogoroditsu* ('O mother of God vigilantly pray-ing'), the two op.6 violin pieces and the orchestral fan-tasy *Utyos* ('The rock'), which bears a quotation from Lermontov's poem but was in fact inspired by Chekhov's short story *Na puti* ('On the road'). Tchaikovsky wanted to conduct the piece during the following season; but in November he died, and Rakhmaninov immediately devoted himself to writing a second *Trio élégiaque* to his memory, clearly revealing the sincerity of his grief in the music's overwhelming aura of gloom.

In January 1895 he began work on his first substan-tial piece, the Symphony no.1 in D minor (which has no connection with a D minor symphonic movement writ-ten in 1891). The symphony occupied him until September, and during 1896 Belyayev agreed to include it in one of his Russian Symphony Concerts. The per-formance, conducted by Glazunov, was on 27 March 1897, and was a disaster: Cui likened the work to 'a programme symphony on the Seven Plagues of Egypt', though other critics acknowledged that its poor recep-tion was due as much to the performance as to the piece itself. Rakhmaninov commented (in a letter of 6/18 May): 'I am amazed how such a highly talented man as Glazunov can conduct so badly. I am not speaking now of his conducting technique (one can't ask that of him) but about his musicianship. He feels nothing when he conducts. It's as if he understands nothing'. Years later Rakhmaninov's wife remarked that Glazunov was drunk at the time. Whatever the cause of the failure, it plunged Rakhmaninov into the depths of depression, and was followed by a three-year period completely devoid of any significant composition: sketches for another sym-

phony were abandoned; ideas for an opera, *Francesca da Rimini*, lay fallow for several years. But just then, thanks to the wealthy industrialist Savva Mamontov, Rakhmaninov was launched on his third career, as conductor, when he was engaged by the Moscow Private Russian Opera for the 1897–8 season. Here he acquired a sound knowledge of Russian and Western opera; he also formed a close friendship with Shalyapin (who sang with the company), and during a summer holiday in 1898 they made intensive studies together of the operas of Rimsky-Korsakov and Musorgsky, particularly *Boris Godunov*.

Rakhmaninov made his London début at the Queen's Hall in April 1899, and, returning to Russia, attended the St Petersburg première of *Aleko*, with Shalyapin in the title role. But even these successes did not inspire him to return to composition. Visits to Tolstoy, intended to stimulate creativity, succeeded only in depressing him further, and finally the Satins decided that he should seek medical help from Dr Nikolay Dahl, who for some years had been specializing in treatment by hypnosis. Dahl, an accomplished amateur musician, had a number of protracted sessions with Rakhmaninov to restore (as Sofiya Satina has recorded in her reminiscences) his 'cheerfulness of spirit, energy, a desire to work, and confidence in his abilities'. The treatment had a rapid effect: in the summer, staying in Italy with Shalyapin, Rakhmaninov composed his anthem *Panteley-tselitel'* ('Panteley the healer') and the love duet for *Francesca da Rimini*. Even more important, he began to compose his most enduringly popular work, the Second Piano Concerto. Ideas were put in order on his return to Russia in August, and he performed the second and

third movements on 15 December 1900. Success was such that he was encouraged to add the first movement, and he gave the first performance of the complete concerto on 9 November 1901.

III 1901–17

Finally reassured of his powers to compose, Rakhmaninov completed his Cello Sonata in December 1901, giving also the first performance (with Alexander Ziloti) of a recently composed Second Suite for two pianos. Early the following year he worked at his first important choral piece, *Vesna* ('Spring'), a cantata based on Nekrasov's poem *Zelyoniy shum* ('The verdant noise'), and shortly after completing it announced his engagement to his cousin Natalya Satina. The difficulties of such a marriage were considerable: Rakhmaninov refused to attend church or confession regularly, and in any case the Russian Orthodox Church forbids first cousins to marry. But one of Rakhmaninov's aunts had connections at the Archangel Cathedral in the Kremlin; she made the necessary arrangements, and the wedding took place at an army chapel on the outskirts of Moscow on 12 May.

After a long honeymoon in western Europe, the Rakhmaninovs returned to Moscow, where in May 1903 Natalya gave birth to their first daughter, Irina. During a summer holiday at Ivanovka, Rakhmaninov turned once more to composition, working on his opera *Skupoy rïtsar'* ('The miserly knight'); the piano score was ready by the following spring, when he again took up the threads of his other long-contemplated opera *Francesca da Rimini*. At the same time he agreed to conduct at the Bol'shoy for two seasons (beginning in

September 1904), and he spent the summer in frantic efforts to complete *Francesca* in the hope that both it and *The Miserly Knight* could be staged in December. Largely because of difficulties with the librettist, Modest Tchaikovsky, he managed to complete only the piano score of *Francesca* by August, when he had to devote all his time to learning the operas he was to conduct at the Bol'shoy. His experience with Mamontov's company stood him in good stead for his début in Dargomïzhsky's *Rusalka*; and again Kashkin was complimentary, remarking in *Russkiy listok*: 'the first appearance of the young Kapellmeister this season justified the hopes placed upon him . . . even in the first bars of the overture the audience began to feel a freshness and cheerfulness, clearly revealing the rich and lively temperament of the conductor'.

At Ivanovka in the summer Rakhmaninov worked on the orchestration of *Francesca* and *The Miserly Knight*. Both operas were complete by August, when he again had to prepare for the Bol'shoy; this time his programme included the Moscow première of Rimsky's *Pan Voyevoda*, an interpretation much admired by the composer, who attended the rehearsals and the performance. Rakhmaninov also conducted the premières of *The Miserly Knight* and *Francesca* in January 1906, but in February, because of the increasing political unrest in Russia, he resigned from the Bol'shoy, leaving almost at once for Italy. Staying near Pisa, he contemplated, but abandoned, another opera, *Salammbô*. He then had to return to Russia with his daughter, who from birth had rarely enjoyed good health and had again become ill. She recovered, but the atmosphere in Russia was still not conducive to work, and in the autumn the family

83

decided to leave Russia for a while and take a house in Dresden.

Living there in seclusion for a few months in each of the next few years, Rakhmaninov completed his Second Symphony (1906–8), his First Piano Sonata (1907), his symphonic poem *Ostrov myortvïkh* ('The isle of the dead', 1909) and part of an opera *Monna Vanna*. In May 1907 he took part in Dyagilev's Saison Russe in Paris, then returned to Ivanovka to join Natalya, who in July gave birth to their second daughter, Tatyana.

In 1909 Rakhmaninov made his first American tour, the programmes for which included a new work, the Third Piano Concerto, composed in the previous summer. At the end of the tour, which he loathed, he declined offers of further American contracts, and again he spent the summer at Ivanovka, recently made over to him by his uncle. It was here, during the next two or three summers, that he found the necessary relaxation to compose several important works: the 13 Preludes op.32 (1910), a setting of the *Liturgy of St John Chrysostom* (1910), the *Etudes-tableaux* op.33 (1911), the 14 Songs op.34 (1910, 1912) and the Second Piano Sonata (1913). The remaining months of the year were generally taken up with a taxing schedule of performing engagements; indeed, during the 1912–13 season he undertook so many concerts and became so tired that he cancelled his final appearance and took the family off to Switzerland. From there they went to Rome, where Rakhmaninov began his choral symphony *Kolokola* ('The bells'). Work on the piece was interrupted when Tatyana and Irina contracted typhoid; but, after they had recovered sufficiently in a Berlin hospital, the family returned to Ivanovka, where Rakhmaninov

84

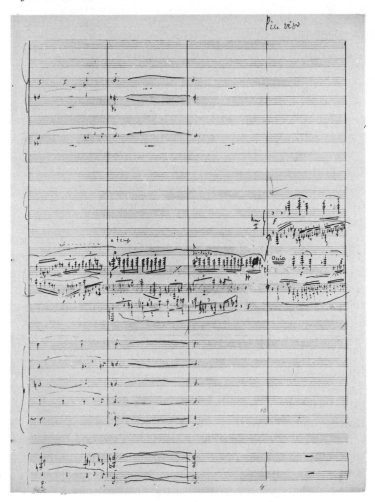

7. *Autograph score from the second movement of Rakhmaninov's Piano Concerto no.3 in D minor, composed 1909; in the printed score the final bar of the piano part is that marked 'Piano I'*

completed the score, conducting the first performance in December.

During autumn 1914 Rakhmaninov toured southern Russia with Koussevitzky, giving concerts for the war effort. Although he composed little after the outbreak of World War I, he did manage to write his finest unaccompanied choral work, the *Vsenoshchnoye bdeniye* ('All-night vigil'), in January and February 1915. By the end of 1916 Russia's internal affairs were in chaos: the country was gripped by strikes, and successive governments seemed able only to augment the popular discontent with the tsar. Rakhmaninov wrote to Ziloti in June 1917 asking if he could get him a visa to leave Russia. But Ziloti could do nothing, and after a concert in Yalta on 18 September Rakhmaninov returned to his flat in Moscow, where he revised the First Concerto, something he had been intending for many years. Just then he received an invitation to play in Stockholm and at once travelled to Petrograd to arrange the journey. Natalya, Irina and Tatyana followed a few days later and just before Christmas the whole family left Russia for the last time.

IV 1918–43

Rakhmaninov lived at first in Stockholm and then settled in Copenhagen. He began to widen his piano repertory, realizing that, without the money and possessions left behind in Russia, his and his family's livelihood depended on a steady income; and he was more likely to achieve that as a concert performer than as a composer. Towards the end of 1918 he received three offers of lucrative American contracts, and, although he declined them all, he decided that the USA

might offer a solution to his financial worries. In November the family arrived in New York, where Rakhmaninov quickly chose an agent, Charles Ellis, and accepted the gift of a piano from Steinway, before giving nearly 40 concerts in four months; at the end of the 1919–20 season he also signed a recording contract with the Victor Talking Machine Company. In 1921 the Rakhmaninovs decided to buy a house in the USA, where they consciously re-created the atmosphere of Ivanovka, entertaining Russian guests, employing Russian servants and observing Russian customs.

For the 1923–4 season Rakhmaninov cut his number of American concerts to allow more time in Europe; and it was while at Dresden in the spring that his elder daughter, Irina, announced her engagement to Prince Pyotr Volkonsky. The wedding was in September, but the marriage ended in tragedy when Volkonsky died less than a year later. It was largely for the benefit of the widowed Irina and for Tatyana that Rakhmaninov founded in Paris a publishing firm, TAIR (derived from his daughters' names), to publish works by Russian composers, particularly himself. Deciding also to limit his American engagements even further and to sell his American property, he found himself with nine months free of all commitments at the end of 1925. His mind turned immediately to composition, for he had long wanted to add another concerto to his repertory; in fact it seems likely that he had been contemplating a fourth concerto as early as 1914. Renting a flat in New York, he worked at the concerto and completed it at Dresden during the summer. Realizing that the piece was too long (he joked to Metner that it would have to be 'performed on successive nights, like the *Ring*'), he made

87

8. *Sergey Rakhmaninov*

a number of cuts before giving the first performance at Philadelphia on 18 March 1927. The highly critical notices made him take another look at the score, and before its publication by TAIR he made many more alterations and cuts. But it still failed to impress audiences, and he withdrew it from his programmes until he could examine the faults in detail.

In 1931 Rakhmaninov made a rare venture into politics: he had usually avoided comment on the Russian regime, but in January, together with Ivan Ostromislensky and Count Ilya Tolstoy, he sent a letter to *The New York Times* (12 January 1931) criticizing various Soviet policies. This was countered by a bitter attack in the Moscow newspaper *Vechernyaya Moskva* (9 March 1931) and a ban on the performance and study of his works in Russia (the ban lasted for only two years, and his music was restored to favour in 1933). During summer 1931 he revised his Second Sonata and also composed his last solo piano work, the Variations on a Theme of Corelli, performing them at Montreal on 12 October. In the following summers at his Swiss villa (called Senar, from *Se*rgey and *Na*talya *R*akhmaninov) he composed the Rhapsody on a Theme of Paganini (1934) and the Third Symphony (1935–6, revised 1938); and in 1937 Fokin approached Rakhmaninov with the idea of a ballet based on the Paganini legend, using Rakhmaninov's music. The ballet was first given at Covent Garden on 30 June 1939, a performance that the composer could not attend as he had slipped at his home and was lame. In fact he was never again to be in England; he had given his last concert on 11 March 1939, and during the summer the family decided that, in view of the threat of war, it would be safer to leave

Europe and return to the USA. There, in the autumn of 1940, he completed his last work, the Symphonic Dances; and in the following year he revised the Fourth Concerto.

Rakhmaninov decided that his 1942–3 season would have to be his last: every year since his arrival in the USA he had undertaken exhausting tours, and recently had been suffering from lumbago, arthritis and extreme fatigue. By January 1943, while on tour, he was clearly unwell. The doctor diagnosed pleurisy, but Rakhmaninov insisted that the tour should continue. On 17 February he gave what was to be his last concert, at Knoxville, becoming so ill afterwards that the family had to return to Los Angeles. There, at his house in Beverly Hills, it became evident that he was suffering from cancer, and he died early on the morning of 28 March.

V Rakhmaninov as a performer
Rakhmaninov pursued his three careers – as pianist, composer and conductor – with almost equal success, admitting, however, that he found it difficult to concentrate on more than one at any given time: certainly the demands of his performing career in his later life precluded much composition. His concert manner was austere, contrasting sharply with the warm and generous personality he revealed in the company of his family and close friends. He possessed a formidable piano technique, and his playing (like his conducting) was marked by precision, rhythmic drive, a refined legato and an ability for complete clarity in complex textures – qualities that he applied with sublime effect in his performances of Chopin, particularly the B♭ minor sonata.

As a performer

The rest of his comparatively small repertory comprised, besides his own works, many of the standard 19th-century virtuoso pieces as well as music by Beethoven, Borodin, Debussy, Grieg, Liszt, Mendelssohn, Mozart, Schubert, Schumann and Tchaikovsky. Whatever music he was playing, his performances were always carefully planned, being based on the theory that each piece has a 'culminating point'. 'This culmination', as he told the poet Marietta Shaginian, 'may be at the end or in the middle, it may be loud or soft; but the performer must know how to approach it with absolute calculation, absolute precision, because, if it slips by, then the whole construction crumbles, and the piece becomes disjointed and scrappy and does not convey to the listener what must be conveyed'.

CHAPTER TWO

Works

Understandably, the piano figures prominently in Rakhmaninov's music, either as a solo instrument or as part of an ensemble. But he used his own skills as a performer not to write music of unreasonable, empty virtuosity, but rather to explore fully the expressive possibilities of the instrument. Even in his earliest works (the three nocturnes of 1887–8, the four pieces probably written in 1887, and the first version of the First Piano Concerto, 1890–91) he revealed a sure grasp of idiomatic piano writing and a striking gift for melody. Some of his early works presage finer achievements: the Prelude in C♯ minor, for example, though less subtle than his mature works, is couched in the melancholy, nostalgic idiom that pervades much of his music. And in some of his early orchestral pieces – *Prince Rostislav* (1891) and, to a lesser extent, *The Rock* (1893) – he showed the first signs of that ability for tone-painting which he was to perfect in *The Isle of the Dead* (1909) and in some of his later piano pieces and songs. In these early years, though, the textures (usually opaque and chordal) lack the variety of later works; his orchestration is often colourless and heavy; and the musical language (notably in his student opera *Aleko*, 1892, and in his D minor symphonic movement of 1891) is often redolent of other Russian composers, particularly Tchaikovsky.

With his works of the mid-1890s Rakhmaninov

began to strike a more individual tone: the six *Moments musicaux* (1896) have the characteristic yearning themes, combined with a rise and fall of dynamics and intricate passage-work. Even his First Symphony (1895), however 'weak, childish, strained and bombastic' (as Rakhmaninov himself described it), has many original features. Its brutal gestures and uncompromising power of expression (particularly in the finale) were unprecedented in Russian music; and, although it must be said that the work has a tendency to ramble, nevertheless its flexible rhythms, sweeping lyricism and stringent economy of thematic material ('the meaningless repetition of the same short tricks', Cui called it) were features used with greater subtlety and individuality later on.

After the three vacuous years that followed the poor reception of the symphony in 1897, Rakhmaninov's style began to develop significantly. In the Second Piano Concerto (1900–01) the headstrong youthful impetuosity of the symphony has largely given way to Rakhmaninov's predilection for sumptuous harmonies and broadly lyrical, often intensely passionate melodies. And there are certain technical developments. In place of the often garish orchestration of the symphony, the colours of the concerto are subdued and more subtly varied; the textures are carefully contrasted; and Rakhmaninov's writing is altogether more concise. The idiom of the concerto rubbed off on the other works of the period, notably the Suite no.2 for two pianos (1900–01), the Cello Sonata (1901), the Ten Preludes op.23 (1901, 1903), the cantata *Spring* (1902), and the 12 Songs op.21 (1900, 1902). In these songs he began to achieve a perfect balance between voice and accompaniment,

using the piano to echo the sentiments of the text. (Some of the piano parts are, in effect, separate instrumental studies of the poems, and it is significant that Rakhmaninov later transcribed one of the finest, *Siren'* ('Lilacs', no.5), for piano solo.) This same sensitivity to mood is seen again in his two operas of the period, *The Miserly Knight* (1903–5) and *Francesca da Rimini* (1900–05); but here, despite Rakhmaninov's keen dramatic sense – particularly in the central scene of *The Miserly Knight* and in the love-duet of *Francesca* – the librettos defy successful stage performance (the former being an almost word-for-word setting of one of Pushkin's 'little tragedies', never intended for the stage; the other an anaemic adaptation by Modest Tchaikovsky of the fifth canto of the *Inferno*).

The years immediately following the premières of the two operas, spent partly in Russia, partly in Dresden, were Rakhmaninov's most fruitful as a composer, and it was during this period that his style reached full maturity. The Second Symphony (1906–8) and the Third Piano Concerto (1909) display his fully-fledged melodic style (particularly in the slow movement of the symphony), his opulent but infinitely varied and discerning use of the orchestra (notably in the symphony's scherzo), and a greater confidence in the handling of large-scale structures. Like those of the First Symphony, the opening bars of the Second contain pithy ideas that act as unifying elements, but here the material is allowed a far more leisurely expansion and development than in the First Symphony; the long-breathed themes need space to display themselves fully, and the cuts sometimes made in performances of the symphony and the concerto serve only to throw them off balance.

Works

The Third Concerto is structurally a more ingenious piece than the Second, not only in the greater continuity achieved through the elimination of the abrupt full stops that occur before important themes in the First and Second Concertos, but also in the subtle recollection and metamorphosis of the first movement material: the fast central section of the slow movement, for example, is a rhythmic mutation of the opening theme.

Certain characteristics of the Third Concerto are brought to mind by the 13 Preludes op.32 (1910), just as the op.23 preludes owe much in style to the Second Concerto. The preludes have the concerto's complexity of texture and flexibility of rhythm, its pungent, chromatic harmony; and, like the concerto, they make extreme demands of agility and power on the pianist. There are extreme emotional demands too, particularly in the more introspective preludes, a mode of expression towards which Rakhmaninov had been developing in the more contemplative of the op.23 preludes and in some of the *Moments musicaux*: the B♭ minor prelude (op.32 no.2), the B minor (no.10) and the D♭ major (no.13) are among the most searching and harrowing music that Rakhmaninov composed. Even the more lyrical preludes have the same hazy quality of his last set of songs (op.38, 1916), while the more ostentatiously dramatic pieces are set in the intense, impassioned idiom of some of the op.39 *Etudes-tableaux* (1916–17). Varied though these pieces are, they all have a common characteristic in that they show Rakhmaninov's ability to crystallize perfectly a particular mood or sentiment: each prelude grows from a tiny melodic or rhythmic fragment into a taut, powerfully evocative miniature. They are, in effect, small tone poems, and it is this vivid

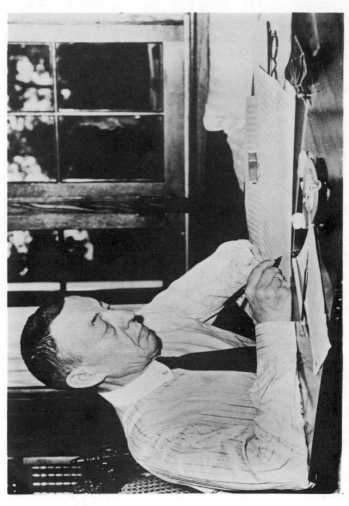

9. Sergey Rakhmaninov

portraiture that, in orchestral music, reached a peak in *The Isle of the Dead*. Here the awesome gloom of Böcklin's picture is reflected in the dark colours of the opening section (where the motion of Charon's oars is imitated by the persistent 5/8 metre), enhanced, as in so much of Rakhmaninov's music, by references to the *Dies irae*; indeed, the dénouement of the piece consists of a battle between the chant (symbolizing death) and another, more wistful melody that Rakhmaninov called the 'life' theme. Similarly doom-laden is the long finale of his choral symphony *The Bells* (1913), where he was able to express, with an emotional intensity he never surpassed, the fatalistic sentiments that imbue many other works. In *The Bells* the effectiveness of the subdued finale is heightened by the other three, more vivid, movements; and in all four movements he applied the discriminating orchestration, evident in his other mature works, to convey Poe's sharply contrasting campanological symbols: silver bells for birth, golden bells for marriage, brazen bells for terror, iron bells for death. In the tenor, soprano and baritone solos he also showed the perceptive response to poetry and the sympathetic vocal writing of his two last sets of songs, opp.34 and 38.

For the 14 Songs op.34 (1910, 1912) he chose poems by some of the principal representatives of Russian Romanticism: Pushkin, Tyutchev, Polonsky, Khomyakov, Maykov and Korinfsky, and also the more modern Bal'mont. Most of the songs are tailored to the individual talents of certain Russian singers: the dramatic, declamatory ones, like *V dushe u kazhdovo iz nas* ('In the soul of each of us', no.2), *Ti znal evo* ('You knew him', no.9), *Obrochnik* ('The peasant', no.11) and

Voskresheniye Lazarya ('The raising of Lazarus', no.6), are dedicated to Shalyapin; the powerful *Dissonans* ('Discord', no.13) to Felia Litvin; the more lyrical songs, like *Kakoye schast'ye* ('What happiness', no.12), to Sobinov; and the wordless *Vocalise* (no.14) to Nezhdanova. Certain features of the op.34 songs (simple vocal lines; sensitive accompaniments that emphasize certain words and phrases by melodic inflections and harmonic shadings) were developed further in the six last songs (op.38). For these Rakhmaninov chose texts exclusively from the works of contemporary poets – Blok, Belïy, Severyanin, Bryusov, Sologub and Bal'mont – all of whom were prominent in the symbolist movement predominant in Russia in the late 19th century and early 20th. Here, as in the op.39 *Etudes-tableaux*, Rakhmaninov was concerned less with pure melody than with colouring; and his almost impressionist style perfectly matches the symbolists' mellifluous, elusive poetry in its translucent piano writing, constantly fluctuating rhythms and ambiguous harmonies.

The op.38 songs and the op.39 studies were the last important pieces that Rakhmaninov wrote before leaving Russia (apart from the substantial revision of the First Piano Concerto, done in 1917). And his friend Vladimir Wilshaw, in a letter written shortly after the Soviet ban on his works had been lifted, perceptively remarked on the difference in style between the extrovert studies (during a performance of which Rakhmaninov had broken a string on the piano) and the Variations on a Theme of Corelli, his last piano work, composed in 1931. In these 20 variations (not, in fact, based on a theme of Corelli, but on the tune *La folìa* which Corelli had used in his Sonata op.5 no.12) the

piano textures have an even greater clarity than in the op.38 songs, combined with biting chromatic harmony and a new rhythmic incisiveness. These were to be the characteristics of all the works composed during this Indian summer of the 1930s and 1940s, and the Corelli Variations were in a sense preparatory exercises for the Rhapsody on a Theme of Paganini (1934), a much more tautly constructed piece than the often diffuse Fourth Piano Concerto (1926). Like the Paganini Rhapsody, the other late works with orchestra – the Three Russian Songs (1926) and the Third Symphony (1935–6) – reveal Rakhmaninov's interest in individual instrumental tone qualities, and this is highlighted by his use of an alto saxophone in his last work, the Symphonic Dances (1940). In the curious, shifting harmonies of the second movement, and in the rhythmic vitality and almost Prokofiev-like grotesquerie of the first and last, the Symphonic Dances are entirely representative of his late style; and they also sum up his lifelong fascination with ecclesiastical chants, for he not only quoted (in the first movement) the principal theme from the First Symphony (derived as it is from motifs characteristic of Russian church music), but he also used in the finale the *Dies irae* and the chant *Blagosloven esi, Gospodi* ('Blessed be the Lord') from his *All-night Vigil* (1915), writing at the end of the score the sadly appropriate line 'I thank thee, Lord'.

Numbers in right-hand margins denote reference in the text.

OPERAS

op.

— Esmeralda (after Hugo: Notre Dame de Paris), 1888; Introduction to Act 1 and frag., of Act 3 only, all in pf score — 76

— Aleko (1, V. Nemirovich-Danchenko, after Pushkin: Tsïganï [The gypsies]), 1892; Moscow, Bol'shoy, 9 May 1893 — 78, 81, 92

24 Skupoy rïtsar' [The miserly knight] (3 scenes, Pushkin), 1903–5; Moscow, Bol'shoy, 24 Jan 1906 — 82, 83, 94

25 Francesca da Rimini (prol, 2 scenes, epilogue, M. Tchaikovsky, after Dante: Inferno), 1900, 1904–5; Moscow, Bol'shoy, 24 Jan 1906 — 81, 82, 83, 94

— Salammbô (7 scenes, M. Slonov after Flaubert), 1906, scenario only — 83

— Monna Vanna (Slonov, after Maeterlinck), 1907; pf score of Act 1 and sketches for Act 2 only; concert perf. of Act 1, orchd I. Buketoff, Saratoga, NY, Saratoga Performing Arts Center, 11 Aug 1984 — 84

CHORAL

— Deus meus, motet, 6vv, 1890 — 77

— V molitvakh neusïpayushchuyu bogoroditsu [O mother of God vigilantly praying], 4vv, 1893 — 80

— Chorus of spirits and Song of the Nightingale from Don Juan (A. K. Tolstoy), unacc., ?1894

15 6 Choruses, female or children's vv, 1895–6: Slav'sya [Be praised] (Nekrasov); Nochka [Night] (V. Lodïzhensky); Sosna [The pine] (Lermontov); Zadremali volnï [The waves slumbered] (K. Romanov); Nevolya [Slavery] (N. Tsïganov); Angel (Lermontov)

— Panteley-tselitel' [Panteley the healer] (A. K. Tolstoy), unacc., 1901 — 81

20 Vesna [Spring] (Nekrasov: Zelyonïy shum [The verdant noise]), cantata, Bar, chorus, orch, 1902 — 81, 93

31 Liturgiya svyatovo Ioanna Zlatousta [Liturgy of St John Chrysostom], unacc., 1910 — 84

35 Kolokola [The bells] (Bal'mont, after Poe), choral sym., S, T, Bar, chorus, orch, 1913; vocal parts of 3rd movt partially rev. — 84, 86, 97

ORCHESTRAL

41 3 Russian Songs, chorus, orch, 1926; Cherez rechku [Across the river]; Akh tï, Van'ka [Oh, Ivan]; Belelitsï, rumyanitsï vï moy [Whiten my roughed cheeks] — 99

— Scherzo, d, 1887 — 76

— Piano Concerto, c, 1889, sketches only — 77

— Manfred, sym. poem, 1890–91, lost — 77

1 Piano Concerto no.1, f♯, 1890–91, rev. 1917 — 77, 78, 86, 92, 95, 98

— Symphony, d, 1891, 1st movt only — 82, 92

— Knyaz' Rostislav [Prince Rostislav], sym. poem after A. K. Tolstoy, 1891 — 77, 92

7 Utyos [The rock], fantasy for orch. after Chekhov: Na puti, 1893 — 80, 92

12 Kaprichchio na tsïganskiye temï [Capriccio on gypsy themes] (Capriccio bohémien), 1892, 1894

— 2 episodes after Byron: Don Juan, 1894, lost

13 Symphony no.1, d, 1895 — 80, 93, 94, 99

— Symphony, 1897, sketches only — 80–81

18 Piano Concerto no.2, c, 1900–01 — 81–2, 93, 95

27 Symphony no.2, e, 1906–8 — 84, 94

29 Ostrov myortvïkh [The isle of the dead], sym. poem after Böcklin, 1909 — 84, 92, 97

30 Piano Concerto no.3, d, 1909 — 84, 85, 94, 95

40 Piano Concerto no.4, g, 1926, rev. 1927, 1941 — 87, 89, 90, 99

43 Rhapsody on a Theme of Paganini, pf, orch, 1934 — 89, 99

44 Symphony no.3, a, 1935–6, rev. 1938 — 89, 99

45 Symphonic Dances, 1940 — 90, 99

CHAMBER

— String Quartet, 1889, 2 movts only — 77

— Romance, a, vn, pf, c1880–90

— Romance, f, vc, pf, 1890 — 77

— Melodie, D, vc, pf, ?1890; arr. M. Altschuler (1947)

— Trio élégiaque, g, pf trio, 1892 — 78
2 2 Pieces, vc, pf, 1892: Prélude, F [rev. of pf piece, 1891], Danse orientale, a
6 2 Morceaux de salon, vn, pf, 1893: Romance, Danse hongroise — 80
9 Trio élégiaque, d, pf trio, 1893, rev. 1907, 1917 — 80
19 Sonata, g, vc, pf, 1901 — 82, 93

PIANO

— ?Study, F♯, ?1886 — 76, 92
— Song without words, d, ?1887
3 Nocturnes: no.1, f♯, 1887; no.2, F, 1887; no.3, c, 1887–8 — 92
— 4 Pieces, ?1887: Romance, f♯; Prélude, e♭; Mélodie, E; Gavotte, D — 92
— Piece (Canon), d, 1890–91
— 2 Pieces, 6 hands: Waltz, A, 1890; Romance, A, 1891
— Prélude, F, 1891, rev. 1892 as Prélude, vc, pf
— Russian Rhapsody, 2 pf, 1891 — 77
3 Morceaux de fantaisie, 1892: Elégie, e♭; Prélude, c♯, arr. 2 pf 1938; Mélodie, E, rev. 1940; Polichinelle, f♯; Sérénade, b♭, rev. 1940 — 78, 92
— Romance, G, 4 hands, ?1894
5 Fantaisie-tableaux (Suite no.1), 2 pf, 1893 — 78
10 Morceaux de salon, 1893–4: Nocturne, a, Valse, A; Barcarolle, g; Mélodie, e–E; Humoreske, G, rev. 1940; Romance, f; Mazurka, D♭
— Romance, G, pf 4 hands, ?1894
11 6 Morceaux, 4 hands, 1894: Barcarolle, g; Scherzo, D; Thème russe, b; Valse, A; Romance, c; Slava [Glory], C
16 6 Moments musicaux, 1896: Andantino b♭; Allegretto, e♭, rev. 1940; Andante cantabile, b; Presto, e. Adagio sostenuto, D♭; Maestoso, C — 93, 95
— Improvisations, 1896, for 4 Improvisations, collab. Arensky, Glazunov and Taneyev
— Morceau de fantaisie, g, 1899
— Fughetta, F, 1899
17 Suite no.2, 2 pf, 1900–01 — 82, 93
22 Variations on a Theme of Chopin, 1902–3 — 93, 95
23 10 Préludes, 1903 (except no.5, 1901)
— Polka italienne, pf 4 hands, ?1906
28 Sonata no.1, d, 1907 — 84

32 13 Préludes, 1910 — 84, 95
33 Etudes-tableaux, 1911: no.1, f; no.2, C; no.3 (6), e♭; no.4 (7), E♭; no.5 (8), g; no.6 (9), c♯; 3 other pieces instended for op.33 withdrawn before publication; of these, no.4, a, pubd as op.39 no.6; no.3, c–C, and no.5, d, pubd posthumously — 84
36 Sonata no.2, b♭, 1913, rev. 1931 — 84, 89
39 Etudes-tableaux, 1916–17: no.1, c; no.2, a; no.3, f♯; no.4, b; no.5, e♭; no.6, a; no.7, c; no.8, d; no.9, D; see also op.33 — 95, 98
— Oriental Sketch, B♭, 1917
— Prelude, d, 1917
— Fragments, A♭, 1917
— Cadenza for Liszt: Hungarian Rhapsody no.2, ?1919 — 89, 98–9
42 Variations on a Theme of Corelli, 1931 — 77, 92

SOLO VOCAL

(for 1v, pf, unless otherwise stated)

— U vrat obiteli svyatoy [At the gate of the holy abode] (Lermontov), 1890 — 77
— Ya tebe nichevo ne skazhu [I shall tell you nothing] (A. Fet), 1890
— Opyat' vstrepenulos' ti, serdtse [Again you leapt, my heart] (N. Grekov), 1890
2 monologues from Boris Godunov (Pushkin), ?1891: Ti, otche patriarkh [Thou, father patriarch]; Eshcho odno posledneye skazan'ye [One last story]
— Noch provedennaya bezsna, Arbenin's monologue from Maskarad (Lermontov), ?1891
— Mazepa (Pushkin: Poltava), 4vv, frag.
— C'était en avril (E. Pailleron), 1891
— Smerkalos' [Twilight has fallen] (A. K. Tolstoy), 1891
— Gryanem ukhnem [Russian boatmen's song], before 1892
— Pesnya razocharovannovo [Song of the disillusioned] (D. Rathaus), 1893
— Uvyal tsvetok [The flower has faded] (Rathaus), 1893
— Ti pomnish' li vecher [Do you remember the evening (A. K. Tolstoy), 1893
4 6 Songs, 1890–93: O net, molyu, ne ukhodi [Oh no, I beg you, forsake me not] (D. Merezhkovsky), 1892; Utro [Morning] (M. Yanova), 1892; V molchan'i nochi taynoy [In the silence of the secret night] (Fet), 1890; Ne poy, krasavitsa, pri mne [Sing not — 78

to me, beautiful maiden] (Pushkin), 1892; Uzh ti, niva moya [Oh thou, my field] (A. K. Tolstoy), 1893; Davno l', moy drug [How long, my friend] (A. Golenishchev-Kutuzov), 1893

8 6 Songs (trans. A. Pleshcheyev), 1893: Rechnaya lileya [The waterlily] (Heine); Ditya! kak tsvetok, ti prekrasna [Child, thou art as beautiful as a flower] (Heine); Duma [Brooding] (Shevchenko); Polyubila ya na pechal' svoyu [I have grown fond of sorrow] (Shevchenko); Son [The dream] (Heine); Molitva [A prayer] (Goethe)   78

14 12 Songs, 1896 (except no.1, 1894): Ya zhdu tebya [I wait for thee] (M. Davidova); Ostrovok [The isle] (Shelley), trans. Bal'mont); Davno v lyubvi otradi malo [For long there has been little consolation in love] (Fet); Ya bil u ney [I was with her] (A. Koltsov); Eti letniye nochi [These summer nights] (Rathaus); Tebya tak lyubyat vse [How everyone loves thee] (A. K. Tolstoy); Ne ver' mne, drug! [Believe me not, friend] (A. K. Tolstoy); O, ne grusti [Oh, do not grieve] (A. Apukhtin); Ona, kak polden', khorosha [She is as lovely as the noon] (N. Minsky); V moyey dushe [In my soul] (Minsky); Vesenniye vodi [Spring waters] (Tyutchev); Pora! ['Tis time] (S. Nadson)

— Ikalos' li tebe [Were you hiccoughing] (P. Vyazemsky), 1899

— Noch' [Night] (Rathaus), 1900

21 12 Songs, 1902 (except no.1, 1900): Sud'ba [Fate] (Apukhtin); Nad svezhey mogiloy [By the fresh grave] (Nadson); Sumerki [Twilight] (J.-M. Guyot, trans. M. Tkhorzhevsky); Oni otvechali [They answered] (Hugo, trans. L. Mey); Siren' [Lilacs] (E. Beketova), arr. pf 1914, rev. 1941; Otrivok iz A. Myusse [Fragment from Musset] (trans. Apukhtin); Zdes' khorosho [How fair this spot] (G. Galina); Na smert' chizhika [On the death of a linnet] (V. Zhukovsky); Melodiya [Melody] (Nadson); Pred ikonoy [Before the icon] (Golenishchev-Kutuzov); Ya ne prorok [No prophet I] (A. Kruglov); Kak mne bol'no [How painful for me] (Galina)   93–4

26 15 Songs, 1906: Est' mnogo zvukov [There are many sounds] (A. K. Tolstoy); Vsyo otnyal u menya [He took all from me] (Tyutchev); Mi otdokhnyom [Let us rest] (Chekhov); Dva prosh-   94

chaniya [Two partings] (Koltsov), Bar, S; Pokinem, milaya [Beloved, let us fly] (Golenishchev-Kutuzov); Khristos voskres [Christ is risen] (Merezhkovsky); K detyam [To the children] (A. Khomyakov); Poshchadi ya molyu! [I beg for mercy] (Merezhkovsky); Ya opyat' odinok [Again I am alone] (Shevchenko, trans. I. Bunin); U moyevo okna [Before my window] (Galina); Fontan [The fountain] (Tyutchev); Noch' pechal'na [Night is mournful] (Bunin); Vchera mi vstretilis' [When yesterday we met] (Polonsky); Kol'tso [The ring] (Koltsov); Prokhodit vsyo [All things pass by] (Rathaus)

— Letter to K. S. Stanislavsky, 1908   84, 97–8

34 14 Songs, 1912 (except no.7, 1910, rev. 1912): Muza [The muse] (Pushkin); V dushe u kazhdovo iz nas [In the soul of each of us] (A. Korinfsky); Burya [The storm] (Pushkin); Veter perelyotniy [The migrant wind] (Bal'mont); Arion (Pushkin); Voskresheniye Lazarya [The raising of Lazarus] (Khomyakov); Ne mozhet bit'! [It cannot be] (A. Maykov); Muzika [Music] (Ya. Polonsky); Ti znal evo [You knew him] (Tyutchev); Sey den', ya pomnyu [I remember that day] (Tyutchev); Obrochnik [The peasant] (Fet); Kakoye schast'ye [What happiness] (Fet); Dissonans [Discord] (Polonsky); Vocalise, rev. 1915; arr. S, orch, c1916; orch, c1919

— Iz evangeliya ot Ioanna [From the Gospel of St John], 1915

38 6 Songs, 1916: Noch'yu v sadu u menya [In my garden at night] (Isaakian, trans. Blok); K ney [To her] (A. Beliy); Margaritki [Daisies] (I. Severyanin), arr. pf 1940; Krisolov [The rat-catcher] (V. Bryusov); Son [A dream] (F. Sologub); A-u! (Bal'mont)   95, 97, 98, 99

— Molitva [Prayer] (Romanov), 1916

— Vsyo khochet pet [All things wish to sing] (Sologub), 1916

ARRANGEMENTS
(for piano)

Tchaikovsky: Manfred, 4 hands, 1886, lost
Tchaikovsky: The Sleeping Beauty, 4 hands, 1890–91
Glazunov: Symphony no.6, 4 hands, 1896
Bizet: Minuet from L'Arlésienne Suite no.1, 1900, rev. 1922   77

Behr: Lachtäubchen op.303, pubd as Polka VR, 1911
Rakhmaninov: Lilacs op.21 no.5, 1914, rev. ?1941
J. S. Smith: The Star-spangled Banner, 1918
Kreisler: Liebesleid, ?1921
Musorgsky: Hopak from Sorochintsy Fair, 1924
Kreisler: Liebesfreud, 1925
Schubert: Wohin?, 1925
Rimsky-Korsakov: Flight of the Bumble Bee, ?1929
Bach: Prelude, Gavotte and Gigue from Violin Partita, E, 1933

Mendelssohn: Scherzo from A Midsummer Night's Dream, 1933
Rakhmaninov: Daisies op.38 no.3, 1940
Tchaikovsky: Lullaby op.16 no.1, 1941

(for piano and violin)
Musorgsky: Hopak from Sorochintsy Fair, 1925

Principal publishers: Gutheil, Jürgenson, Edition Russe de Musique, Fischer, TAIR, Belwin Mills, Boosey & Hawkes, Muzgiz

BIBLIOGRAPHY

V. Belyayev: *Sergey Rakhmaninov* (Moscow, 1924); Eng. trans. in *MQ*, xiii (1927), 359

S. Rakhmaninov: 'Some Critical Moments in my Career', *MT*, lxxi (1930), 557

A. J. and K. Swan: 'Rachmaninoff: Personal Reminiscences', *MQ*, xxx (1944), 1, 174

G. Kogan: 'Rakhmaninov – pianist', *SovM sbornik*, iv (1945), 58

K. A. Kuznetsov: 'Tvorcheskaya zhizn' S. V. Rakhmaninova' [Rakhmaninov's creative life], *SovM sbornik*, iv (1945), 25

D. Zhitomirsky: 'Fortepianniye tvorchestvo Rakhmaninova' [Rakhmaninov's piano works], *SovM sbornik*, iv (1945), 80

I. F. Belza, ed.: *S. V. Rakhmaninov i russkaya opera* (Moscow, 1947)

V. M. Bogdanov-Berezovsky, ed.: *Molodïye godï Sergeya Vasil'yevicha Rakhmaninova* [Rakhmaninov's early years] (Leningrad and Moscow, 1949)

J. Culshaw: *Sergei Rachmaninov* (London, 1949)

Z. A. Apetian, ed.: *S. V. Rakhmaninov: pis'ma* [Letters] (Moscow, 1955)

E. Bortnikova, ed.: *Avtografï S. V. Rakhmaninova v fondakh gosudarstvennovo tsentral'novo muzeya muzïkal'noy kulturï imeni M. I. Glinki: katalog-spravochnik* [Rakhmaninov's autographs in the archives of the State Central Glinka Museum of Musical Culture: a reference catalogue] (Moscow, 1955, rev. and enlarged 2/1980)

S. Bertensson and J. Leyda: *Sergei Rachmaninoff: a Lifetime in Music* (New York, 1956, 2/1965)

Z. A. Apetian, ed.: *Vospominaniya o Rakhmaninove* [Reminiscences of Rakhmaninov] (Moscow, 1957, enlarged 4/1974)

N. Bazhanov: *Rachmaninov* (Moscow, 1966; Eng. trans., 1983)

V. N. Bryantseva: 'Gde rodilsya S. V. Rakhmaninov?' [Where was Rakhmaninov born?], *Muzïkal'naya zhizn'* (1969), no.19, p.20

——: *Detstvo i yunost' Sergeya Rakhmaninova* [Rakhmaninov's childhood and youth] (Moscow, 1970, 2/1973)

Z. A. Apetian, ed.: *N. K. Metner: pis'ma* [Letters] (Moscow, 1973) [incl. Rakhmaninov's letters to Metner]

Yu. V. Keldïsh: *Rakhmaninov i evo vremya* [Rakhmaninov and his time] (Moscow, 1973)

——: 'Tvorcheskiy put' velikovo muzïkanta' [The creative path of a great musician], *SovM* (1973), no.4, p.74

G. Norris: 'Rakhmaninov's Second Thoughts', *MT*, cxiv (1973), 364

——: 'Rakhmaninov's Student Opera', *MQ*, lix (1973), 441

R. Threlfall: 'Rachmaninoff's Revisions and an Unknown Version of his Fourth Concerto', *MO*, xcvi (1972–3), 235

Bibliography

N. D. Uspensky: 'Sergey Vasilievich Rakhmaninov', *Journal of the Moscow Patriarchate* (1973), no.8, p.79; no.9, p.76

P. Piggott: *Rachmaninov Orchestral Music* (London, 1974)

V. Bryantseva: *S. V. Rakhmaninov* (Moscow, 1976)

G. Norris: *Rakhmaninov* (London, 1976)

Z. A. Apetian, ed.: *S. Rakhmaninov: literaturnoye naslediye* [Literary heritage] (Moscow, 1978–80)

R. Threlfall and G. Norris: *Catalogue of the Compositions of S. Rachmaninoff* (London, 1982)

G. Norris: 'Rakhmaninov's Apprenticeship', *MT*, cxxiv (1983), 602

R. Palmieri: *Sergei Vasil'evich Rachmaninoff: a Guide to Research* (London and New York, 1985)

SERGEY PROKOFIEV

Rita McAllister

Russia: 1891–1918

Sergey Sergeyevich Prokofiev, composer and pianist, was born in Sontsovka, in the Ekaterinoslav district of the Ukraine, on 27 April 1891 (this is the date on his birth certificate, although Prokofiev himself believed that he was born on 23 April). His early works, whimsical, wilful and often heavily ironic, reflect the artistic ferment of the last years of tsarist Russia. After the Revolution he moved to the USA, then to Paris, and his style became more settled, broader and more lyrical. The last 17 years of his life he spent in the USSR, both stimulated and restricted by the cultural policies of the Stalin regime. Throughout his life his greatest involvement was with music for the stage; he was an instinctive musical dramatist, with a sharp sense of theatre and character. His orchestral works, concertos and piano sonatas have also, however, made a significant impact on the concert repertory, and he remains one of the most frequently-performed composers of the 20th century.

Prokofiev's parents were affluent and cultured. His father was an agricultural engineer, who managed a large estate in the Ukrainian steppe. His mother was well-educated, sociable and a good pianist. Her devotion to music, especially to the works of Rubinstein, Chopin and Beethoven, had the greatest influence in his early years. An adored only child, Prokofiev was musically

precocious. He wrote his first piano piece at the age of five; at nine he was playing the easier Beethoven sonatas; and by summer 1902, when Glier went to Sontsovka to tutor the boy, he was already the composer of two operas and numerous short piano pieces.

From Glier he learned the rudiments of harmony, form and orchestration and, with help, he soon completed a four-movement symphony. The first of the Little Songs date from that summer, too. Over the next five years he was to compose 60 of these short mood pieces for piano, most of them in simple three-part form, and of all the music of Prokofiev's childhood these pieces most clearly contain the seeds of future developments. The earliest of them are still childish and imitative, but increasingly they form a diary of his musical experiments. By 1904 he was writing scherzos and marches with unusual metres and uncommon tonalities, dance movements with wild and capricious rhythms, and many of the later pieces are full of his distinctive brand of musical humour.

Sontsovka may have been musically as well as geographically isolated, but Prokofiev was kept in touch with the current musical repertory through both Glier's teaching, which continued spasmodically until 1904, and annual winter visits with his mother to Moscow. On these visits he played his latest pieces to Taneyev; by 1903 his impressive list of works included a violin sonata, part of a piano sonata and a new opera, *Pir vo vremya chumï* ('A feast in time of plague'). It was now necessary to his development as a composer that he should have more continuous contact with the professional musical world, and also that his general education should become formal. The matter hung in the air for

some time: the Prokofievs were loath to commit him so early to a musical career. In spring 1904, however, he was taken to St Petersburg and, on the advice of Glazunov, he applied for entrance to the conservatory.

The following September Prokofiev passed the entrance examination. He was to spend the next ten years at the St Petersburg Conservatory, and was to prove one of its most unruly students. The conservatory itself was far from settled in those years. 'Bloody Sunday' and the first rumblings of revolution in January 1905 had immediate repercussions among the musical intelligentsia in the city. Rimsky-Korsakov was dismissed from his conservatory post for anti-government activities, and several of his colleagues, including Glazunov and Lyadov, resigned in sympathy. The building was closed completely for six months, and the following session, 1905–6, was repeatedly disrupted by staffing problems. But the lack of continuous teaching was not the sole cause of Prokofiev's unhappiness. A self-willed and arrogant boy, much younger than his classmates, he made few friends. More than that, he was sadly disillusioned with the teaching. Lyadov's harmony class he found dull and creatively inhibiting, and his relationship with him often developed into open clashes. His later lessons in orchestration with Rimsky-Korsakov he found equally tiresome; he was clearly too young to derive much benefit from Rimsky's experience. It was as well, then, that Lyadov's counterpoint class of 1906 introduced him to two men whose friendship – which was to be lifelong – more than compensated for the general lack of attention accorded his talent. They were Boris Asaf'yev and Nikolay Myaskovsky.

Myaskovsky, who was then 25, had a profound influence on Prokofiev over the next few years. Most of all he gave him encouragement, and it was to Myaskovsky, rather than Lyadov, that Prokofiev showed his latest pieces, the opera *Undina* and a series of piano sonatas (two of which were later remodelled into the sonatas opp.1 and 28). His friendship with Myaskovsky also marked the beginning of his regular contact with new music in St Petersburg. Together they explored the works of Skryabin (whose influence it was difficult for any young Russian composer to escape), Reger, Strauss and Debussy. They procured an introduction to the Evenings of Contemporary Music, the rallying ground of the St Petersburg musical avant garde. These concerts were established under the auspices of some of the leaders of Dyagilev's 'World of Art' movement, Karatïgin, Alfred Nurok and Walter Nuvel; here the works of Schoenberg, Strauss and Stravinsky had their first performances in Russia, and here too, on 31 December 1908, Prokofiev made his public début as a composer–pianist. He played some of his short piano pieces of 1907–8, among them the fiery *Navazhdeniye*, or *Suggestion diabolique*, and took the audience by storm. The press pronounced his music 'unintelligible' and 'ultra-modern'; and in the next few years he did his best to maintain this image of the 'enfant terrible'.

Undoubtedly, it was in these short piano pieces – later grouped into his opp.3 and 4 – that the most startlingly individual features of Prokofiev's early style first emerged. Composed, as they were, for his own performance, they reflect both the uncompromising personality of the young man and the nervous intensity of

his playing, qualities which imparted a sense of almost physical shock to many of his contemporary commentators, Stravinsky and Asaf'yev amongst them. Texturally, rhythmically, and even stylistically, they seem moulded by the preferred sensations of Prokofiev the pianist: his liking for the 'white' keys of C major and the modally-inflected minors of D, E and A, but with sudden shifts to and from the 'black' keys of Db major and Bb minor; his involvement with mounting pace, quick changes of hand direction and intricately-patterned finger movements, resulting in innumerable fast toccatas, dynamic sequential passages, tenuously stretched melodies, chromatic 'blurring' inner lines to the textures, repetitive ostinatos of all sorts, and the frequent propulsion of his music by either strong, hammer-like accents or by jolting contrasts. With the pieces of opp.3 and 4, almost all these characteristic ingredients of his style are already there, if in basic form. The earlier set is technically simpler and emotionally cooler than the spectacular pieces of op.4, a series of miniature musical cabarets of exaggerated gestures and caricatural climaxes, which contain a greater intensity of harmonic dissonance than anything in his music to date.

At the end of the 1908–9 session Prokofiev graduated from the composition course at the conservatory. He had enjoyed little enough of it, and his grades were far from brilliant. In his disillusionment with the composition teaching he had become interested in piano performance, and his first public appearances made him realize that it was as an exponent of his own piano music that he might become better known. And so he decided, for the time being, to continue at the conser-

vatory in the piano and conducting courses.

Prokofiev spent summer 1909, as usual in Sontsovka, composing; his method of working and his attitude to his music were already established. He repeatedly revised and rearranged his scores. Not only did he make substantial revisions to earlier works, but he would frequently adapt movements and whole pieces for new combinations of instruments; piano and orchestral suites appeared from ballet and opera scores, orchestral movements from chamber pieces, and vocal lines were adapted for violin, mostly to attract performances, but also because, for him, a musical idea did not necessarily have a specific context. Moreover, completely new works were composed using thematic ideas from earlier scores. The music of an unfinished string quartet went into the opera *Ognenniy angel* ('The fiery angel') before being rewritten as the Third Symphony; the main musical ideas of the Fourth Symphony had their origins in the ballet *Bludniy sïn* ('The prodigal son'). Of the three works written in summer 1909 only one, the Four Etudes op.2, achieved its final form at once. The First Piano Sonata op.1 was a revision of an earlier work (it was to receive short shrift from the new-music circles – despite the remarkable poise and maturity of its compositional technique – because it sounded like Rakhmaninov), and the Sinfonietta op.5 was to go through two more versions before its eventual publication in 1931.

Prokofiev began his piano course with Anna Esipova in autumn 1909 and, as ever, differences soon developed between pupil and teacher. Prokofiev's training as a pianist had been a haphazard business. From his early

lessons with his mother, and later with Alexander Winkler, he had acquired remarkable dexterity and pan-ache, but no sense of discipline. He disdained the Classical repertory, and if he played Mozart or Schubert at all it was with his own doublings and 'im-provements'. Only when faced with expulsion from the course did Prokofiev accept the rigours of Esipova's methods, and much to his benefit; these four years were decisive to his later career as a pianist, and also to the evolution of certain aspects of his compositional style. The strength of his playing, its precision and steely brilliance – these assets of his personal technique – con-tinued to be predominant influences on his musical thinking for at least the next decade. Esipova, however, developed in him an appreciation of gentler, more lyrical melodic shapes and a geater sensitivity to tone colour; the Ten Piano Pieces of op.12, completed in 1913, are clear evidence of the expansion in his ex-pressive range. And he even grew to appreciate Mozart and Schubert.

Nikolay Tcherepnin's conducting course was of tremendous importance to Prokofiev, not because he was ever more than a competent conductor, even of his own music, but because Tcherepnin, the 'modernist' on the conservatory staff, further promoted his urge to experi-ment with musical sounds. It was an influence not superseded until Prokofiev's introduction to the heady world of Dyagilev's Ballets Russes in 1914. Tcherepnin himself composed in a style that owed much to both Debussy and late Skryabin; the sensuousness of such sounds, mixed with his current attraction to the poems of the symbolist writers Bal'mont and Blok – their

mysteriousness, above all – led Prokofiev to compose a series of intense and atmospheric works, which contrast strongly with most of his pieces hitherto.

The highly charged Romanticism of late Skryabin and early Strauss is not a quality one immediately associates with Prokofiev, but in fact it is clearly in evidence in certain works written over the next ten years or so, works like the symphonic poems *Snï* ('Dreams') and *Osenneye* ('Autumnal sketch'), both of 1910, the cello Ballade (1912), the one-act opera *Maddalena* (1911–13) – strongly influenced by Strauss's *Elektra* and *Salome* – the songs of opp.9, 23 and 27, and much of *The Fiery Angel*. Prokofiev's personal brand of Romanticism communicates itself to the listener most strongly as constant underlying tension, only-just-contained energy; the music of *Maddalena*, in particular, seems continually on the point of eruption. Technically, the emotional charge of these works seems a product of Prokofiev's textural layering; their melodic and harmonic style is not in itself markedly different from his other music of the time. In comparison with, say, *The Tale of the Buffoon* or *The Love for Three Oranges*, both *Maddalena* and *The Fiery Angel* (1919–27) are more densely scored, full of chromatic, blurring, inner parts, often doubled in 3rds and 6ths, against obsessive pedal basses, and of wedge-shaped textures whose angularly-widening melodic shapes wrench themselves against chromatic bass lines. Their often clashing harmonic dissonances are the result of the superimposition of sonorous textural strands – sometimes chordal in themselves – along with measured chromatic glissandos and tremolo effects of all sorts. In his later years, Prokofiev was to achieve emotional intensity by less extrovert means – his scoring

became clearer and more linear, the outlines of his textural shapes softened considerably; but the strong sense of 'atmosphere' created in these earlier works was to remain as an almost physical presence in the most personal of his large scores.

In 1910 Prokofiev's father died, and the circumstances of the 19-year-old composer's life were drastically changed. The estate at Sontsovka had to be given up; his mother gave him a home in St Petersburg and continued to support him as best she could, but the young man who had known no financial hardship was now faced with making his own way in life. The tragedy coincided with the beginnings of his recognition as a composer: 1911 was something of a landmark in his career. He had his first public symphony concert, when *Dreams* and *Autumnal Sketch* were performed in Moscow that July; his works appeared in print for the first time when Jürgenson issued the First Piano Sonata and the pieces of op.3; and he began his first 'more or less mature composition, both as regards the conception and its fulfilment' (as he later wrote), the First Piano Concerto. This was also to be his first truly controversial work, bringing him to the forefront of critical opinion in musical circles in both St Petersburg and Moscow. His initial notion was to write a short concertino for piano and orchestra which he could perform himself, and which might also be a reasonable financial proposition. It was to be expanded into a brilliant, dynamic single-movement work, with an incisive and virtuoso part for the soloist. Though unique in its structure, the concerto immediately established Prokofiev's attitude to the genre. His approach is noticeably unsentimental and un-intimate. He deliberately sim-

117

plifies the conventional conflict between soloist and orchestra; the combination of piano and orchestra is a gloriously bigger-and-better keyboard sonority. The sectional form of the work is undisguised, and its thematic material seems deliberately unsubtle. The compelling power of the score is undeniable, a product not only of its relentless rhythmic drive, but also of the whimsy of its melodic detail – the 'unending' tonal switches in its main sections, the stylized decorations of its central Andante.

The première of the First Piano Concerto in Moscow caused something of a furore, and it was most probably the violent reactions of some of its critics, along with his own love of pianistic bravura, that urged Prokofiev to compose some of the boldest piano pieces of his youth in 1912, among them the Toccata op.11, the *Humoresque Scherzo* of op.12 and the first of the *Sarcasms* op.17. And if the First Piano Concerto caused a sensation, the Second (completed early in 1913) left its listeners, according to the critic Karatïgin, 'frozen with fright, hair standing on end'. It was undoubtedly the frenetic intensity of its middle movements which caused alarm, along with the aggressive excitement of the long cadenza–development for the soloist in the first movement. This passage, virtuoso in the extreme and one of the most iconoclastic in all early Prokofiev, culminates in a wild explosion of ostinato-based dissonance, in which tonality is not so much absent as irrelevant. Despite the poise and even introversion of much of the Concerto's outer movements (probably in part a result of the 1923 rewriting of the score), it must have seemed to the audience at its first performance in St Petersburg like a futurist imperti-

nence. Prokofiev had created a major scandal; most critics could hardly find strong enough terms for condemnation.

The year 1913–14 was Prokofiev's last at the conservatory, and he was to leave with characteristic aplomb. He coveted the Rubinstein Prize, the highest award offered to a student pianist, and he set out to attain it by unorthodox means. Instead of the customary classical concerto, he offered his own First Concerto and had Jürgenson print it for the occasion. His gambit succeeded and, although his examiners, Glazunov among them, were far from unanimous, he won the prize, a grand piano.

Immediately after his graduation, in June 1914, Prokofiev made a trip to London, in the company of Walter Nuvel. He was by then 23, and clearly on the threshold of fame in Russia, as both pianist and composer. Admired in new-music circles, he was also beginning to find acceptance by the musical establishment: he had recently performed his First Concerto at one of Koussevitzky's subscription matinées. His compositional style was already distinctive and well formed. But he now came into contact with the fashionable musical sct, not of Russia but of all Europe: Dyagilev, Stravinsky and the Ballets Russes. Dyagilev's charisma he found irresistible, and musically he fell under the spell of Stravinsky's stage works. In London he saw *The Nightingale*, *The Firebird* and *Petrushka*, but it was, not surprisingly, *The Rite of Spring* which had most impact on his works of the following years. Stravinsky was possibly the only contemporary composer to have a direct influence on Prokofiev's music, on works like *Ala i Lolli*, *Skazka pro shuta* ('The tale of the buffoon'), the

cantata *Semero ikh* ('They are seven') and the Second Symphony, though it was one Prokofiev was curiously unwilling to acknowledge. He admired Stravinsky, but there were obviously personal rivalries between them.

Prokofiev met Dyagilev in London and played him his Second Piano Concerto. Ever on the lookout for new Russian exotica, Dyagilev thought of presenting the work as a ballet but then decided to commission a new score from Prokofiev, for a ballet on a prehistoric theme. Prokofiev's relations with the Ballets Russes were to be unproductive for some time to come; it was not until 1921 that one of his ballets was staged by the company. *Ala i Lolli*, begun in 1914, was doomed from the start. Both Prokofiev and Gorodetsky, who wrote the scenario, were totally inexperienced in writing for the ballet stage, and Stravinsky's 'paganism' in *The Rite of Spring* was not easy to match. Dyagilev arranged a concert in Rome for Prokofiev in March 1915, but he rejected his score. A second ballet was commissioned; *The Tale of the Buffoon*, or *Chout*, begun in 1915, was to be one of Prokofiev's brightest and wittiest works, but war prevented its immediate performance.

Despite the stature of his later symphonies, it was in his ballets that Prokofiev's (like Stravinsky's) orchestral thought found its most natural and characteristic outlet. And from these first scores, apart from the audible reminders of Stravinsky's influence, it is clear that Prokofiev's fundamental impulses were in reality quite different from those of his older contemporary, especially in the realm of rhythm. Prokofiev's rhythms are almost entirely external: they evolve around unchanging, metric beat, and are characteristically unsyncopated. At their extreme, in *Ala i Lolli*, the rhyth-

mic force of the music is carried in repetitive patterns of metric downbeats. As a result, the larger rhythmic structures are almost always periodic. Prokofiev's melodies, too – again unlike Stravinsky's – are both strongly metrical and fall into recognizable phrase structures; almost all of his linear figurations tend to function as, and to sound like, tunes – though of a highly distinctive nature. Inevitably, then, his typical longer structures are of the sectional and lyrical sort; hence the complex permutations of 'arch' and rondo forms that underlie much of his music of all periods. And even his experimental earlier ballet scores are much more recognizably music for dancing than any of Stravinsky's stage works before *The Soldier's Tale*.

Most of the war period Prokofiev spent in Petrograd, avoiding conscription by enrolling once more as a student at the conservatory, this time in the organ class. Since his contact with Dyagilev he had become something of a fashionable figure in musical Petrograd, and his recent works had several performances. With the première of *The Tale of the Buffoon* postponed, he took up an idea that had been in his mind for some time, to compose an opera based on Dostoyevsky's *The Gambler*. Since Dyagilev's departure from Russia the younger members of the Mariinsky Theatre directorate were keen to match his successes on home ground, and the new conductor of the theatre orchestra, Albert Coates, promised to perform Prokofiev's opera. Aware that a sensation was expected of him, Prokofiev allowed his imagination free play; in its original form *Igrok* ('The gambler') is his most violent and impulsive score, at the furthest extreme from the conventions of traditional opera, with its formal divisions and set numbers.

The impression is of complete spontaneity – a kaleidoscopic array of new ideas following one another breathlessly, and bound together only by dramatic appropriateness and rhythmic energy. There are recurring motifs, but in effect these are swept on by the opera's headlong rush towards its climax, the wonderful scene in the gaming-hall, which Prokofiev 'permitted [himself] to consider entirely new in the literature of opera', and which is certainly one of his finest achievements as a composer. He worked quickly on the score, and rehearsals began in January 1917. There were difficulties almost at once; the singers were unhappy in their roles, the director resigned, the orchestra revolted, and with the first Revolution at the end of February 1917 the performance had to be cancelled.

The February Revolution caused no major disruptions in the musical life of Petrograd, however; the theatres remained open and concerts continued. Prokofiev spent that summer in a village on the outskirts of the city at work on the First Violin Concerto and the Classical Symphony. These two works, dissimilar though they are, give some of the earliest indications of future clarifications in Prokofiev's musical style. True to its original conception as a concertino, the Violin Concerto is deliberately unsensational and unshowy: the music of the solo line grows from and merges with an unusually transparent (for the time) orchestral texture in a relationship not of tension, but of cohesion. The climactic coda of the final movement is, indeed, one of the most rhapsodic passages Prokofiev ever wrote. The Classical Symphony was begun as an experiment in composing without the piano; it was deliberately close to Haydn in style, with the addition of 'something new'.

The title is the composer's own, chosen partly to 'tease the geese', but also in the hope that the work would become a classic. His hopes were fulfilled: it was among the first of his works to gain international recognition.

Meanwhile Petrograd was reaching a state of crisis. In September it was rumoured that the city was about to fall to the Germans, and Prokofiev left to join his mother in the Caucasus. On 7 November 1917 the Bolsheviks under Lenin seized power from the provisional government. In the wake of revolution came civil war, dividing the country into several fronts on which the Red Army fought the Whites. Kislovodsk in the Caucasus, where Prokofiev was staying, remained in White hands until March 1918, when it was occupied by the Red Army. Prokofiev then returned north, first to Moscow then to Petrograd. He gave some concerts, including the first performances of the Classical Symphony and the Third and Fourth Piano Sonatas, but by this time he had decided to go abroad. It seemed to him that Russia, in its present unsettled state, had little use for new music. In May 1918 he left for the USA, apparently with the intention of returning after a few months.

CHAPTER TWO

USA: 1918–22

As a composer of 27, Prokofiev was well justified in regarding his immediate future outside Russia with optimism. Within Russia his career had been strikingly successful. He had been able to compose almost entirely on his own impulse, with few financial difficulties and no more than an encouraging amount of opposition from his critics. His contacts with western Europe, if not yet productive, were at least encouraging. A performance of *The Tale of the Buffoon* was still promised by Dyagilev, and Prokofiev hoped, now that the work was completed, that *The Gambler*, too, might be staged. America, with its reputation for artistic open-mindedness, must have seemed to offer exciting prospects in his present situation.

The journey to New York, by way of Vladivostok, Tokyo and San Francisco, took over four months. On board ship he occupied himself with fresh compositional plans. A libretto for a new opera, *Lyubov' k tryom apel'sinam* ('The love for three oranges'), was sketched out; a two-movement string quartet was begun (and soon discarded). His reputation, he found, had indeed arrived before him, but he was soon to encounter the attendant pressures. As a composer and as a phenomenon from 'Godless Russia' he was expected to outdo the novelty value of a Stravinsky, to satisfy the critics; and as a performer he would have to compete in tech-

nical virtuosity with artists like Rakhmaninov, to satisfy his promoters and audiences.

Prokofiev began well enough. His first solo recital, in the Aeolian Hall, New York, on 20 November, created an appropriate sensation; the manufacturers of Steinway–Duo-art player pianos immediately requested recordings from him, and a New York publishing house commissioned some new piano pieces, *Skazki staroy babushki* ('The tales of an old grandmother') op.31 and the Four Pieces op.32. These new pieces, delicate, lyrical, almost simplistic in mood, seem to hark back to the style of some of his earliest piano miniatures, and they made little impression on any potential American publishers. Two concerts given by Frederick Stock in Chicago, including the First Piano Concerto and the *Scythian Suite* (from *Ala i Lolli*), were so successful, however, that the directors of the Chicago Opera offered to produce one of his stage works. They approved the plans for his new opera, and a contract for *The Love for Three Oranges* was signed in January 1919; the work was to be completed by October for inclusion in the winter season.

The prospect of a performance must have filled Prokofiev with elation, but in the event it was to be short-lived. Despite his lifelong attraction to opera, uncomplicated success in this medium continually eluded him. He spent long periods, often against all creative and financial odds, at work on at least ten opera scores; the disappointments he encountered in trying to have them staged must have been among the saddest blows in his composing career. Three of the ten, *Maddalena* (1911–13), *Khan Buzay* (1942) and *Dalyokiye morya* ('Distant seas', 1948), had to be aban-

125

doned for lack of support before they were finished. Three more, *The Fiery Angel* (1919–27), *Voyna i mir* ('War and peace', 1941–52) and *Povest' o nastoyash-chem cheloveke* ('The story of a real man', 1947–8), had no complete staged performances in his lifetime. *Sem-yon Kotko* (1939), his first Soviet opera, survived initial production difficulties and reached the stage in 1940, but was soon dropped because of its 'inappropriate' subject matter.

Only *The Love for Three Oranges* gained truly inter-national acclaim for Prokofiev during his lifetime. Its success is entirely justifiable; of all his operas the plot of *Oranges* seemed best suited to the composer's natural talents. Prokofiev wrote what was, above all, an opera to amuse, a refined and sophisticated extravaganza. The volatile nature of the fairy-tale he recreated, in musical terms, in an entirely characteristic and wholly individual way. His score is built up, like a highly colourful mosaic, in patterns of very short, epigrammatic musical figures, as varied in their shape as in their instrumentation; these figures work up considerable energy and momentum for as long as they are relevant to the dramatic situation; they are immediately superseded when their impetus is exhausted. Most of the thematic ideas are instantly recognizable; they are in themselves repetitive, and are typically extended into cumulative ostinatos. Moments of extended lyricism are rare in the work, but for that very reason such moments are both sweet and pungent: here, Prokofiev's sense of theatre is unerringly effective. Even with this opera, however, there were initial per-formance problems. Despite a near-fatal illness in spring 1919 Prokofiev completed the work in time, and by December rehearsals were well under way; then the

conductor Campanini died and the première was postponed until the following season. A wrangle over financial compensation resulted, along with another postponement, and the opera was not performed until December 1921.

In the process Prokofiev's American career had reached a low ebb. By devoting all his energies to the opera he had sacrificed his contacts in the performing world, and in any case his promoters were unwilling to risk the bad publicity he might gain by performing too much of his own music. He was in financial difficulty. His decision to leave the USA was becoming inevitable, but having no desire to return to Russia with a sense of failure, he set his sights on Paris, where Dyagilev's Ballets Russes had now resumed their seasons of opera and ballet. Even in the middle of this disillusionment, however, he began work on another opera. *The Fiery Angel*, uncommissioned and in any light an unwise proposition, may well have been sheer escapism. This strange, though musically powerful work seems certainly to have fulfilled a strong inner need in Prokofiev; on only one other score, *War and Peace*, did he ever lavish so much time and care.

The Fiery Angel is perhaps the most difficult of all his operas to place in context. In its concern with characters about whom we learn little that is personal, and whose behaviour seems entirely ritualistic, it seems far removed from any traditions of Russian opera. In addition, Prokofiev's means of musical structuring (the entire opera is formed as an extended, thematically-taut, sonata structure, into which are interpolated a series of self-contained action episodes) is unique in his music, and would seem to have some affinity with that of

Wagnerian–Straussian music drama. The general chromatic richness of its harmonic language, too, owes much to Germanic tradition. Yet the opera sounds quite unlike the work of any other composer and, indeed, in the raw intimacy and sustained intensity of its personal expression, it is also exceptional in Prokofiev's own output.

In April 1920 Prokofiev went to Paris. His contact with the USA continued; in the short term, he had still to attend to the production of *The Love for Three Oranges*, and until 1938 he gave prolonged concert tours throughout North America. As a composer, however, he was to meet with much more ready acceptance in Europe, and it was in France that he wrote most of his music over the next 16 years. Straight away he renewed his association with Dyagilev and Stravinsky, and as a result spent summer 1920 in Mantes-la-Jolie revising the ballet *The Tale of the Buffoon* for its inclusion in the company's next summer season. In December he made a long concert tour of California, which he found delightful; there he wrote the Five Songs without Words op.35 for the soprano Nina Koshits.

The Tale of the Buffoon opened in Paris on 17 May 1921 as the novelty of the season. It was a lavish production, which pleased the Parisian audiences, but soon shocked the London critics. Well pleased with the excitement he had created, Prokofiev retired for the summer to Etretât on the coast of Brittany to work on the Third Piano Concerto. The idea of composing a large virtuoso concerto, for his own performance, had been in his mind for several years, and many of the main themes were already sketched out. Part of the first movement dates from 1911; the main melody of the

128

second movement was written in 1913; the two main first-movement themes and two of the central variations date from 1916–17; and part of the finale came from his discarded string quartet of 1918. But in spite of its diverse origins, this was to be one of Prokofiev's most attractive and satisfying scores; it is still the most popular of his five piano concertos. In each of its three movements, and in the work as a whole, the composer succeeded in finding both a poetic and a structural balance between moments of 'confrontation' (which he found irresistible) and overall continuity. It is also one of his most truly inventive scores, in terms of the sheer quality of its thematic ideas.

In Brittany Prokofiev renewed his friendship with Bal'mont, who had emigrated to France. He had been captivated by Bal'mont's 'cosmic and barbarous exotic images' at the height of the symbolist vogue in pre-war St Petersburg, and had set several of his poems, both then and later, in his songs of opp.7, 9 and 23, and in the dramatic cantata *They are Seven* op.30. In the course of the summer of 1921 he set five new poems in his cycle of op.36; Bal'mont reciprocated with a sonnet on the Third Piano Concerto.

At the end of October Prokofiev was back in Chicago for the rehearsals of *The Love for Three Oranges*. The première, given in French, was warmly received in Chicago, perhaps simply from civic pride, but it was by no means appreciated by the critics in New York, who heard it a few weeks later. There were similar responses from the two cities to the Third Piano Concerto, given by the composer in December and January. Indeed, his American season, which had begun promisingly enough, had collapsed completely by spring 1922, when Mary

Garden, his supporter with the Chicago Opera, resigned her directorship. With this his hopes for a performance of *The Fiery Angel* faded, and he had once more to retreat from the American scene, 'with a thousand dollars in my pocket and an aching head'.

CHAPTER THREE

Paris: 1922–36

Prokofiev left the USA and returned to Europe in
March 1922, with a fervent desire for peace, quiet and
time to compose. He went first to Paris to join his
mother, who had left Russia in spring 1920. Then, along
with her and the poet Boris Verin, he rented a house in
the village of Ettal, near Oberammergau in the Bavarian
Alps. This was to be his first real home after four years
of travelling, and the 18 months he spent there were in
many ways of crucial importance to his future. Financed
by the proceeds of his American trip and the concerts he
continued to give throughout the European centres, he
was for a time able to devote most of his energies to
composition. Some of this activity was directed towards
profitable ends – he arranged the piano scores of *The
Love for Three Oranges* and *The Tale of the Buffoon* for
publication and extracted a symphonic suite from the
ballet – but mainly he worked on *The Fiery Angel*. The
atmosphere of the surrounding countryside was conducive to work – the witches' sabbaths portrayed in *The
Fiery Angel* must have happened thereabouts – and by
the beginning of 1923 he had completed the opera in
piano score. He then revised the Second Piano
Concerto, the original score having been lost, and began
the Fifth Piano Sonata.

In spring 1923 Prokofiev received his first official
invitation to return to Russia, when the Leningrad PO

offered him a series of concert engagements. Over the preceding five years he had kept in touch with musical affairs in the USSR through his correspondence with personal friends. He was in contact with Myaskovsky and Meyerhold, who loyally defended his decision to stay abroad to the Soviet musical establishment. In May 1923 a report on his activities appeared in the journal *K novïm beregam*, and around the same time some of his recent works were performed in Leningrad and Moscow. Three of the songs of op.36 had their première in Moscow in October 1923; the Third Piano Concerto and the *Scythian Suite* were both given there in 1925; and in February 1926 *The Love for Three Oranges* opened in Leningrad, where it ran for 49 performances. But in 1923 Prokofiev was not yet ready to return to Russia. His career in western Europe was just beginning, and the future looked promising. He had strong family ties there; his mother was ill and largely dependent on him (she died in December 1924). In September 1923 he married the Spanish-born singer Lina Llubera, and in 1924 his son Svyatoslav was born; his second son, Oleg, was born in 1928. So he declined the offer from Leningrad, and a similar invitation the following year, but he kept the possibility open for the future.

After his marriage Prokofiev moved with his family to Paris. Over the next few months several of his works had their first performances there – the First Violin Concerto, the Fifth Piano Sonata, the revised Second Piano Concerto and *They are Seven* – but with mixed success. Perhaps because of certain anomalies in the idiom of his music, its mixture of sophisticated elements with a sort of home-grown innocence, of steely dissonance with almost tender lyricism, perhaps also because

10. Sergey Prokofiev with his wife, Lina

of his personality, Prokofiev must have found the Paris of the early 1920s a difficult world to conquer, to shock or to amuse. To be Russian was in itself no longer chic. Stravinsky may still have been a fashionable figure in musical circles, but he was by now truly Parisian, and Prokofiev could not approve of his recent music, his 'pseudo-Bachism', as Prokofiev later described it. Milhaud, Poulenc and the other members of Les Six were very much in vogue, and although Prokofiev was personally friendly with the group he could not share their musical attitudes. However, in summer 1924, the year of Honegger's *Pacific 231*, he set out to write his own work 'of iron and steel'.

This was the Second Symphony, perhaps his most startling, certainly – its first movement, at least – his most complicated score. Determined to cause a sensation with the work, he laboured over its composition for more than nine months, finding the task unusually difficult. The result was a two-movement symphony of large dimensions (its structure was modelled on Beethoven's Piano Sonata op.111), which contains some of the most densely-textured music Prokofiev wrote. The first movement is seethingly energetic and aggressive, its main theme surely one of the most angular of its day. The following Theme and Variations begins quietly enough (its material dates back to the months the composer spent in Japan in 1918), but the internal tensions of the music remain unrelieved, and there is no true resolution in its quiet ending. The uncompromising effort behind Prokofiev's intentions seems still to linger in the Second Symphony, even if time has mellowed the harshness of its outlines. It is indicative that Prokofiev himself, most untypically, had doubts about the worth of

his achievement – doubts that the première in June 1925 did little to dispel. The work was far from successful; and Prokofiev would have been thrown into deep despair had not Dyagilev just then approached him with a new, and most surprising, commission.

With its formal recognition by most of the major countries of western Europe, Soviet Russia and the life of its people had suddenly become topical, and Dyagilev now proposed to stage a ballet on a Soviet theme. The constructivist painter Yakulov, who had only recently left Russia, was to write the scenario. The theme of the new work was to be industrialization; it was to be a ballet of construction, with a 'wielding of hammers big and small . . . and a flashing of light signals'. Prokofiev was delighted by the idea, and began work on *Stal'noy skok* ('The steel step'), or *Le pas d'acier*, Dyagilev's title, with great enthusiasm. Most of the music was composed over a two-month period, in August and September 1925.

Towards the end of that year Prokofiev and his wife left Europe for a concert tour of the USA. It was his first visit for almost four years, and by comparison with his last it was comfortably successful. The following spring the couple gave a recital tour in Italy. It was on his travels at this time that Prokofiev devised a new system of orchestrating his scores that allowed him to carry out the process even on rough train journeys. With practice he found it possible to indicate not only the instrumentation, but also details of accent and bowing by expanding his original piano score on to one or more additional staves. Most of his later works were notated in this way, with the transcription into full score left to an amanuensis.

The orchestration of *The Steel Step* was completed by spring 1926. Its première was postponed until the following year, but in the meantime Bruno Walter had accepted *The Fiery Angel* for performance in Berlin. Prokofiev accordingly spent summer 1926 revising the music and reorganizing the dramatic structure of the opera. At the same time he worked on the 'American' Overture, op.42, a work interesting in the combination of its instrumental timbres, but one which, like some few of its time, met with a cool response from both audiences and critics. In the autumn he was once more in correspondence with concert authorities in the USSR; this time he accepted their invitation to make an extensive tour in western Russia.

On 18 January 1927 Prokofiev arrived in the USSR after an absence of almost nine years. His tour lasted for three months, during which he gave 21 concerts in Moscow, Leningrad, Khar'kov, Kiev and Odessa. He conducted or performed most of his recent works, among them the suites from *The Love for Three Oranges* and *The Tale of the Buffoon*, the Second and Third Piano Concertos and his piano sonatas and songs. The 'American' Overture and the Quintet op.39 had their premières in Moscow, and Prokofiev attended the Leningrad production of *The Love for Three Oranges*. Everywhere he was received as a celebrity; indeed the great success of the tour, along with his renewal of personal friendships, must have made the prospect of a permanent return very attractive.

Rehearsals for *The Steel Step* had already begun in Paris, however, and its successful première was on 7 June 1927. Dyagilev had spared no expense; the production played up the Bolshevik subject matter to

the full, and Prokofiev's music sounded authentically 'constructivist'. Partly in an attempt to produce music that he thought 'could convey the spirit of modern times', that would be forthright and direct, in keeping with the nature of the subject, and no doubt partly as a reaction against the complications of the Second Symphony, the music of the new ballet was 'in large measure diatonic and many of the themes were composed on white notes only'. In fact, with its rhythmic repetitions and its obsessive small intervals, *The Steel Step* owes more to the influence of *The Rite of Spring*, *The Wedding* and to the machine music of Les Six than to anything specifically Soviet, a fact not lost on the Russian Association of Proletarian Musicians (RAPM) when they auditioned, and rejected, the ballet in Moscow in 1929. But the novelty value of the whole spectacle was considerable, and its success was repeated a month later in London.

With the orchestration of *The Fiery Angel* completed, but with its Berlin performance postponed indefinitely, Prokofiev began a similar process of revision on his early opera *The Gambler*. Meyerhold had long been eager to stage the première of the work, and in the course of 1926 and 1927 he went to Paris to discuss the possibility of producing it as a follow-up to the Leningrad production of *The Love for Three Oranges*. Prokofiev's revisions, carried out over the winter of 1927–8, were extensive. By now an experienced theatre-composer, his views on opera had modified considerably since those of 1917. He discarded those portions of the score which were 'sheer padding disguised by thunderous chords', clarified the orchestration, and imposed a greater degree of order on the work's overall structure. The result,

however, is by no means tamer than the original; the revolutionary nature of Prokofiev's concept is, rather, more clearly and effectively realized. *The Gambler* had its first, successful, performance in April 1929, but it was in Brussels. In Leningrad, 'interest in the project had gradually waned' in the light of the RAPM's disapproval of the opera.

Two large and important works occupied Prokofiev throughout the remainder of 1928: the Third Symphony and the ballet *The Prodigal Son* (*L'enfant prodigue*). The symphony was a product of Prokofiev's unshakable faith in the worth of *The Fiery Angel*. In June 1928 the second act of the opera was given a concert performance under Koussevitzky in Paris, and Prokofiev decided that, rather than make an orchestral suite from the music, he might develop its thematic material symphonically. The drama and intensity of the resultant Third Symphony op.44 are the only hints to the listener of its operatic origins. Prokofiev insisted that, in its new context, his music should not be considered programmatic or merely illustrative, and indeed his atmospheric textures and their dramatic contrasts seem to acquire greater musical stature in the symphony. The composer considered it one of his best scores, and one in which, he felt, he had 'succeeded in deepening [his] musical language'.

Dyagilev's request for a ballet on the biblical theme of the prodigal son was as surprising to Prokofiev as his last commission, but it was a task he found 'both easy and pleasant'. Aided by a strong, dramatic plot, he wrote and orchestrated the music in the space of three months (November 1928 to February 1929). The two new works had their first performances within four days

138

in the middle of May 1929 – the ballet not without problems. Dyagilev was already ill (he died only two months later) and had lost enthusiasm for the work; Lifar, in a fit of pique, did not wish to perform the title role. It was only at the last minute that all was made well, and Prokofiev's ballet, given in a programme with Stravinsky's *Renard*, was warmly received.

The production of *The Prodigal Son* marked the height of Prokofiev's success in Paris. The ballet is the work of a composer fully in command of his creative powers. He never produced a more lyrical, nor more melodically beautiful score than this. In that it happened to mark the end of an era, both culturally (the season was Dyagilev's last) and personally for Prokofiev (it was his last major work written specifically for performance in Paris), it is a work of special importance in his output. In strong contrast to the Third Symphony, the ballet is cool and transparent, already closer in spirit to some of the Soviet-period works – *Zolushka* ('Cinderella') or the Sixth Symphony, for instance – than to his earlier ballets. The metamorphosis of his musical idiom was taking place not through struggle, but apparently with marvellous ease.

When he received a commission in summer 1929 for a symphonic work to commemorate the 50th anniversary of the Boston SO, Prokofiev again thought of re-using material from his theatrical music. The Fourth Symphony, extracted partly from the music of *The Prodigal Son* and partly from music he had written for the ballet but not included in it, is less of a success than the Third, however. As a symphony, it seems lacking in momentum, and this despite (or perhaps because of) the wealth and beauty of its thematic ideas.

139

In October 1929 Prokofiev was involved in a motor-car accident, which temporarily injured his hands, so that his visit to Moscow in November was without concert engagements. He was able on this occasion to hear much new Soviet music and to become acquainted with some of the workings of the musical establishment, though still as an outsider. More or less recovered from his accident, he undertook an extensive concert tour of the USA, Canada and Cuba early in 1930. Since his success in Europe, respect for Prokofiev's music had increased immeasurably in the USA, and his reception both by the public and by the press 'was quite serious this time'. A string quartet was commissioned by the Library of Congress, and the Metropolitan Opera in New York showed interest in staging *The Fiery Angel*. His hopes raised, yet again, Prokofiev began a second revision of the opera's dramatic structure; Act 2 was broken up into a number of short, dynamic scenes. But, once more, the production failed to materialize, and the planned revision was never completed.

On his return to Europe, Prokofiev gave a series of concerts in Brussels, Turin, Monte Carlo and Milan before returning to Paris to work on the string quartet, and on a new ballet, commissioned by the Paris Opéra. The ballet, *Na Dnepre* ('On the Dnieper'), or *Sur le Borysthène*, written in collaboration with Lifar, was to be the least memorable of his theatrical works. Its plot, set among the peasants of the Ukraine, was far from gripping. Its music was written as an abstract piece and, though not unlike *The Prodigal Son* in idiom, it is loosely constructed and rather pallid. It survived no more than a few performances at the Opéra in 1932.

Apart from the Fifth Sonata, Prokofiev had

composed practically nothing for the piano in the 1920s. It may be that he had lost confidence in his handling of the medium. Whatever the reason, the group of works that he composed for the piano in the early 1930s – the Fourth Piano Concerto op.53, the two Sonatinas op.54 and the Fifth Piano Concerto op.55 – are not only rather strange pieces but, despite their energetic fast movements, they seem idiomatically tentative and uncertain. The clarification of his style may have happened in some works with ease, but Prokofiev himself later described these years as a period of creative frustration, of searching for a 'new simplicity' – a simplicity 'with its novel forms and . . . new tonal structure' which was, he felt, largely misunderstood. Undoubtedly in the light of Stravinsky's neo-classical explorations (of which Prokofiev disapproved) and Schoenberg's serial systemizations (which were both temperamentally and compositionally alien to Prokofiev), he felt impelled to scrutinize his own techniques; and it was probably more important than ever to him that he should maintain his own musical individuality.

In the short term his searchings were not overtly successful. Neither the Fourth Concerto of 1931 (a commission from the Austrian pianist Paul Wittgenstein and written for the left hand alone) nor the Fifth Concerto of 1932 seems audibly to demonstrate 'novel forms' or whatever 'new tonal structure' he had in mind. The former is a lively four-movement work, modest in scale, but of considerable virtuosity for the pianist; the latter was planned as a non-virtuoso work, originally to be called 'Music for Piano' rather than concerto – though it grew into a suite of five movements, full of vivid moods and sharp contrasts. Both works are more clearly

141

sectional than his works of the 1920s. The forms of their parts are familiar enough – sonata-rondos, rondos and ternary forms, often with highly decorated repeats. Their thematic textures, however, though often densely scored, are less complex and more diatonic than previously, and with this his melodies (always a dominant element in his music) seem to have acquired a kind of studied gaucheness, a whimsy born of deliberation. Neither work made a public impact. The Fourth Concerto was received by Wittgenstein with politeness but a total lack of comprehension, and he never played it, while the Fifth, perhaps because of a certain lack of overall cohesion, has never been as widely performed as the First and Third Piano Concertos.

The years 1932–6, like the period 1918–22, saw great flux and change in Prokofiev's circumstances. It was a time of decision: whether to return to the USSR and become a Soviet citizen, or to remain, as Stravinsky and Rakhmaninov had done, in the West as an émigré. Exactly when he made his decision, or even if he formulated it as such, is unclear; Victor Seroff in his biography of Prokofiev describes a conversation with him in Paris in 1932 which implied that his mind was already made up; other sources disagree. It is easier to speculate on the reasons why he decided to return. Perhaps naively, he seems to have disregarded the political implications of such a move. Prokofiev had never held any strong political views; he may well have assumed that the Soviet authorities would respect this, and that if any pressures were being brought to bear on composers, of all people, they somehow would not apply to him. Quite simply, he wanted to go home. Throughout his stay in the West he had never ceased to be, above all, a

Russian. He had made many close acquaintances, but his real friends were Russians, and most of them, Myaskovsky, Derzhanovsky, Meyerhold and Asaf'yev, were in the USSR. He missed the support and confidence of these people; most of all he missed the vital stimulus of being in the company of Russians in Russia.

The process of his return was a gradual one; it was not until spring 1936 that he was permanently resident in Moscow. Until then both he and his wife held Nansen passports. Although his trips to the USSR became increasingly frequent after 1932, and from 1933 he had the use of an apartment in Moscow, his home was still in Paris. His family lived there, all his belongings were there, and most of the music he wrote between 1932 and 1936 was composed in Paris.

Gradually the sources of Prokofiev's commissions changed. Of the works of this period only two had their origins in France: the Sonata for two violins (1932) was written for the Triton chamber concerts in Paris, and the Second Violin Concerto (1935) was a commission from the French violinist Robert Soetans. The concerto had its first performance in Madrid on a tour Soetans made with Prokofiev to Spain, Portugal and north Africa at the end of 1935. Two more works, the *Symphonic Song* op.57 and the Cello Concerto in E minor op.58, though written for performance in Paris, had their premières in Moscow, in 1934 and 1938. The remainder, all large-scale pieces, were written for Soviet performance.

Of these works only the Second Violin Concerto exhibits both the creative confidence and technical mastery of the best of Prokofiev's music. He decided from the outset that it would be entirely different from

143

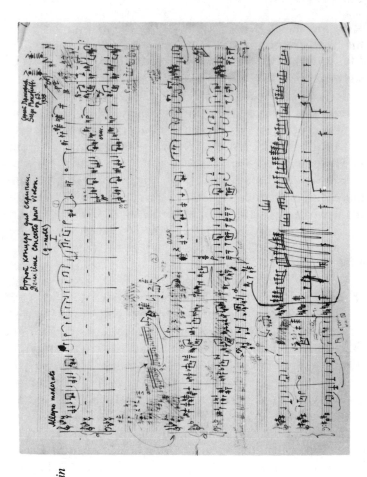

11. Autograph sketches for the opening of Prokofiev's Violin Concerto no. 2, composed 1935

the First Violin Concerto of 17 years earlier; it was
conceived as an intimate work, a 'concert sonata for
violin and orchestra'. The format was expanded in the
writing of the piece, but the consequences of Prokofiev's
initial impulses were to remain: compared with its
predecessor, this concerto is much more personal, more
meditative and even more restrained. The lyricism of its
first two movements – the mellow richness of the central
Andante in particular – has strong affinities with the
love music of *Romeo and Juliet*, written during the same
summer months of 1935. And while its exhilarating
finale seems entirely propelled by the wilful whimsy of
the composer's earlier years, this is the work which most
nearly marks the beginning of Prokofiev's later compositional style.

Prokofiev's first Soviet commissions came in 1933.
That year he made two trips to the USSR, to Moscow
in April and to the Caucasus for an extensive concert
tour in the autumn. In the spring the Leningrad film
director Feinzimmer approached him with the request
for music for his film *Poruchik Kizhe* ('Lieutenant Kije').
This satirical tale, of the soldier who never was, perfectly matched Prokofiev's sense of humour, and he
spent that summer in Paris working on the delightfully
frivolous score which was to become perhaps his most
popular work. Then he received a commission from the
Moscow Kamernïy Theatre for music for a dramatic
extravaganza in which it was planned to combine ex-
tracts from Shaw's *Caesar and Cleopatra*,
Shakespeare's *Antony and Cleopatra* and Pushkin's
Egyptian Nights. Less inspired by this idea, Prokofiev
wrote some rather undistinguished music for chamber
orchestra, which accompanied the play in its short run

145

in April 1935. The best of the music he included in the orchestral suite *Egipetskiye nochi* ('Egyptian nights') op.61.

Towards the end of 1934 a suggestion came from the Kirov Theatre in Leningrad to stage a new ballet by Prokofiev. The choice of subject, *Romeo and Juliet*, proved controversial from the start, and soon the project was taken over by the Bol'shoy Theatre in Moscow. The problem was the ending to the story; as Prokofiev later put it, 'living people can dance, the dying cannot'. A happy ending, with Romeo arriving in the nick of time, seemed the only solution, and it was with this dénouement that the first version of the score was composed. It was the longest ballet Prokofiev had ever written, and the most intensely dramatic. Its 52 separate numbers, despite being almost all 'closed' structural units, and a significant proportion of them rhythmically conventional dances (waltzes, galops, minuets, gavottes), are in performance remarkably cohesive. It is an immensely compelling piece of musical theatre. Even so, its composition took him only four months, and at the end of summer 1935 his piano score was heard by the theatre directorate. The work was rejected out of hand as being unsuitable for dancing. Prokofiev carried out large-scale revisions to the music in the months that followed. The choreographers found a way of restoring the original tragic ending to the drama. But it was to be some years before *Romeo i Dzhul'yetta* was seen in Moscow.

CHAPTER FOUR

USSR: 1936–53

Prokofiev took up permanent residence in the USSR with the arrival of his wife and family in Moscow in the spring of 1936. His move to the USSR coincided with a critical period for Soviet music. With the dissolution of the RAPM in 1932 and the subsequent establishment of the Union of Soviet Composers, the administration of musical affairs throughout the country was, in effect, subject to government control. The Party Central Committee had also recommended general guidelines for composers and these, on the surface at least, probably seemed not unreasonable to Prokofiev. Composers were advised to pay heed to the social content of their music and its appeal to the people at large; as a basis for their idiom they might look to the traditions of the past and to folk resources within the countries of the USSR.

In practice, however, this was the beginning of Russia's artistic isolation from western Europe, as one important result was the disappearance from concert programmes within the USSR of much recent music by progressive composers in the West. None of this as yet directly affected Prokofiev, although he had already felt the effects of censorship with *The Steel Step* and *The Gambler*. In January, only months before his family moved to Moscow, came *Pravda*'s overt condemnation of

Shostakovich. Again, while Prokofiev was not directly involved, the implications of such an attack could not have escaped him. Whether as a reaction to such events, or because of his disappointment over *Romeo and Juliet*, or simply as a change from the scale of his recent scores, he concentrated his attention in the meantime on a number of short pieces, many of them written for children. From this period date the Music for Children, a series of easy pieces for piano, the Three Children's Songs op.68 and *Petya i volk* ('Peter and the wolf').

By the middle of 1936 preparations were being made for two important jubilees the following year, the 20th anniversary of the Revolution and the centenary of Pushkin's death. Prokofiev wrote his Three Romances op.73 to texts by Pushkin during summer 1936, and at the same time he worked on three separate commissions he had received in connection with the Pushkin celebrations. He had been asked by the director Romm to provide music for a film version of *The Queen of Spades*; Meyerhold had commissioned a 'stormy background' for his projected experimental production of *Boris Godunov*; and from the Kamerniy Theatre came the request for incidental music to a new stage adaptation of *Evgeny Onegin*. Since all three had famous operatic settings, Prokofiev regarded the task as a challenge, and it is clear from his manuscripts that he took great care in composing the music. He was prompted to write an article on the question of combining music with spoken dialogue, and he was concerned, as he was in his later operas, to find musical equivalents for the characters as they develop dramatically. For various reasons, however, none of the Pushkin productions materialized. Prokofiev was to re-use many of his thematic ideas in

later scores, notably in *Semyon Kotko* and *War and Peace*.

For the other celebrations he composed his mammoth *Cantata for the Twentieth Anniversary of the October Revolution*, to texts by Marx, Lenin and Stalin, and for a total of 500 performers. It was a sincere attempt to approach the concept of socialist realism, and in fact its performance calls for such 'realistic' sound-effects as gun shots, machine-gun fire and sirens. Prokofiev had begun the work early in 1936 in Paris, though some of its themes date from years earlier; its orchestration occupied him through summer 1937. Once again, however, its hoped-for performance never took place. Its critics suspected Prokofiev's motives in writing such a work, and there were accusations of vulgarity. Such accusations were, in fact, quite unfounded. It may have been naive on Prokofiev's part to set texts of such fundamental ideological importance, but he responded to their drama with music which is both haunting and emotionally stirring, comparable with his best of that time. The build-up of its ten large sections is evidence, once more, of the composer's sure sense of dramatic effect and the direct appeal of his creative ideas. The cantata was not performed until 1966, but it is surely only the somewhat unexportable nature of its subject matter that has prevented its international recognition.

Prokofiev made two concert tours abroad during this period, the first in December 1936 through western Europe and the USA, the second at the beginning of 1938 to Czechoslovakia, France, Britain and the USA. These were his last tours outside the USSR – a further trip, planned for 1940, had to be cancelled – and in the

course of his stay in the USA he visited the studios in Hollywood to study film music techniques. He was able to make use of the experience in his next important commission, to work with Sergey Eisenstein on the music for *Alexander Nevsky*. It was an ideal collaboration: from the start the two men were able to combine their talents and deal intuitively with each other's art. The result needs no description here. *Alexander Nevsky* is now a film classic, and in 1939 Prokofiev rearranged his music in the form of the dramatic cantata which is one of his best-known works.

The film score occupied most of Prokofiev's time between May and October 1938, but in the course of the summer he found a subject for a new opera. It was Valentin Katayev's civil war story *I am the Son of the Working People*. The idea of writing a specifically Soviet opera, with relevance to everyday life, had attracted Prokofiev for some time, but he realized that there were problems involved. As he put it, 'a recitative for a commisar trying to dial a telephone could cause the raising of eyebrows'. Indeed, in *Semyon Kotko* he did not entirely overcome such problems, and although the score contains quantities of fine music, the drama as a whole rarely raises itself above the level of a bad western.

There were more problems over the production of the work. Its première was planned for the 1939–40 season at the Stanislavsky Theatre, where Meyerhold was the principal producer. But this collaboration between Prokofiev and Meyerhold was to prove as abortive as the others, and it was to be Meyerhold's last project. In June 1939, before the opera was finished, he was arrested and later executed 'as a result of a slanderous

150

report'. After several postponements *Semyon Kotko* had its first performance in June 1940. Both the plot and the music of the opera were found to be suspect, however, and the following year it was dropped from the repertory.

In 1939, besides his work on the opera, Prokofiev began three new piano sonatas and composed the cantata *Zdravitsa* ('Hail to Stalin') op.85. He worked on all these pieces, and even on their separate parts, simultaneously, to avoid losing time. The Sixth Sonata was completed in spring 1940; the others he continued to compose spasmodically during the years of the war. In these sonatas, Prokofiev's long search for a 'new simplicity' in both language and form found one of its most positive rewards. In idiom they are a consistent and mature amalgam of the less wilful features of his earlier piano music and the greater structural and tonal clarity of his music of the late 1920s and early 1930s. The textures are less complex and more coherent; greater attention to, and independence of, line replaces his former techniques of textural layering; the ostinatos which remain a strong feature of the music are thematically and harmonically more functional. An underlying sense of nervous energy persists, however, and it is felt most potently in the driving rhythms of the fast movements; only in his last (Ninth) sonata do his musical ideas sound remotely submissive. Perhaps most significantly, the later sonatas indicate that Prokofiev's melodic gift had lost none of its power to fascinate.

In May of 1940, before *Semyon Kotko* had had its première, he started on two new stage works, the ballet *Zolushka* ('Cinderella') and the opera *Obrucheniye v monastïre* ('Betrothal in a monastery'), or *The Duenna*.

Cinderella was to be a long-term project; the outbreak of war in June 1941 interrupted its composition, and other commissions then took precedence. *The Duenna* he finished by the beginning of 1941. Sheridan's play, with its heady mixture of humour and romance, had fired his imagination, and he planned a bright, lyrical work in the manner of Mozart or Rossini. In this he succeeded. *The Duenna* is in many respects the Soviet counterpart to *The Love for Three Oranges*. Its musical idiom is simpler, its humour more restrained and its pervasive dances and dance rhythms make of the work almost a hybrid opera-ballet. And if, in comparison with *Oranges*, the sophisticated contemporary spectator might seek in it a little more to bite on, the charm and elegance of the work could hardly elude him.

The events of 1941 altered the circumstances of both Prokofiev's career and his personal life. That spring he suffered the first of a series of heart attacks which badly affected his health over the next few years. With the outbreak of war the Soviet government evacuated large numbers of artists, Prokofiev among them, away from the capital to the comparative safety of the southern republics. He spent varying periods of time over the next year or two in the Caucasus, in Georgia and in Kazakhstan. His family life in Moscow was completely disrupted, though there were other reasons for this, too.

Prokofiev became acquainted with Mira Mendel'son, who was then 24 years old and a senior student at the Moscow Literary Institute, towards the end of 1938. Their relationship led to the break-up of his marriage to Lina. The situation was undoubtedly complicated, and its nature and outcome have provoked vastly differing explanations – including suggestions of political

dealings. The composer's marriage had certainly been far from happy in the years following his return to the USSR; by the spring of 1941 he had become estranged from his wife, and was to spend the rest of his life with Mira Mendel'son. She became of crucial importance to his professional as well as to his personal life, and was to collaborate with him on the texts of many of his later works. In his correspondence with close friends, certainly by 1944, Prokofiev referred to Mira as his second wife. By then Lina, as a foreigner, was *persona non grata* in wartime Moscow with a precarious chance of survival. In 1948 she was to be arrested on charges of espionage and thereafter spent nine years in labour camps in the Soviet north. Prokofiev's marriage certificate to Mira Mendel'son, by coincidence or not, also dates from 1948.

The outbreak of war gave impetus to a project Prokofiev had sketched out in spring 1941, for an opera based on *War and Peace*. His initial plan for a small-scale, intimate opera which would highlight the personal dramas in the novel was expanded, the war aspects in particular, and on his arrival in Nalchik in August 1941 he began the music. At the same time he completed the symphonic suite *1941-y god* ('The year 1941') and composed the Second String Quartet, in which he used, to wonderful effect, material from local Kabardinian folksongs and folkdances. The quartet was the first of his wartime compositions to reach performance, in September 1942.

In November Prokofiev was moved from Nalchik to Tbilisi. There, the following April, he finished *War and Peace* in piano score and also completed his Seventh Piano Sonata. He sent the score of the opera to Moscow

for approval, and in the meantime began its orchestration. In May 1942 he travelled to Alma-Ata at Eisenstein's invitation to work on the music for the film *Ivan Groznïy* ('Ivan the Terrible'). Eisenstein's wartime studios were elaborate, and Prokofiev found the environment stimulating. During his year's stay there he worked on several very different projects. The music for Part I of the film was composed between June and November; he wrote the *Ballada o malchike, ostavshemsya neizvestnïm* ('Ballad of an unknown boy') and made extensive sketches, including a complete libretto, for a new opera, *Khan Buzay*, which, like his recent quartet, was to use local folk material; and in March 1943 he completed the orchestration of *War and Peace*.

Following the advice of the Committee on the Arts in Moscow, Prokofiev had drastically revised the opera in the process; the war scenes had been extended and the patriotic elements strengthened. It was no longer an intimate opera but an epic and heroic work. Prokofiev's incentive in revising the score was the promise of a production of the opera at the Bol'shoy at the end of 1943, for which Eisenstein was to design the sets. After a summer spent in Perm, in the Urals, working on *Cinderella* and the Flute Sonata op.94, he returned to Moscow for the rehearsals. But, as had happened so often, the performance was first cancelled, then postponed indefinitely. Throughout the rest of his life Prokofiev continually made revisions and additions to *War and Peace*, including the composition of two new scenes, in a series of attempts to secure performances. It was only in 1957, however, after his death, that anything like a complete version of the opera was staged.

Spanning, as it did, the last 12 years of his life, *War*

and Peace both typifies and epitomizes the music of Prokofiev's Soviet period. The huge score, as the composer left it, is too unwieldy for an uncut one-evening performance, and it has been produced in a variety of versions. In all but the most insensitive productions, the strength, beauty and dramatic vision of the opera are compellingly effective. In the more intimate scenes of Peace, the directness of his musical invention results in remarkably immediate portraits of Tolstoy's characters. The heady atmosphere of their surroundings is encapsulated in music for the dance, concentrated in the two Ball scenes (ii and iv), with their waltzes, mazurkas and polonaises, so reminiscent of similar scenes in Tchaikovsky's *Eugene Onegin* and *The Queen of Spades*. The War scenes have close stylistic and thematic ties with his Soviet film scores and cantatas, yet Prokofiev's overall concept of these scenes is often surprisingly close to that of Musorgsky in his stage works. They are full of poetic detail; moments of musical intimacy vie in effect with broadly melodic choruses in a musical montage of great power. The techniques of thematic and textural confrontation, at the basis of so many of his musical structures, are seen clearly here for perhaps what they always were, a product of his essential Russianness.

During spring 1944 the orchestration of *Cinderella* was at last completed and for the summer Prokofiev moved to the large country house run by the Union of Composers on Ivanovo estate, some 80 km west of Moscow. There he finished the Eighth Piano Sonata, begun as long ago as 1939, and composed the Fifth Symphony. It was 15 years since his last essay in symphonic form, and even longer – the Second Symphony

was composed in the mid-1920s – since he had written a completely abstract work of these dimensions; his orchestral works of the intervening years had consisted mainly of suites from his stage pieces. He now saw his new symphony as 'the culmination of a long period of my creative life . . . a symphony of the grandeur of the human spirit'. He had long planned the work – some of its themes date back to the 1930s – and in Moscow much was expected of it. The Fifth Symphony is a work of stature and dignity, from its majestic opening to its exuberant finale. There are moments of humour and bright lyricism, but most of all it impresses one as an essentially sombre and introspective score. It is thought by many to be his greatest symphony, and it is probably his most frequently performed. Certainly, it is his most conventional, and on that count alone it is not his most characteristic work.

On 13 January 1945 Prokofiev conducted the première of the symphony in Moscow, to a rapturous reception. This was to be his last public appearance on the concert platform. Shortly afterwards he had a bad fall and suffered concussion. His doctors prescribed complete rest, and he spent the next four months in a sanatorium near Moscow; but the repercussions of the accident affected him, often severely, until his death. He was forced to ration his energies and gradually, in the late 1940s, his prodigious rate of composition slowed down. In the short term, however, Prokofiev recovered his spirits, and during the summer, which he again spent at Ivanovo, he worked on a typically wide range of compositional projects. He finished his experimental (and unsuccessful) *Ode to the End of the War*, scored for eight harps, four pianos and a variety of wind and

percussion instruments. He composed a number of themes for use in his future Ninth Piano Sonata, and sketched out a Sixth Symphony. Between June and November the music for Part 2 of *Ivan the Terrible* was assembled. His health deteriorated again during the winter, and another period in hospital left him weak. He wrote little new music in the months that followed, but he arranged the music of his ballet *Cinderella* into three separate symphonic suites.

In spring 1946 he was advised, for the sake of his health, to leave Moscow, and in June he moved with Mira Mendel'son to the village of Nikolina Gora, to the west of the city. There he occupied a villa in the middle of the country, and for the rest of his life this virtually became his home. During winter 1946–7 he finished the Sixth Symphony, one of his most poignant scores. By comparison with the Fifth it is modest in scale, purer in tone, and totally devoid of pretentiousness. The symphony seems to have had a particular personal significance for Prokofiev. Its opus number, 111, is the same as that of Beethoven's last sonata, and the symphony has something of that work's sense of tragedy. The first two movements undoubtedly had their source in Prokofiev's experiences of war; they are explicitly emotional. They are also perhaps the most truly 'symphonic' movements he ever wrote. In the opening Allegro the sense of an unstaged scenario, common to all Prokofiev's symphonies, is still to the fore; but the drama here is grimly personal, and the powerful atmosphere of the music is a product of a highly integrated musical structure. Nothing could contrast more strongly with the characteristic music of his youth, but comparisons are invalid here; in 1947 the quality of his creative thought was unimpaired.

The Sixth Symphony and the Ninth and last Piano Sonata had their premières in autumn 1947, and for the 30th anniversary of the Revolution Prokofiev wrote the 'festive poem' *Tridtsat' let* ('30 Years') op.113 and the cantata *Rastsvetay, moguchiy kray* ('Flourish, mighty land') op.114. The official response to these works was subdued: it was the calm before the furious storm which broke on the Soviet musical world at the beginning of 1948. During the war, in the face of more pressing matters, the party's concern for the arts had been relaxed; now state intervention was felt necessary to rectify the unhealthy state of musical affairs. A decree of the party central committee was published on 10 February which declared the works of most prominent Soviet composers, Prokofiev among them, 'marked with formalist perversions ... alien to the Soviet people'. *War and Peace* came under special fire, and many of Prokofiev's earlier works were banned from performance.

At the time Prokofiev was working on a new opera, *Povest' o nastoyashchem cheloveke* ('The story of a real man'), about the heroism of the World War II pilot Alexey Meres'yev; this, he was confident, would restore the balance. The opera was given a 'closed preview' to party and Union of Composers officials in the Kirov Theatre in Leningrad on 3 December 1948; it was presented without sets, costumes or props. The reaction was almost unanimously unfavourable, and though Prokofiev strongly defended his opera it was withdrawn from the Kirov's programme; it was not staged publicly until the years of ideological 'thaw' after Stalin's death.

After 1948, and doubtless partly as a result of its events, Prokofiev's health failed rapidly. More and more

12. Sergey Prokofiev, 1951

he sought the seclusion of Nikolina Gora, venturing into Moscow only for occasional performances of his music. His detachment increased with the deaths of his closest friends – Asaf'yev died in 1949, Myaskovsky in 1950 and Pavel Lamm in 1951 – and his creative spirit seemed broken. Many of the works of these last years were in response to official commissions: for the children's radio division he wrote the choral suite *Zimniy kostyor* ('Winter bonfire', 1949–50), the oratorio *Na strazhe mira* ('On guard of peace', 1950) and the Seventh Symphony (1951–2); the symphonic poem *Vstrecha Volgi s Donom* ('The meeting of the Volga and the Don', 1951) was composed for the opening of the Volga–Don canal. All these works are a sad reflection of his talent.

Prokofiev's last ballet, *Skaz o kamennom tsvetke* ('The tale of the stone flower'), begun in autumn 1948, was an exotic fantasy, based on Bazhov's collection of legends from the Urals. In this something of his characteristic enthusiasm was revived, and he created a rich, colourful and energetic score, which makes much of the scenario's outlandish setting. The strongest work of his last years, however, was perhaps the Symphony-Concerto for cello and orchestra, which he wrote in close collaboration with Mstislav Rostropovich, and which incorporated much of the best music from his Cello Concerto op.58. In its revised form, the work is altogether more expansive and more rhetorical. Its structure is at once broader and more conventional. Each of the three movements was extended to contain a greater proportion of rhapsodic, lyrical melody. Prokofiev's remaining reserves of creative energy – and they were surprisingly substantial considering his very poor state of health – were poured into his Seventh Sym-

phony, commissioned by the State Radio as a simple and appealing work for young listeners. However uneven the musical quality of this last symphony, it more than fulfilled the demands of the commission, and has endured in the concert repertory. Not surprisingly, it is by no means a symphony of struggle in the Beethovenian sense. Rather, it seems a statement of serene tranquillity, realized in an uncomplicated succession of constrasting lyrical ideas which retain the imprint of the composer's highly distinctive musical personality.

During his last winters Prokofiev lived in Moscow so that he might keep in daily contact with his doctors. In October 1952 he attended his last concert, for the première of his Seventh Symphony, and five months later – on 5 March, the day of Stalin's death – he died of a brain haemorrhage. The irony of the coincidence would not have escaped him.

WORKS

Numbers in right-hand margins denotes references in the text.

OPERAS

op.		
—	Velikan [The giant] (3), vocal score, 1900, unpubd	125
—	Na pustïnnïkh ostrovakh [On desert islands], ov. and 3 scenes of Act 1, 1900–02, unpubd	110
—	Pir vo vremya chumï [A feast in time of plague] (1, after Pushkin), vocal score, 1903, 1 scene rev. 1908–9, unpubd	110
—	Undina (4, M. Kilstett, after de la Motte Fouqué), 1904–7, unpubd	112
13	Maddalena (1, after M. Lieven), 1911–13, inc., unpubd; BBC, London, 25 March 1979 [orchd E. Downes]	116, 125
24	Igrok [The gambler] (4, Prokofiev, after Dostoyevsky), 1915–17, rev. 1927–8; Brussels, Monnaie, cond. M. Corneil de Thoran, 29 April 1929; see orch works, op.49	121–2, 124, 137–8, 147
33	Lyubov' k tryom apel'sinam [The love for three oranges] (prol, 4, after Gozzi), 1919; Chicago, Auditorium, cond. Prokofiev, 30 Dec 1921; see orch works, opp.33bis, pf works, op.33ter	116, 124, 125, 126–7, 128, 129, 131, 132, 136, 137, 152
37	Ognennïy angel [The fiery angel] (5, after Bryusov), 1919–23, rev. 1926–7; Act 2 in concert perf., Paris, cond. Koussevitzky, 14 June 1928; complete, Paris, Champs Elysées, cond. Bruck, 25 Nov 1954; see orch works, op.44, vocal orch works, op.37bis	114, 116, 126, 127–8, 130, 131, 136, 137, 138, 140
81	Semyon Kotko (5, V. Katayev, Prokofiev, after Katayev), 1939; Moscow, Stanislavsky, cond. M. N. Zhukov, 23 June 1940; see orch works, op.81bis	126, 149, 150–51
86	Obrucheniye v monastïre [Betrothal in a monastery] (The Duenna) (4, Prokofiev, M. Mendel'son, after Sheridan), 1940–41; Leningrad, Kirov, cond. B. Khaikin, 3 Nov 1946; see orch works, op.123	151, 152
—	Khan Buzay, 1942–, inc., unpubd	125, 154
91	Voyna i mir [War and peace] (5, epigraph, Prokofiev, after Tolstoy), 1941–3, rev. 1946–52; concert perf., Moscow, 16 Oct 1944; 8 scenes. Leningrad, Malïy, cond. S. A. Samosud, 12 June 1946; complete, with cuts, Moscow, Stanislavsky, cond. A. Shaverdov, 8 Nov 1957; see orch works, op.110, pf works, op.96	126, 127, 149, 153, 154–5, 158
117	Povest' o nastoyashchem cheloveke [The story of a real man] (4, Prokofiev, Mendel'son, after B. Polevoy), 1947–8; private concert perf., Leningrad, Kirov, cond. Khaikin, 3 Dec 1948; staged, Moscow, Bol'shoy, cond. M. F. Ermler, 8 Oct 1960	126, 158
—	Dalyokiye morya [Distant seas] (Prokofiev, after V. A. Dïkhovichnïy), 1948–, inc., unpub; planned as op.118	125

BALLETS

op.		
20	Ala i Lolli (Gorodetsky, Prokofiev), 1914–15, withdrawn, unpubd; see orch works, op.20	119, 120–21
21	Skazka pro shuta [The tale of the buffoon] (Chout) (6 scenes, Prokofiev, after Afanas'yev), 1915, rev. 1920; Paris, Gaîté Lyrique, cond. Prokofiev, 17 May 1921; see orch works, op.21bis	116, 120, 121, 124, 128, 131
39	Trapetsiya [Trapeze] (1), 1924; Berlin, Romanov Company, late 1925; music also as Quintet, op.39	120–21
41	Stal'noy skok [The steel step] (Le pas d'acier) (2 scenes, Prokofiev, G. Yakulov), 1925–6; Paris, Sarah Bernhardt, cond. Désormière, 7 June 1927; see orch works, op.41bis	135, 136–7, 147
46	Bludnïy sïn [The prodigal son] (L'enfant prodigue) (3 scenes, Kochno), 1928–9; Paris, Sarah Bernhardt, cond. Prokofiev, 21 May 1929; see orch works, opp.46bis, 47	114, 138–9, 140
51	Na Dnepre [On the Dnieper] (Sur le Borysthéne) (2 scenes, Lifar, Prokofiev), 1930–31; Paris, Opéra, cond. P. Gaubert, 16 Dec 1932; see orch works, op.51bis	140
64	Romeo i Dzhul'yetta [Romeo and Juliet] (4, Prokofiev, others, after Shakespeare), 1935–6; Brno, cond. Q. Arnoldi, 30 Dec 1938; see orch works, opp.64bis, 64ter, 101, pf works, op.75	145, 146, 148
87	Zolushka [Cinderella] (3, N. D. Volkov), 1940–44; Moscow, Bol'shoy, cond. Y. Fayer, 21 Nov 1945; see orch works, opp.107–10, chamber works, op.97bis, pf works, opp.95, 97, 102	139, 151, 152, 154, 155, 157
118	Skaz o kamennom tsvetke [The tale of the stone flower] (4, L. Lavrovsky, Mendel'son, after P. Bazhov), 1948–53; Moscow, Bol'shoy, cond. Fayer, 12 Feb 1954; see orch works, opp.126–9	160

OTHER DRAMATIC WORKS
(*incidental music*)

—	Egipetskiye nochi [Egyptian rights] (Pushkin, Shakespeare, Shaw), 1934; Moscow, Kamerniïy, April 1935; see orch works. op.61	145–6
70bis	Boris Godunov (Pushkin, produced Meyerhold), 1936; Moscow, Central Children's Theatre, April 1957; selected nos. from opp.70, 70bis and 71 arr. as Pushkiniana by Rozhdestvensky (1962)	148
71	Evgeny Onegin (Pushkin), 1936; BBC, London, 1 April 1980	148
77	Gamlet [Hamlet] (Shakespeare), 1937–8; Leningrad, 15 May 1939; see pf works, op.77bis	

(*film scores*) 155

—	Poruchik Kizhe [Lieutenant Kije] (dir. Feinzimmer), 1933, unpubd; see orch works, op.60, other vocal works, op.60bis	145
70	Pikovaya dama [The queen of spades] (after Pushkin), 1936; film unrealized	148
—	Alexander Nevsky (dir. Eisenstein), Mez, chorus, orch. 1938, unpubd; see vocal orch works, op.78, other vocal works, op.78bis	150
—	Lermontov, 1941, unpubd; see orch works, op.110, pf works, op.96	
—	Kotovsky, 1942, unpubd	
—	Partizanï v stepyakh ukrainï [The partisans in the Ukrainian steppes], 1942, unpubd	
—	Tonya, 1942, unpubd; film unrealized	
116	Ivan Grozniïy [Ivan the Terrible] (dir. Einsenstein), part 1, 1942–4, part 2, 1945; arr. as oratorio by A. Stasevich, 1961	154, 157

ORCHESTRAL

—	Symphony, G, 1902, unpubd	110
—	Symphony no.2, e, 1908, unpubd, reworked in Piano Sonata no.4	
5	Sinfonietta, A, 1909, rev. 1914–15, unpubd; rev. as op.48	114
6	Snï [Dreams], sym. tableau, 1910, unpubd	116, 117
8	Osenneye [Autumnal sketch], small orch, 1910, rev. 1915, 1934	116, 117
10	Piano Concerto no.1, D♭, 1911–12	117–18, 119, 125, 142

16	Piano Concerto no.2, g, 1912–13, unpubd; rev. 1923	118–19, 120, 131, 132, 136
19	Violin Concerto no.1, D, 1916–17	122, 132, 145
20	Suite from Ala i Lolli (Scythian Suite), 1915	125, 132
21bis	Suite from The Tale of the Buffoon, 1920	131, 137
25	Symphony no.1 'Classical', D, 1916–17	122–3
26	Piano Concerto no.3, C, 1917–21	128–9, 132, 136, 142
29bis	Andante from Piano Sonata no.4, 1934	
33bis	Suite from The Love for Three Oranges, 1919, rev. 1924	136
34bis	Overture on Hebrew Themes [after chamber work], 1934	
40	Symphony no.2, d, 1924–5; see also op.136	120, 134–5, 137, 155–6
41bis	Suite from The Steel Step, 1926	
42	'American' Overture, B♭, chamber orch, 1926	136
42bis	'American' Overture, B♭, full orch, 1928	
43	Divertissement, 1925–9; see pf works, op.43bis	
44	Symphony no.3, c [material from The Fiery Angel], 1928	114, 138, 139
46bis	Suite from The Prodigal Son, 1929	
47	Symphony no.4, C [material from The Prodigal Son], 1929–30, unpubd; rev. as op.112	114, 139
48	Sinfonietta, A [rev. of op.5], 1929; see pf works, op.52	
49	Four Portraits and Dénouement from The Gambler, 1931	
50bis	Andante from String Quartet no.1, str, ?1930, unpubd	
51bis	Suite from On the Dnieper, 1933	
53	Piano Concerto no.4, B♭, left hand, 1931	141–2
55	Piano Concerto no.5, G, 1931–2	141–2
57	Symphonic Song, 1933, unpubd	143
58	Cello Concerto, e, 1933–8	143, 160
60	Suite from Lieutenant Kije, with Bar ad lib, 1934	
61	Suite from Egyptian Nights, 1934	145
63	Violin Concerto no.2, g, 1935	143, *144*, 145
64bis	Suite no.1 from Romeo and Juliet, 1936	
64ter	Suite no.2 from Romeo and Juliet, 1936	
65bis	Letniy den [Summer day], children's suite [after nos.1, 9, 6, 5, 10–12 of pf work op.65], small orch, 1941	
69	Four Marches, military band, 1935–7	
72	Russian Overture, with quadruple ww, 1936; rev. with triple ww, 1937, unpubd	

Songs, 1st ser., 12 pieces, 1902; Bagatelle no.2, a, 1902; Little Songs, 2nd ser., 12 pieces, 1903; Sonata, Bb, 1903–4; Little Songs, 3rd ser., 12 pieces, 1903–4: Variations on 'Chizhika', 1904; Little Songs, 4th ser., 12 pieces, 1905; Polka mélancolique, f♯, 1905 — 110, 110

Little Songs, 5th ser., 12 pieces, 1906; Song without Words, Db, 1907; Intermezzo, A, 1907; Humoresque, f, 1907; [untitled work] bb, 1907; Oriental Piece, g, 1907; [untitled work], c, 1907; Sonata no.2, f, 1907, reworked in op.1; Sonata no.3, a, 1907, reworked in op.28; 4 Pieces, 1907–8, rev. as op.3; Sonata no.4, ?1907–8, lost; 4 Pieces, 1908, rev. as op.4; Sonata no.5, 1908, reworked in op.29; Examination Fugue, 1908; Andante, c, 1908, inc.; 2 Pieces, 1908; Study, c, 1908; Piece on Es–C–H–E, 1908, Sonata no.6, ?1908–9, lost — 112

For 4 hands: March, C, 1897; March C, 1898/9; March, F, 1899; Piece, F, 1899; Piece, d, 1900; Piece, with zither, 1900, inc.; Bagatelle no.1 c, 1901

(mature works)

1   Sonata no.1, f [after Sonata no.2, 1907], 1909 — 112, 114, 117

2   Four Etudes, 1909 — 114

3   Four Pieces [rev. of 4 Pieces, 1907–8], 1911: Skazka [Story], Shutka [Jest], Marsh [March], Prizrak [Phantom] — 112–13, 117

4   Four Pieces [rev. of 4 Pieces, 1908], 1910–12: Vospominaniya [Reminiscenes], Poriv [Elan], Otchayaniye [Despair], Navazhdeniye (Suggestion diabolique) — 112–13

11 Toccata, d, 1912 — 112

12 Ten Pieces, 1906–13: March [after Little Songs, 5th ser., no.6], Gavotte, Rigaudon, Mazurka, Capriccio, Legend, Prelude, Allemande, Humoresque Scherzo, Scherzo; see chamber works, op.12bis — 118, 115, 118

14 Sonata no.2, d, 1912

17 Sarcasms, 5 pieces, 1912–14

22 Mimoletnosti (Visions fugitives), 20 pieces, 1915–17 — 118

28 Sonata no.3 (from old notebooks), a [after Sonata no.3, 1907], 1917 — 112, 123

29 Sonata no.4 (from old notebooks), c [after Sonata no.5, 1908 and Sym., 1908], 1917 — 123

31 Skazki staroy babushki [The tales of an old grandmother], 4 pieces, 1918 — 125

32 Four Pieces, 1918: Dance, Minuet, Gavotte, Waltz — 125

33ter March and Scherzo from The Love for Three Oranges, 1922

38 Sonata no.5, C, 1923, rev. as op.135 — 131, 132, 140

43bis Divertissement [after orch work], 1938

45 Veshchi v sebe [Things in themselves], 2 pieces, 1928

52 Six Pieces, 1930–31: Intermezzo, Rondo, Etude [all from The Prodigal Son], Scherzino [from 5 Songs, op.35], Andante [from Str Qt no.1, op.50], Scherzo [from Sinfonietta, op.48]

54 Two Sonatinas, e, G, 1931–2 — 141

59 Three Pieces, 1933–44: Progulka [Promenade], Peyzazh [Landscape], Pastoral Sonatina, C

62 Misli (Pensées), 3 pieces, 1933–4

65 Music for Children, 12 pieces, 1935; see orch works, op.65bis — 148

75 Ten Pieces from Romeo and Juliet, 1937

77bis Gavote [from Hamlet], 1938

82 Sonata no.6, A, 1939–40 — 151

83 Sonata no.7, Bb, 1939–42 — 151, 153

84 Sonata no.8, Bb, 1939–44 — 151, 155

95 Three Pieces from Cinderella, 1942

96 Three Pieces, 1941–2: Waltz [from War and Peace], Contredanse, Mephisto-waltz [both from Lermontov]

97 Ten Pieces from Cinderella, 1943

102 Six Pieces from Cinderella, 1944

103 Sonata no.9, C, 1947 — 151, 157, 158

135 Sonata no.5, C [rev. of op.38], 1952–3

137 Sonata no.10, c, inc., unpubd

138 Sonata no.11, unrealized

— Dumka, after 1933, unpubd

OTHER WORKS

Music for gymnastic exercises, 1935, inc., unpubd

Arrs.: D. Buxtehude: Organ Prelude and Fugue, pf, 1920/?1918:
F. Schubert: Waltzes, suite, pf, 1920/?1918, pf 4 hands, 1923

Principal publishers: Boosey & Hawkes, Edition Russe de Musique, Gutheil, Jürgenson, Muzgiz

BIBLIOGRAPHY

MONOGRAPHS AND COLLECTIONS OF ESSAYS

I. V. Nest'yev: *Prokofiev: his Musical Life* (New York, 1946)
Tempo, no.20 (1949) [special no.]
S. I. Shlifshteyn, ed.: *S. S. Prokof'yev: materialï, dokumentï, vospominaniya* [Materials, documents, reminiscences] (Moscow, 1956, 2/1961; Eng. trans., 1960, 2/1968; Ger. trans., 1965)
I. V. Nest'yev: *Prokof'yev* (Moscow, 1957, enlarged 2/1973; Eng. trans., 1961)
I. Martïnov: *Laureat leninskoy premii Sergey Prokof'yev* [Sergey Prokofiev: Winner of the Lenin Prize], (Moscow, 1958)
M. Sabinina: *Sergey Prokof'yev* (Moscow, 1958)
L. Gakkel: *Fortep'yannoye tvorchestvo S. S. Prokof'yeva* [Prokofiev's piano works] (Moscow, 1960)
L. Polyakova: *'Voyna i mir' Prokof'yeva* (Moscow, 1960, rev. 2/1971)
C. Samuel: *Prokofiev* (Paris, 1960; Eng. trans., 1971)
T. Boganova: *Natsional'no-russkiye traditsii v muzïke S. S. Prokof'yeva* (Moscow, 1961)
A. Klimovitsky: *Opera Prokof'yeva 'Semyon Kotko'* (Moscow, 1961)
L. Berger, ed.: *Chertï stilya S. Prokof'yeva* [Aspects of Prokofiev's style] (Moscow, 1962)
S. Katanova: *Baletï S. Prokof'yeva* (Moscow, 1962)
G. Ordzhenikidze: *Fortep'yanne sonatï Prokof'yeva* (Moscow, 1962)
S. I. Shlifshteyn, ed.: *Notograficheskiy spravochnik S. S. Prokof'yeva* [Reference list of Prokofiev's works] (Moscow, 1962)
P. R. Ashley: *Prokofiev's Piano Music: Line, Chord, Key* (diss., Rochester U., 1963)
L. Danko: *Operï S. Prokof'yeva* (Moscow, 1963)
M. R. Hofmann: *Serge Prokofiev* (Paris, 1963)
Y. Soroker: *Kamerno-instrumental'noye ansambli S. Prokof'yeva* (Moscow, 1963)
H. A. Brockhaus: *Sergej Prokofjew* (Leipzig, 1964)
L. and E. Hanson: *Prokofiev* (London, 1964)
I. V. Nest'yev and G. Y. Edelman, ed.: *Sergey Prokof'yev: stat'i i materialï* [Articles and materials] (Moscow, 1965)
M. Rayment: *Prokofiev* (London, 1965)
S. I. Shlifshteyn, ed.: *Sergey Prokof'yev/Sergei Prokofiev* (Moscow, 1965)
L. Danko: *S. S. Prokof'yev* (Moscow and Leningrad, 1966)
Yu. Kremlyov: *Esteticheskiye vsglyadï S. Prokof'yeva* [Prokofiev's aesthetic standpoint] (Moscow, 1966)
T. Ter-Martirosyan: *Nekotorïye osobennosti garmonii Prokof'yeva*

167

[Features of Prokofiev's harmony] (Moscow and Leningrad, 1966)
M. H. Brown: *The Symphonies of Prokofiev* (diss., Florida State U., 1967)
Ya. Kholopov: *Sovremennïye chertï garmoniya Prokof'yeva* [Contemporary aspects of Prokofiev's harmony] (Moscow, 1967)
S. Morozov: *Prokof'yev* (Moscow, 1967)
V. Seroff: *Sergei Prokofiev: a Soviet Tragedy* (New York, 1968)
M. Tarakanov: *Stil simfoniy Prokof'yeva* [Prokofiev's symphonic style] (Moscow, 1968)
M. Aranovsky: *Melodika S. Prokof'yeva* (Leningrad, 1969)
R. McAllister: *The Operas of Sergei Prokofiev* (diss., U. of Cambridge, 1970)
V. Blok, ed.: *S. S. Prokof'yev: stat'i i issledovaniya* [Articles and researches] (Moscow, 1972)
O. Stepanov: *Teatr masok v opere S. Prokof'yeva 'Lyubov' k tryom apel'sinam'* (Moscow, 1972)
V. Blok: *Violonchel'noye tvorchestvo Prokof'yev* (Moscow, 1973)
S. Prokofiev: *Autobiografiya*, ed. M. G. Kozlova (Moscow, 1973)
I. I. Martïnov: *S. S. Prokof'yev* (Moscow, 1974)
S. Moisson-Franckhauser: *Serge Prokofiev et les courants esthétiques de son temps* (Paris, 1974)
V. Blok, ed.: *Sergei Prokofiev: materials, articles, interviews* (Moscow, 1978)
V. Blok: *Metod tvorcheskoy rabotï S. Prokof'yeva* [The working methods of Prokofiev] (Moscow, 1979)
M. I. Nest'yeva, ed.: *S. S. Prokof'yew* (Moscow, 1981)
N. P. Savkina, *S. S. Proko'yev* (Moscow, 1982)

ARTICLES ON PARTICULAR WORKS
(*operas*)

M. Sabinina: '"Voyna i mir"' *SovM* (1953), no.12, p. 29
C. Bruck: '"Ognennïy angel" v Parizhe', *SovM* (1955), no.7, p. 128
Ya. Keldïsh: 'Eshcho ob opere "Voyna i mir"' [More about the opera 'War and Peace'], *SovM* (1955), no.7, p. 33
D. Mitchell: 'Prokofiev's "Three Oranges": a Note on its Musical-dramatic Organisation', *Tempo*, no.41 (1956), 20
H. Swarsenski: 'Prokofieff's "The Flaming Angel"', *Tempo*, no.39 (1956), 16
A. Zolotov: 'Ode to Heroism: "The Story of a Real Man" at the Bolshoy Theatre', *Current Digest of the Soviet Press* (1960), no.48
J. Renate: 'Von "Spieler" zur "Erzählung von Wahren Menschen"', *Musik und Gesellschaft*, xi (1961)
D. Lloyd-Jones: 'Prokofiev and the Opera', *Opera*, xiii (1962), 513
A. Porter: 'Prokofiev's Early Operas', *MT*, ciii (1962), 528

168

Bibliography

M. Sabinina: 'Ob opere kotoraya na bïla napisana' [On the opera that was never written], *SovM* (1962), no.8, p.41 [on *Khan Buzay*]

L. Polyakova: 'O poslednem opernom zamïsle S. Prokof'yeva "Dalekie morya" ' [On Prokofiev's last operatic creation 'Distant seas'], *SovM* (1963), no.3, p.53

A. Jefferson: ' "The Angel of Fire" ', *Music and Musicians*, xiii/12 (1964–5), 32

E. Mnatsakanova: 'Neskol'ko zametok ob opere "Igrok" ' [Some notes on the opera 'The Gambler'], *Muzïka i sovremennost*, iii (1965), 122

——: 'Prokof'yev i Tolstoy', *Muzïka i sovremennost*, iv (1966)

G. Pugliese: 'The Unknown World of Prokofiev's Operas', *High Fidelity*, xvi (1966), 44

A. Porter: 'Prokofiev's Late Operas', *MT*, cviii (1967), 312

R. McAllister: 'Prokofiev's Early Opera "Maddalena" ', *PRMA*, xcvi (1969–70), 137

——: 'Natural and Supernatural in "The Fiery Angel" ', *MT*, cxi (1970), 785

——: 'Prokofiev's Tolstoy Epic', *MT*, cxiii (1972), 851

M. H. Brown: 'Prokofiev's *War and Peace*: a Chronicle', *MQ*, lxiii (1977), 297–326

R. McAllister: 'Prokofiev's *Maddalena*: a première', *MT*, cxx (1979), 205

(other dramatic works)

P.-O. Ferroud: 'The Ballets of Sergei Prokofiev', *The Chesterian*, xv (1933–4), 89

P. Hope-Wallace: 'Prokofiev's Music for "Cinderella" ', *Ballet* (1949), 34

U. Seelmann-Eggebert: 'Prokofjew und die Filmmusik', *NZM*, Jg.125 (1964), 522

G. Troïtskaya: 'Prokof'yev: kompositor kino', *SovM* (1978), no.9, p.95

C. Bennett: 'Prokofiev and Eugene Onegin', *MT*, cxxi (1980), 230

(orchestral works)

M. Montagu-Nathan: 'Prokofiev's First Piano Concerto', *MT*, lviii (1917), 12

A. Frank: 'Piano Concerto no.3', *The Concerto*, ed. R. Hill (Harmondsworth, 1952), 382

E. Lockspeiser: 'Prokofieff's Seventh Symphony', *Tempo*, no.37 (1955), 24

W. W. Austin: 'Prokofiev's Fifth Symphony', *MR*, xvii (1956), 205

I. Yampol'sky: 'Prokofiev's Third Symphony', *Musical Events* (1962), Sept, 22

R. Layton: 'Sergei Prokofiev', *The Symphony*, ed. R. Simpson (Harmondsworth, 1967), 166

A. Shnitke: 'Osbennosti orkestrovovo golosovedeniya S. Prokof'yeva' [Features of orchestral part-writing in Prokofiev], *Muzïka i sovremennost'*, vii (1974), 202

(*piano sonatas*)

F. Merrick: 'Serge Prokofiev's Sixth Piano Sonata', *MT*, lxxxv (1944), 9
——'Prokofiev's Piano Sonatas 1–5', *MT*, lxxxvi (1945), 9
——: 'Prokofiev's Seventh and Eighth Piano Sonatas', *MT*, lxxxix (1948), 234
——: 'Prokofiev's Piano Sonatas', *PRMA*, lxxv (1948–9), 13
——: 'Prokofiev's Ninth Piano Sonata', *MT*, xcvii (1956), 649

M. H. Brown: 'Prokofiev's Eighth Piano Sonata', *Tempo*, no.70 (1964), 9

E. Roseberry: 'Prokofiev's Piano Sonatas', *Music and Musicians,* xix/7 (1970–71), 38

V. Pavlinova: 'Vazhnaya cherta fortep'yannogo tvorchestva S. Prokof'yeva' [An important feature of Prokofiev's piano music], *SovM* (1981), no.4, p.88

OTHER LITERATURE

M. Calvocoressi: 'Sergej Prokofjew', *Musikblätter des Anbruch* (1922), 172

B. de Schloezer: 'Igor Strawinsky und Sergej Prokofjew', *Melos*, iv (1924–5), 469

G. Abraham: 'Prokofiev as a Soviet Composer', *MR*, iii (1942), 241

N. Nabokov: 'Prokofiev, Russian Musician', *Atlantic Monthly* (1942), July, 62

G. Abraham: *Eight Soviet Composers* (London, 1943/R1976)

H. Ottaway: 'Sergei Prokofiev and Benjamin Britten', *MO*, lxiii (1949–50), 576

A. Werth: 'The Real Prokofiev', *The Nation*, clxxvi (1953), 285

H. Swarsenski: 'Prokofieff: Unknown Works with a New Aspect', *Tempo*, no.30 (1953–4), 14

M. Prokofieva: 'Iz vospominaniy' [From reminiscences], *SovM* (1961), no.4, p. 91

S. Prokofiev: Correspondence with V. Alpers, *Muzïkal'noye nasledstvo,* i (1962)

J. Szigeti: 'The Prokofiev I Knew', *Music and Musicians,* xi/10 (1962–3), 10

A. Jacobs: 'A Prokofiev Problem', *Opera*, xvi (1965), 31

R. Zanetti: 'Prokofjew und Diagilew', *Melos*, xxxii (1965), 443

Bibliography

S. Prokofiev: Correspondence with V. Meyerhold, *Muzïkal'noye nasledstvo*, ii (1968)

K. Kh. Adzhemov: *Nezabïvaemoye* [Memoirs] (Moscow, 1972)

D. S. Kabalevsky and others, eds.: *S. S. Prokof'yev i N. Y. Myaskovsky: perepiska* [correspondence] (Moscow, 1977)

DMITRY SHOSTAKOVICH

Boris Schwarz

Laurel E. Fay

CHAPTER ONE

Life

Dmitry Dmitriyevich Shostakovich was born at St Petersburg (now Leningrad) on 25 September 1906. He is widely regarded as the greatest symphonist of the mid-20th century, with 15 symphonies to his credit, from the precocious First in the 1920s, through the epic utterances of the war years to the personal anguish of the later works; a similar range of more private emotion is contained in the 15 string quartets. He also composed some 'official' works, and his relationship to Soviet officialdom, though on the surface sometimes uneasy, rested on his view of the Soviet composer as, first and foremost, a citizen with a moral duty to his fellow citizens. None of this compromised his integrity as an artist of the widest scope.

Shostakovich received his first piano lessons from his mother, a professional pianist, at the age of nine. In 1919 he was admitted to the Petrograd Conservatory, where he studied the piano with Leonid Nikolayev and composition with Maximilian Shteynberg, and where he was given encouragement and material help by Glazunov. Frail and highly strung, the young Shostakovich had to help support his widowed mother and his sisters by playing the piano in a cinema. At the conservatory he completed the piano course in 1923 and the composition course in 1925; for a time he was undecided whether to follow the career of a pianist or

that of a composer. Success came early in both fields: his First Symphony, written as a graduation piece, was acclaimed in Leningrad at the première on 12 May 1926 (under Malko), in Berlin on 5 May 1927 (under Walter) and on 2 November 1928 in Philadelphia (under Stokowski); and Shostakovich won 'honourable mention' as a pianist at the International Chopin Contest in Warsaw in 1927. Although he continued as a postgraduate student in composition until 1930, he rarely consulted his teacher Shteynberg, who admitted that he 'understood nothing' in Shostakovich's more recent works. Indeed, they showed a new musical idiom – astringent, satirical, and highly dissonant – which reflected the modern trends in west European music.

Afraid of becoming academic and epigonal, Shostakovich eagerly broadened his musical horizon. In his Second Symphony (1927), sub-titled 'To October' and commissioned for the tenth anniversary of the Revolution, he attempted to combine a modern idiom with Marxist ideology; but the work did not attain a durable success, though some Soviet critics acclaimed it at the time. Nor did the Third Symphony ('The First of May'), conceived in a similar spirit, enter the permanent repertory. In later years Shostakovich dismissed these two symphonies as 'youthful experiments'. Between 1927 and 1930 he also became involved in all aspects of dramatic music: he wrote an opera (*Nos*, 'The nose'), a ballet (*Zolotoy vek*, 'The age of gold'), a film score (*Noviy Vavilon*, 'New Babylon') and incidental music to Meyerhold's staging of *Klop* ('The bedbug') by Mayakovsky. In these scores humour and cutting satire prevail at the expense of lyricism, and are heightened by the brilliant and imaginative use of orchestral resources.

176

A new and important project, begun in 1930, was the opera *Ledi Makbet Mtsenskovo uyezda* ('Lady Macbeth of the Mtsensk district'), based on a novella by Leskov. Produced on 22 January 1934 in Leningrad and two days later in Moscow (there under the title *Katerina Izmaylova*), the work was hailed as a major achievement of socialist construction; such an opera 'could have been written only by a Soviet composer brought up in the best traditions of Soviet culture'. By 1936 *Lady Macbeth* had been given 83 performances in Leningrad and 97 in Moscow; it also attracted international attention and was heard in New York, Stockholm, London, Zurich and Copenhagen.

Suddenly, in a dramatic reversal, *Pravda* launched a violent attack on Shostakovich's opera. On 28 January 1936 an article entitled 'Chaos instead of Music' denounced the 'fidgety, screaming, neurotic' score and branded it as 'coarse, primitive and vulgar'. While ostensibly directed only against Shostakovich, the article was interpreted as a warning against all modernism in Soviet music. The Union of Soviet Composers (established in 1932) convened hurriedly to chart the future of Soviet music. Shostakovich was denounced by many fellow composers, and even his friends Asaf'yev, Sollertinsky and Shteynberg hardly dared to defend him. He suffered in silence and decided to answer his critics through his music. Thus his new Fifth Symphony (1937) came to be known as 'the creative reply of a Soviet artist to justified criticism'. However, this designation originated with an unidentified commentator, not with Shostakovich, though he accepted it (see *Vechernyaya Moskva*, 25 January 1938). The success of the Fifth Symphony (introduced on 21 November

13. Dmitry Shostakovich

1937) reinstated Shostakovich as the foremost Soviet composer of the young generation. Further official recognition came to him in 1940 when he received the Stalin Prize for his Piano Quintet.

Hitler's invasion of the USSR in June 1941 spurred Shostakovich into an important creative effort. During the first few months of the war he was in besieged Leningrad, and there he composed the first three movements of his Seventh Symphony, which he later dedicated to the city. Evacuated to Kuybïshev in October of that year, he completed the symphony by December. The first performances took place in 1942, on 5 March in Kuybïshev, on 29 March in Moscow, on 9 August in Leningrad. The microfilmed score was flown to the USA, where Toscanini conducted the NBC SO for an audience of millions on 19 July 1942. Shostakovich's work became the symbol of resistance against Nazism – music 'written with the heart's blood', in the words of Carl Sandburg. During the 1942–3 season 62 performances of the 'Leningrad' Symphony were given in the USA alone, and it was heard in every Western country. Two years later Shostakovich wrote another 'war' symphony, no.8, which, though a better work, met with less success.

The victorious end of the war was followed, in the USSR, by tightening ideological controls and artistic repressions. The commissar in charge of the cultural 'purges' was Andrey Zhdanov, who engineered a total reorganization of the Union of Soviet Composers. In a decree dated 10 February 1948 a number of prominent composers, including Shostakovich and Prokofiev, were accused of representing 'most strikingly the formalistic perversions and anti-democratic tendencies in music',

179

namely the 'cult of atonality, dissonance and discord . . . infatuation with confused, neurotic combinations which transform music into cacophony'. The accused composers recanted, each in his own way. Shostakovich admitted that he had tried to eradicate the 'pernicious elements' in his music, but the 'reconstruction' was not complete: 'Certain negative characteristics in my musical style prevented me from making the turn . . . I again deviated in the direction of formalism and began to speak a language incomprehensible to the people . . . I know that the party is right . . . I am deeply grateful for the criticism contained in the resolution'.

The decree of 1948 dealt a stunning blow to the creative life of Soviet music. For the next five years composers displayed great caution so as not to offend the party hierarchy. In practical terms, Shostakovich began to use two musical idioms: one more simplified and accessible to comply with the guidelines of the decree, the other more complex and abstract to satisfy his own artistic standards. To the first belonged such choral works as *Pesn' o lesakh* ('Song of the forests', 1949) and *Nad rodinoy nashey solntse siyayet* ('The sun shines on our motherland', 1952), to the second the Violin Concerto no.1, the Fourth String Quartet and the song cycle *Iz yevreyskoy narodnoy poezii* ('From Jewish folk poetry'). In order to avoid a public controversy, Shostakovich withheld the last three compositions until after 1953, when the death of Stalin brought about a gradual relaxation of cultural regimentation.

After an eight-year pause Shostakovich returned to the symphony with his Tenth (1953). The première, on 17 December, aroused a great deal of discussion, both favourable and unfavourable, in Soviet circles. Some

hailed it as a manifesto of liberalization, others criticized it as a reversal to formalism. But eventually the Tenth Symphony received its recognition as a masterpiece, both at home and abroad. By now Shostakovich had reached the position of unofficial grand master of Soviet music, particularly since Prokofiev had died in 1953. As the trend towards the liberalization of the arts continued, one might have expected Shostakovich to lead the way, especially since he had suffered under official repression. On the contrary, however, he became rather more conservative, praised the government policies, and spoke out against the musical avant garde. As if to prove that the concept of socialist realism was still viable, he wrote two symphonies, no.11 ('The Year 1905') and no.12 ('The Year 1917', dedicated to the memory of Lenin), which can be considered prototypes of the realist style. He even wrote a mildly amusing musical comedy, *Moskva, Cheryomushki* (1958). Counterbalancing this lighter fare are such first-rate works as the Cello Concerto no.1 and two of his finest string quartets, nos.7 and 8 (both 1960), the latter dedicated 'to the memory of the victims of fascism and the war'.

Two important events marked the year 1962: the première of his Symphony no.13 (18 December) and the revival of his long-banished opera *Lady Macbeth* (26 December; the 'official' première took place on 8 January 1963). The symphony, often called 'Babiy Yar' after the first movement, was based on poems by the young Yevtushenko and caused a certain degree of controversy because of the texts; repeat performances were permitted only after Yevtushenko had made several changes. As for *Lady Macbeth*, it was renamed

Katerina Izmaylova and given in a revised version which Shostakovich had begun in 1956; essentially it was the same work, so reviled in 1936, that was now hailed as a masterpiece of theatrical realism. Since then it has been produced as a film and exported to many countries. It was given at Covent Garden in December 1963 and at the New York City Opera in March 1965. The original version of the opera was recorded in England in 1979 and subsequently has been revived in a number of Western cities.

A serious heart ailment developed in 1966 and disabled Shostakovich for a brief time. He never fully recovered, and his health was further weakened by severe arthritis. However, he remained as creative as ever, producing a number of important works. His 14th Symphony (1969) in particular is a work of striking novelty and fierce intensity, dominated by a preoccupation with death. Shostakovich commented on this in 1973 (see Brown):

The entire symphony is my protest against death. Composers such as Mussorgsky have written calm works about death, works that have a soothing effect upon the listener. My intention was just the opposite. That is also why I chose the texts I used which I have known for some time.

While continuing to speak against the 12-note serial system of composition as such, Shostakovich acquired a much more advanced musical idiom in his later works, a fact he freely acknowledged. He paid a last visit to the USA in 1973, and died in Moscow on 9 August 1975, six weeks before his 69th birthday.

CHAPTER TWO

Works

I Early works, 1924–36

Shostakovich's creative career can be divided into three periods: youth, maturity and final years. Broadly speaking, his first period extends to 1936 and culminates in the Fourth Symphony; his second period opens with Symphony no.5 (1937) and extends beyond Symphony no.13 (1962) to 1966; the last period spans the last nine years of his life and reaches its apex with Symphony no.14 (1969). Admittedly, within each period there are subdivisions, contradictions and inconsistencies; but the categorization is helpful in considering Shostakovich's vast output.

Disregarding the adolescent first nine opus numbers, Shostakovich's output begins with op.10, which is the First Symphony. There appears to be no common denominator applicable to the first period, though each work bears the unmistakable imprint of Shostakovich's personality. One can speak of a split focus: concern for tradition against challenge of it. In a way, Shostakovich reflected the free-wheeling and controversial Leningrad atmosphere of the late 1920s. Having established his reputation with the chiselled classicistic First Symphony, he joined the avant-garde camp with the piano *Aforizmï* ('Aphorisms'), the First Piano Sonata, the Second Symphony and *The Nose*, earning himself the approval of modernistic critics. Even the First Piano

Concerto, with its prankish humour, can be explained as a challenge to the traditional Russian concerto style. But there were also moments of reflection where Shostakovich tried to discipline and correlate the opposing forces of tradition and innovation, as in the Cello Sonata and the 24 Piano Preludes op.34. A creative synthesis was achieved most forcefully in *Lady Macbeth of the Mtsensk District* (1930–32) and the Fourth Symphony (1935–6), the two most ambitious works of the first period. The opera (now known as *Katerina Izmaylova*) is a stunning piece of Russian *verismo*, though not unrelated to the 'animal eroticism' of *Wozzeck* (a comparison by Sollertinsky, a close friend of Shostakovich). The Fourth Symphony is Shostakovich's encounter with Mahler, a flawed masterpiece, yet a pivotal work in his evolution. It is tragic to contemplate that both these works were condemned to oblivion for 25 years, *Lady Macbeth* by party-inspired interference, the Fourth Symphony by Shostakovich's self-criticism.

Within Shostakovich's orchestral writing, particularly in the symphonies, it is possible to see a gradual change from the delicate transparency of the First Symphony to the over-inflation of the Fourth, a tendency that he learnt to control in later symphonies. He experimented with form, using the traditional four movements in the First Symphony, an integrated one-movement form (with final chorus) in nos.2 and 3, and a three-movement form in no.4. (In later years he admitted that he found it difficult to write a solid first-movement *allegro* in traditional form.) He seems to have been particularly at ease in zestful scherzo-like movements, intermingling humour and thumping rhythms.

184

As his symphonies and stage works reached outward, so Shostakovich's music for piano solo probed increasingly inward: he discarded keyboard showmanship and preferred a sparse linear texture. His harmonic language ranges from traditional tonality to polytonality and atonality, using dissonant textures with increasing frequency. His melodic line is often angular and deliberately anti-Romantic. In later years he rejected his early experimental writing as 'erroneous striving after originality' (*Aphorisms*) and 'infants' diseases' (Symphonies nos.2 and 3). Whatever the quality, Shostakovich's musical mind was full of exploratory zest, wavering between exuberance and 'Weltschmerz', basically unsentimental yet receptive to the 'revolutionary romanticism' of the 1920s peculiar to Russia.

II Mature works, 1937–66
Although Shostakovich was jolted by the *Pravda* criticism of *Lady Macbeth* (1936), he continued to work on his Fourth Symphony and completed it on 20 May 1936, some four months after the censure had appeared. There is no apparent stylistic break in that work, and it can be assumed that for a time he chose to disregard the criticism. However, after hearing the Fourth in rehearsal he became dissatisfied (mainly with the Finale) and withdrew it from performance (as late as 1956 he referred to the Fourth as 'a very imperfect, long-winded work that suffers – I'd say – from "grandiosomania" '). During the rest of 1936 he did little composing but apparently much soul-searching. On 18 April 1937 he began a new symphony, the Fifth, which was completed three months later. The première on 21 November 1937 was a triumphal success, and the Fifth has become the

most frequently performed of Shostakovich's symphonies. The critics who acclaimed it in 1937 did not know the composer's Fourth, and Western critics were inclined to belittle it as a 'concession' to political pressure. But, in retrospect, it can be said that Shostakovich made no significant concession of any kind, except, perhaps, for the bombast of the Finale. Had he really wanted to make concessions he could have written a symphony in the terms of socialist realism, a programme symphony or a 'song symphony'. But he challenged the prevailing taste by writing an abstract work and, simply by avoiding some of the excesses that marred the Fourth, he succeeded in making the new symphony a better piece by his own standards. He returned to the traditional four-movement form and a normal-sized orchestra, but, more important, he organized each movement along clear lines, having come to the conclusion that a symphony is not viable without firm architecture. True, the harmonic idiom is less astringent, more tonal, the thematic material more accessible, yet every bar bears his personal imprint. All his best qualities, meditation, humour and grandeur, blend in perfect balance and self-fulfilment.

As if to prove that other solutions were possible, Shostakovich created a new and highly original pattern with his Sixth Symphony: an extended, essentially tragic Largo, followed by two quick movements, an airy Scherzo and a galop-like Finale. The contrast between the philosophical beginning and the flippant ending seemed rather sharp, yet here again Shostakovich was true to himself. At about the same time he turned to chamber music: his First String Quartet, completed and first played in 1938, is a piece of naive sophistica-

tion, challenging the hallowed genre with deliberately shallow material. Infinitely superior is the Piano Quintet op.57 (1940), a work of a neo-classical stance, where the keyboard and the string quartet are juxtaposed in an effective manner. The work received the Stalin Prize; however there were dissenting voices, as for example that of Prokofiev: 'What astonishes me in this Quintet is that so young a composer, at the height of his powers, should be so very much on his guard, and so carefully calculate every note. He never takes a single risk. One looks in vain for an impetus, a venture'. This harsh judgment reflects Prokofiev's low estimate of Shostakovich, dating back to 1935: 'He is a talented but somehow "unprincipled" composer and ... bereft of melodic invention; he is made too much of here' (letter to Dukelsky).

The next two symphonies, nos.7 and 8, are usually brackctcd as 'war symphonies'. The Seventh, the 'Leningrad', received acclaim far beyond its merits, while the Eighth, an intensely moving piece, is generally underrated. The Seventh is a description of war, the Eighth a contemplation of war and its horrors. Begun in besieged Leningrad in September 1941, the Seventh is pictorial, and each of its four movements represents a programmatic idea (the original titles, later discarded by Shostakovich, were 'War', 'Evocation', 'Native Expanse' and 'Victory'). Composed under the immediate impact of Hitler's invasion, it was written at furious speed. 'I saw the struggle of the Russian people and tried to inculcate the pictures of their heroic deeds in my music', Shostakovich remarked. In the first movement is the 'invasion theme', a long episode that has an obsessive quality through sheer repetition and orchestral build-up.

14. *Autograph score of the opening of Shostakovich's* Symphony *no.7 ('Leningrad'), composed 1941*

While the Seventh Symphony is externalized, the Eighth, composed two years later, reflects the pain and anguish of the war, punctuated by anger and a hope for true peace. It has a curious, somewhat lopsided form, consisting of five movements. The first is an immense tripartite structure (Adagio–Allegro–Adagio), and it is followed by two aggressive and savage scherzo-like movements. Linked without break is a Largo in the form of a passacaglia, the ostinato theme being repeated 12 times in the lower instruments while the variations built above are in a mood of desolation and loneliness. The final movement has a more cheerful, pastoral mood, and the coda trails off like a peaceful dream. Critics have called the finale an anticlimax; coming as it does at the end of four tension-filled movements, it disperses the tension rather than resolves it. But there can be no doubt that the Eighth Symphony contains some of Shostakovich's most sincerely felt music.

To celebrate the victorious end of the war Shostakovich wrote his Ninth Symphony, a merry, exuberant, lighthearted work quite contrary to the expectations of his countrymen. 'We were prepared to listen to a new monumental fresco ... but we heard something quite different, something that at first astounded us by its unexpectedness', was the comment of a fellow musician. The irreverence of the new symphony aroused their 'sharply negative attitude'; Shostakovich must have taken a boyish delight in deflating the pompous expectations of his compatriots. The Ninth is, to quote Cardus, 'probably the least symphonic music ever written'.

The resolution of the party in 1948, condemning Shostakovich and other prominent composers for 'for-

malistic distortions and anti-democratic tendencies alien to the Soviet people', forced Shostakovich to certain concessions. There was now a stronger concentration on film scores and vocal music, for which he used a more accessible musical idiom; among them are the prize-winning films *Vstrecha na El'be* ('Encounter at the Elbe') and *Padeniye Berlina* ('The fall of Berlin') and the oratorio *Pesn' o lesakh* ('Song of the forests'), which won the Stalin Prize for 1949; they have imagination and charm and display the usual high standard of crafts-manship. Other works, particularly the Violin Concerto no.1, in a more esoteric and abstract style, were with-held by Shostakovich; this is why the concerto is some-times designated by conflicting opus numbers: 77, assigning it to the period 1947–8, and 99, placing it in the year 1955. Shostakovich reworked only minor de-tails of the concerto before its release in 1955, and the later opus number was eventually reassigned to the film score *Perviy eshelon* ('The first echelon'). As for the song cycle *From Jewish Folk Poetry*, the reason for with-holding it in 1948 was probably the strong anti-semitic bias of the late Stalinist years; it was first performed on 15 January 1955.

Stalin's death in 1953 and a change in political leadership brought about a gradual liberalization. Shos-takovich's contribution of that year was his Tenth Symphony, which contains some of his greatest music. Essentially it is a tragic work, except for the fourth and final movement, whose artificial gaiety seems somewhat out of place in an otherwise beautifully integrated cycle of movements. While the Tenth Symphony was hailed in the West as a kind of musical 'rehabilitation' of Shostakovich, it provoked a heated debate within the

Soviet Composers' Union. The hard-line opposition maintained that the work was 'non-realistic' and deeply pessimistic in approach, but in the end the liberal faction won with the slogan that the new symphony was 'an optimistic tragedy'. Shostakovich had established his right to speak as he pleased. In fact, he proclaimed publicly in 1954 that 'the artist in Russia has more "freedom" than the artist in the West'. The delayed performance in 1955 of the First Violin Concerto, one of his most original works, further widened the gamut of musical expression possible within Soviet music. The concept of socialist realism, far from being abandoned, was simply enlarged to accommodate works of different styles.

Instead of taking advantage of the hard-won freedom, Shostakovich seemed content during the next few years to create within the loose guidelines of socialist realism. As if to prove that the concept was still viable, he created his Symphony no.11 as a prototype of that style. Written in 1957 for the 40th anniversary of the Revolution, it is sub-titled 'The Year 1905' and marks an important departure in compositional technique by the use of folk (or pseudo-folk) material. Because of that, there is a stronger emphasis on tonality and a general accessibility of musical idiom. Depicting the tragic events of the abortive 1905 Revolution, the movements are sub-titled: 'Palace Square', 'Ninth of January', 'Eternal Memory', 'Tocsin'; they are continuous, and the thematic treatment is cyclic. Shostakovich used authentic tunes related to the revolutionary experience, some belonging to the 19th century, some to the year 1905. Not content with mere quotation, he succeeded in integrating them within the fabric of the symphony and

191

15. *Shostakovich (centre), with Prokofiev (left) and Khachaturian in Moscow, 1945*

lending them his own imprint. (Six years earlier he had written Ten Poems on revolutionary texts, which can be considered a preliminary study to this symphony.)

The Symphony no.12 ('The Year 1917', dedicated to the memory of Lenin) is similarly descriptive, but is built on freely invented themes. Nevertheless, the two symphonies belong together, forming a diptych of the Russian Revolution. In the Symphony no.12 the subtitles are 'Revolutionary Petrograd', 'Razliv', 'Aurora' and 'The Dawn of Mankind'. The work is more traditional in form, perhaps, than any of Shostakovich's previous symphonies. In spirit, too, it is closer to 'old Russia', mainly to Borodin and his epic Second Symphony. Acclaimed at home (especially no.11), the two latest symphonies were harshly criticized in the West and dismissed as 'monumental trivialities'. Yet to Shostakovich and his compatriots, they contained a definite social message.

Though the Symphonies nos.11 and 12 represent a somewhat lower level of purely musical accomplishment, Shostakovich made up for them by giving his best thoughts to the genres of string quartet and concerto – an interesting shift in focus. Of the quartets nos.6–8, composed between 1956 and 1960, the Eighth is undoubtedly the finest. It has been called 'autobiographical' because the dominating theme is Shostakovich's musical signature D–S–C–H (D–E♭–C–B), a motif that he had already used in the First Violin Concerto and the Tenth Symphony. He also quoted from some of his earlier works, the First Symphony, the Piano Trio no.2 and the First Cello Concerto, as if to re-live his experiences. A hauntingly beautiful page is the

quotation in the fourth movement of the revolutionary Russian song *Tortured by Heavy Bondage*, followed by a melody from Act 4 of *Lady Macbeth*. The work is an uninterrupted sequence of five movements: Largo, Allegro molto, Allegretto, Largo, Largo. Written 'in memory of the victims of fascism and war', it is intensely poignant and personal in the slow movements, bitter and driven in the faster sections. There are relationships with the Eighth Symphony, equally an outcry against war. Despite its heterogeneous components, the Eighth Quartet is beautifully integrated and balanced in its use of homophonic and polyphonic textures. A year before composing the work, in 1959, Shostakovich had completed his First Cello Concerto, one of his most important works, though perhaps less probing than the First Violin Concerto. Rostropovich received the dedication and gave the first performance in Leningrad in October 1959, followed a month later by the American première in Philadelphia in the presence of Shostakovich.

The liberalizing trend in Soviet culture reached a highpoint in 1962 (the year when permission was granted to publish Solzhenitsïn's *A Day in the Life of Ivan Denisovich*). Shostakovich became interested in the courageous poetry of Yevtushenko and selected five of his poems for the Symphony no.13. Scored for solo bass, a chorus of basses and orchestra, the work is properly a symphonic cantata, yet the orchestral framework is so strong, the form so symphonic, that Shostakovich's designation is fully justified. The poems form a perfect symphonic cycle: a strongly dramatic first movement ('Babiy Yar'), a Scherzo ('Humour'), two slow movements ('In the Shop' and 'Fears') and a Finale ('A

Career'). The music, far from being merely descriptive, has a life and logic all its own, yet is closely welded to the texts. The chorus is used consistently in unison and often creates the effect of a choral recitation; the solo part, too, tends to resemble a 'speech-song'. At the première on 18 December 1962, the effect of music and words was overwhelming; the meaning of the text, an oblique criticism of the Stalinist past, was not lost on the audience. In the meantime, the political wind had changed in Moscow, and the anti-liberal forces mounted a concerted attack on the Symphony no.13. The score was withdrawn for revision, and Yevtushenko was forced to rewrite certain lines, particularly in 'Babiy Yar'. No change in music was involved, since the substituted lines fitted exactly, but even in the revised version the symphony remained under a cloud, receiving only a few performances in the next years. Now it is fully accepted and reveals the composer in a stark and bitter mood, using dark and brooding orchestral colours, to which the exuberant humour of the scherzo and the pastoral serenity of the finale serve as welcome contrasts. Shostakovich and Yevtushenko collaborated on another important work, the vocal-symphonic poem *Kazn' Stepana Razina* ('The execution of Stepan Razin') for bass solo, mixed chorus and orchestra (1964), effective but musically less original.

Shostakovich's second period came to a close with three more string quartets (nos.9–11) and the Second Cello Concerto op.126 (1966).

III Late works, 1967–75
Shostakovich's third and last creative period can be said to extend from op.127 (the seven Blok songs) to

op.147 (the Viola Sonata). It includes two symphonies (nos.14 and 15), two shorter orchestral works, four string quartets (nos.12–15), the Second Violin Concerto, two sonatas, two film scores, five vocal cycles (one for unaccompanied chorus, the others of songs) and an orchestral version of an earlier song cycle. The significantly large proportion of vocal works is enlarged by the Symphony no.14, which consists of 11 settings of poems. The list is impressive for its length, variety and content. There is no noticeable slowing down of Shostakovich's creative power. Only some of the early flamboyance seems to be gone; there is also a preoccupation with sombre thoughts, a premonition of death; and a lugubrious mood suffuses entire works, such as the String Quartet no.15, with its six uninterrupted adagios. But there are also instances of high spirits, as in the first movement of the Symphony no.15, where the repeated references to Rossini's *Guillaume Tell* overture invariably provoke laughter.

A preoccupation with death hovers over the Symphony no.14 (1969), a work of anguish and pessimism, relieved occasionally by sardonic humour or pensive lyricism. Shostakovich defied every established tradition: the whole concept is non-symphonic and lacks firm architecture or musical continuity; the selection of 11 poems is challenging, all but one being by west European poets (Apollinaire, Lorca, Rilke) and far removed from the psyche of the Soviet listener. Their tortured imagery is captured in a musical idiom of bleak colours, dissonant atonality and surcharged emotionalism. The only lyrical respite is provided by the lone Russian poet, Küchelbecker, a schoolfellow of Pushkin who languished in prison for 20 years. His words,

'What comfort is there for talent among villains and fools?', are quietly defiant. Did Shostakovich identify with these lines? Certainly he created a score that goes against every tenet of socialist realism, and in trying to come to terms with its stark pessimism, Soviet critics drew parallels with Musorgsky's *Songs and Dances of Death*. In scoring the Symphony no.14, Shostakovich used 19 strings, ten percussion instruments and two solo voices (soprano and bass), keeping the texture transparent and intimate, yet capable of achieving strong climaxes. The symphony is dedicated to Benjamin Britten, for whom Shostakovich felt friendship and admiration.

With his last symphony, no.15, Shostakovich returned to the purely instrumental concept. It is scored for a normal-sized orchestra of strings and wind, but with an important percussion section of 14 instruments. These are used not only for incidental colour and rhythm but to musical purpose; the coda of the finale, for instance, brings a delicate interplay of celesta, triangle, xylophone and bells with a few rhythm instruments, all set against an immobile string chord. (Shostakovich's creative interest in percussion instruments was not new; one may recall the percussion interlude in *The Nose*.) After the searing intensity of the Symphony no.14, Shostakovich appears rather subdued and contemplative in his last symphony, and the work does not sustain the listener's interest, nor does it reveal significant new facets in the composer's personal style. Just as the jaunty quote from *Guillaume Tell* characterizes the first movement, so the quotation of the sombre 'fate motif' from *Die Walküre* colours the finale.

A trend towards transparent scoring is also noticeable

in the Second Violin Concerto, where percussion and other instruments are drawn into interplay with the solo violin (similar procedures can be observed in the Second Cello Concerto). While the First Violin concerto has greater scope, the Second is by no means an inferior work: it has beautiful cantilena and technical inventiveness, though on the whole it is less 'difficult' than no.1. Both concertos are dedicated to Oistrakh, who gave the premières.

Among Shostakovich's late works, the song cycles on Blok and Tsvetayeva deserve special attention. The Blok cycle is for soprano and piano trio, yet each of the songs uses a different instrumentation: voice and one instrument in the first three, voice and two instruments in the next three, and the full complement in the last. Five of the songs are pensive, and the mood is beautifully realized; the remaining two are somewhat strident. A richer instrumental setting is used in the second version (op.143a) of the six Tsvetayeva songs: a chamber orchestra forms the background for the mezzo-soprano line. Here, too, the mood of the music is mostly sombre, yet the orchestral colours (including xylophone and bells) add charm and life to the musical texture, which otherwise tends to be somewhat monochrome.

The Violin Sonata op.134 (1968) is a rather stark work, written for David Oistrakh. The first movement is a sensitive piece with non-tonal and tonal writing in juxtaposition. The first theme is a 12-note one, and there is artful interweaving of piano and violin. The second movement, as a contrast, is a relentless pounding on both instruments, over-long for its material. In the finale (Largo–Andante) a chaconne-like theme is used, but eventually the movement turns into a stylistic

medley with solo cadenzas. The different moods do not fuse into a unified entity.

That same year (1968) Shostakovich wrote his 12th String Quartet and used similar technical procedures. Like the Violin Sonata, the quartet begins with a 12-note statement and continues immediately with a strong affirmation of tonality, a dichotomy that persists throughout the work. Questioned on this point, Shostakovich replied (see Brown, 1973): 'I did use some elements of dodecaphony in both works. Of course, if you use solely this theory, I have a very negative attitude towards this kind of approach. But if a composer feels that he needs this or that technique, he can take whatever is available and use it as he sees fit'. His procedures are not serial, but they lead to an astounding widening of his musical vocabulary, abandoning tonality for long stretches in pursuit of linear logic. The Quartet no.12 is but one example of this evolution characteristic of his last period: skirting atonality, he was prevented by his innate conservatism from making the ultimate break and always returned in the end to tonal affirmation. While characteristic of the late compositions, the tonal–atonal polarity can be traced in some of his earlier works, as far back as the Second Symphony.

The remaining three string quartets testify to Shostakovich's continued preoccupation with the genre. No.13 is a highly unified one-movement work in palindromic form; the basic tempo is *adagio* and the middle section moves at double speed. Percussive effects are used by tapping the bow against the body of the instrument. The principal theme is again of 12 notes, and the feeling of tonality is obscured through much of

the piece. In keeping with the dedication to Borisovsky, the original violist of the Beethoven Quartet, the viola is assigned an important part. In no.14 it is the cello that has a leading role (the dedicatee was Shirinsky, the cellist of the Beethoven Quartet). Indeed, Shostakovich's concern for the individual talents of the four quartet players is, in a way, characteristic of his quartet style. His last quartet, no.15 (without dedication), is an elegiac work in six continuous adagios entitled 'Elegy', 'Serenade', 'Intermezzo', 'Nocturne', 'Funeral March' and 'Epilogue'. The texture is extremely transparent, often reduced to one or two lines, conveying a mood of brooding grief with little of change or of rhythmic variety.

Contrasting with the sombreness of the Quartet no.15, Shostakovich's last completed work, the Viola Sonata op.147 (1975), is a beautifully balanced piece in three movements (Moderato, Allegretto, Adagio). The prevailing mood is one of subdued serenity, with the playful Allegretto separating the lyrical outer movements. Particularly moving is the final Adagio, the most extended of the three movements. The veiled timbre of the viola colours the work, though the technical demands are, in places, quite considerable. There is a mysterious reminiscence of Beethoven's 'Moonlight' Sonata, fleeting but unmistakable; it is a poignant farewell, resigned but not sad.

CHAPTER THREE

Summary of achievement

Shostakovich belonged to the first generation of Russian composers educated entirely under the Soviet system. His loyalty to his country and its government was unquestioned. Even at a time of personal disfavour, after the party resolution of 1948, he was willing to represent the USSR at the Peace Congress in New York in 1949 and at similar congresses in Warsaw in 1950 and Vienna in 1952. With a high sense of civic duty, he served as a deputy member of the Supreme Soviet, both of the RSFSR and of the USSR. He was a member of the directorate of the Union of Soviet Composers from 1939 to 1948 and later served as first secretary of the Russian chapter of the union, relinquishing that post in 1968 because of ill-health. He was made a People's Artist of the RSFSR in 1948 and of the USSR in 1954. The Order of Lenin was conferred on him in 1956 and 1966, and he received the Lenin Prize in 1958 for his Symphony no.11. Among foreign honours bestowed on him were membership in the Royal Musical Academy of Sweden (1954), honorary membership in the Accademia di S Cecilia in Rome (1956) and the gold medal of the Royal Philharmonic Society (1966); he was also a corresponding member of the Academy of Arts of the German Democratic Republic. Honorary doctorates of music were conferred on him by the

201

University of Oxford (1958), Trinity College, Dublin (1972) and Northwestern University (1973).

Throughout most of his life, Shostakovich was a dedicated teacher, his pupils including Karayev, Sviridov, Karen Khachaturian, Tishchenko and many others. Most of his teaching was done at the Leningrad Conservatory: he was a member of the composition faculty (1937–41, 1945–8) and he accepted a class of postgraduate students in 1961. He also taught at the Moscow Conservatory from 1943 to 1948. He lived in Leningrad until 1941 and in 1943 settled in Moscow. His son Maxim has become a well-known conductor and a noted interpreter of his father's music.

Shostakovich the composer can be described as an eclectic progressive, rooted in tradition and tonality, yet using dissonance and occasional atonality as expressive means without adhering to any particular school. He spoke out sharply against dodecaphony and serialism, but considered their occasional use 'entirely justified if it is dictated by the idea of the composition'. His background was many-sided: at the Leningrad Conservatory the curriculum was dominated by the theories of Rimsky-Korsakov, but he broke away as soon as he left the classroom. Among the Russian 'classics', he felt closest to Musorgsky and Borodin. As a young man he rejected Skryabin but felt attracted by the daring of Prokofiev and Stravinsky, Krenek and Hindemith; *Wozzeck* impressed him, to which may be added his growing involvement with Mahler. These heterogeneous elements left their imprint on his personality, where three basic strands can be identified: high-spirited humour, introspective meditation and declamatory grandeur. Whenever these elements were balanced he

could produce genuine masterpieces; whenever one or the other aspect prevailed, he could become shallow or blatant. His quick method of working allowed his self-criticism to weaken occasionally, resulting in works not quite worthy of his talent. His enormous technical facility encouraged rapid work, yet at no time in his career did he allow shoddy workmanship. His artistic conscience was strong, but he did not brood over a less successful work; there was always the next composition which, he hoped, would be better. His advice to young composers was to work more slowly.

It has been said that Shostakovich wrote deliberately facile music under political pressure. This is a misconception. No outside pressure was needed to make him write 'facile' music: he enjoyed it; it was part of his multi-faceted personality. He has been reproached for having accepted public castigation too submissively and for having admitted 'errors' too willingly. True, he was sensitive to criticism, be it from laymen, professionals or politicians. As a creative artist he was attuned to the needs and responses of his audiences. Shifts in his musical style were not always meant to placate ideological opponents; more probably they represented an almost intuitive reaction to the environment and the mood of the country. Despite a certain flexibility, he maintained his artistic integrity and independence to a greater degree than any of his fellow composers. His absolute sincerity is never in doubt. Had Shostakovich lived outside the USSR, there is no question that his talent would have developed differently. But to reproach him for not having followed Western-style 'modernism' is to misjudge the artist's social role and responsibility as he envisioned them. He accepted the principle of

'paternal concern' for the arts as demonstrated by the party. What he disliked was the bureaucratic meddling of the 'apparatchiki' in artistic matters, and in later years, particularly after 1953, he protested against it. His controversial 'memoirs', published in the USA after his death, would seem to bear out his discontent with Soviet officialdom, but their authenticity is disputed by both Soviet and Western authorities.

Twice in his lifetime, Shostakovich was subjected to massive musico-political pressures: in 1936, when *Lady Macbeth* was forced off the stage by criticism in *Pravda*, and in 1948, when he and a group of distinguished fellow composers were denounced in a party resolution. The first attack was personal, the second collective. The 1936 affair became a test case, 'the first clear demonstration of what Communist totalitarianism in art meant' (Abraham). More far-reaching was the resolution of 1948, because it imposed ideological controls on Soviet composers (some of the most scurrilous accusations were withdrawn by the resolution of 1958, but not the underlying principles). Rostropovich remembered the year 1948: 'How much nonsense was written about those giants of our music, Prokofiev and Shostakovich. . . . Now, when one looks back at the newspapers of those years, one becomes unbearably ashamed' (open letter to *Pravda*, 31 October 1970). In December 1962 Shostakovich's name was again drawn into an ideological controversy in connection with his Symphony no.13 'Babiy Yar', but it was the poetry of Yevtushenko, not the music, which came under criticism. The few textual changes did not affect the musical setting. Eventually Shostakovich reached a plateau beyond ideological criticism; even his most 'expressionistic'

16. Dmitry Shostakovich

work, the Symphony no.14 (1969), was accepted on its own terms.

Shostakovich's total output shows an astounding variety. Among his 147 opus numbers are 15 symphonies, 15 string quartets, two operas and an operetta, six concertos for various instruments, chamber music for piano and strings, music for piano solo, several cantatas and oratorios, three ballets, 36 film scores, incidental music

for 11 plays, and vocal music of all kinds. In addition, there are a number of orchestral suites fashioned from his own scores for films, ballets or incidental scores. His productivity never slowed. Living under the open-handed patronage of the arts in the USSR, he was free of worries about fees, royalties, performances and publications. His material needs were taken care of in a generous way. Among his friends and admirers were the leading Soviet artists, and their devotion was rewarded with dedications of major works: the conductor Mravinsky, the pianists Gilels and Richter, the violinist Oistrakh, the cellist Rostropovich, the soprano Vishnevskaya, the Beethoven String Quartet. Thus he was always assured of superb performances in accordance with his own ideas, and these performances were captured on records. Also a complete edition was begun during his lifetime. The few setbacks in his career were more than counterbalanced by decades of unparalleled recognition, both national and international. Yet none of the honours bestowed on him changed his basic personality: he was shy and inhibited, unassuming and self-critical, nervous and highly-strung, though fun-loving in his younger years. He was unfailingly helpful and encouraging towards younger colleagues and had a high sense of fairness. Because of his reputation for honesty and integrity, his opinions carried enormous weight everywhere. He often appeared as a pianist in his own works and played with technical finish, avoiding any show of emotion; it was 'objective' playing. As a public speaker and writer of critical commentaries he was a man of few words, limiting himself to the essentials, expressing his thoughts in a direct and simple manner without adornment.

Achievement

Shostakovich will be remembered primarily as a composer of symphonies. His imagination needed the stimulus of orchestral colours; his melodic invention (generally not his strongest point) acquired originality through the use of instrumental timbres; his sense of form is enhanced by the skilful manipulation of orchestral masses. He had the grand gesture of the born symphonist, mastering such diverse concepts as the purely orchestral, the programmatic and the vocal-instrumental. With Stravinsky and Prokofiev Shostakovich represents the culmination of 20th-century Russian music but, unlike his two older contemporaries, he is alone in having composed his entire oeuvre within the framework of Soviet aesthetics. When forced on to the defensive, he did not argue; but through the strength of his genius he overcame the limitations of socialist realism to the point where it no longer inhibited free musical creation, in the battle for which it was Shostakovich who ultimately emerged victorious.

WORKS

Edition: *D. Shostakovich: Sobraniye sochineniy v soroka dvukh tomakh* [Collected works in 42 volumes] (Moscow, 1980–)

Numbers in right-hand margins denote references in the text.

	OPERAS AND BALLETS	
op.		
15	Nos [The nose] (opera, 3, D. Shostakovich, Ye. Zamyatin, G. Ionin, A. Preys, after Gogol), 1927–8; Leningrad, Maliy Opera Theatre, 18 Jan 1930	176, 183, 197
22	Zolotoy vek [The age of gold] (ballet, 3, A. Ivanovsky), 1929–30; Leningrad, Academic Theatre of Opera and Ballet, 26 Oct 1930	176
27	Bolt (ballet, 3, V. Smirnov), 1930–31; Leningrad, Academic Theatre of Opera and Ballet, 8 April 1931	
29	Ledi Makbet Mtsenskovo uyezda [Lady Macbeth of the Mtsensk district] (opera, 4, Shostakovich, Preys, after Leskov), 1930–32; Leningrad, Maliy Opera Theatre, 22 Jan 1934; rev. as op.114	177, 181–2, 184, 185, 194, 204
39	Svetliy ruchey [The limpid stream] (ballet, 3, F. Lopukhov, A. Piotrovsky), 1934–5; Leningrad, Maliy Opera Theatre, 4 June 1935	
—	Igroki [The gamblers] (opera, after Gogol), 1941–2, inc.; Leningrad Philharmonic Bol'shoy Hall, 18 Sept 1978	181
105	Moskva, Cheryomushki (operetta, 3, V. Mass, M. Chervinsky) 1958; Moscow Operetta Theatre, 24 Jan 1959	
114	Katerina Izmaylova [rev. of op.29], 1956–63; Moscow, Stanislavsky and Nemirovich-Danchenko Theatre, 8 Jan 1963	181–2
—	Mechtateli [The dreamers] (ballet, 4) [adaptation of opp.22 and 27], 1975; Moscow, Stanislavsky and Nemirovich-Danchenko Theatre, 19 Jan 1976	

	OTHER DRAMATIC WORKS	
	(incidental music)	
19	Klop [The bedbug] (V. Mayakovsky), 1929; Moscow, Meyerhold Theatre, 13 Feb 1929	205–6
24	Vïstrel [The shot] (A. Bezïmensky), 1929, lost; Leningrad, Working Youth Theatre, 14 Dec 1929	176
25	Tselina [Virgin soil] (A. Gorbenko, N. L'vov), 1930, lost; Leningrad, Working Youth Theatre, 9 May 1930	
28	Prav', Britaniya [Rule, Britannia] (A. Piotrovsky), 1931; Len-	

	ingrad, Working Youth Theatre, 9 May 1931	
31	Uslovno ubitïy [Conditionally killed] (stage revue, V. Voyevodin, E. Riss), 1931; Leningrad Music Hall, 20 Oct 1931	
32	Gamlet [Hamlet] (W. Shakespeare), 1931–2; Moscow, Vakhtangov Theatre, 19 March 1932	
37	Chelovecheskaya komediya [The human comedy] (P. Sukhotin, after Balzac), 1933–4; Moscow, Vakhtangov Theatre, 1 April 1934	
44	Salyut, Ispaniya [Hail, Spain] (A. Afinogenov), 1936; Leningrad, Pushkin Theatre of Drama, 23 Nov 1936	
58a	Korol' Lir [King Lear] (Shakespeare), 1940; Leningrad, Gor'ky Bol'shoy Dramatic Theatre, 24 March 1941	
63	Otchizna [Native country] (spectacle), suite 'Rodnoy Leningrad' [Native Leningrad], 1942; Moscow, Dzerzhinsky Central Club, 7 Nov 1942	
66	Russkaya reka [Russian river] (spectacle), 1944; Moscow, Dzerzhinsky Central Club, Dec 1944	
72	Vesna pobednaya [Victorious spring] (spectacle), 2 songs (M. Svetlov), 1945; Moscow, Dzerzhinsky Central Club, May 1946	
—	Gamlet [Hamlet] (Shakespeare) [incl. music from op.58a], 1954; Leningrad, Pushkin Theatre of Drama, April 1954	

	(film scores)	
18	Novïy Vavilon [New Babylon], 1928–9 [for live perf. with silent film]	
26	Odna [Alone], 1930–31	
30	Zlatïye gorï [Golden mountains], 1931	
33	Vstrechnïy [Counterplan], 1932	
36	Skazka o pope i rabotnike yevo Balde [The tale of the priest and his worker, Blockhead], 1933–4, inc.; rev. as comic opera by S. Khentova, 1980	
38	Lyubov' i nenavist' [Love and hatred], 1934	
41	Yunost' Maksima [The youth of Maxim], 1934 [no.1 of 'Maxim' trilogy]	

(concertos, miscellaneous symphonic)

No.	Work	Pages
1	Scherzo, f♯, 1919	205
3	Theme and Variations, B♭, 1921–2	183
7	Scherzo, E♭, 1923–4	183
23	Two pieces for E. Dressel's opera Der arme Columbus, 1929	183
35	Piano Concerto no.1, c, pf, tpt, str, 1933; D. Shostakovich, A. Schmidt, Leningrad PO, cond. F. Stiedry, Leningrad Philharmonic Bol'shoy Hall, 15 Oct 1933	183–4
42	Five Fragments, 1935, perf. 1965	
—	Solemn March, military band, 1942	
77	Violin Concerto no.1, a, 1947–8; D. Oistrakh, Leningrad PO, cond. Mravinsky, Leningrad Philharmonic Bol'shoy Hall, 29 Oct 1955	180, 190, 191, 193, 194, 198
—	Three Pieces for Orchestra, 1947–8	
96	Festive Overture, A, 1954	
102	Piano Concerto no.2, F, 1957; M. Shostakovich, USSR SO, cond. N. Anosov, Moscow Conservatory Bol'shoy Hall, 10 May 1957	
107	Cello Concerto no.1, E♭, 1959; M. Rostropovich, Leningrad PO, cond. Mravinsky, Leningrad Philharmonic Bol'shoy Hall, 4 Oct 1959	181, 193, 194
—	Novorossiyskiye kuranti (Ogon' vechnoy slavï) [Novorossiisk chimes (The flame of eternal glory)], 1960	
115	Overture on Russian and Khirghiz Folk Themes, 1963	
126	Cello Concerto no.2, G, 1966; Rostropovich, USSR State SO, cond. Ye. Svetlanov, Moscow Conservatory Bol'shoy Hall, 25 Sept 1966	195, 198
129	Violin Concerto no.2, c♯, 1967; Oistrakh, Moscow PO, cond. Kondrashin, Moscow, Bol'shoy Palace of Culture, 13 Sept 1967	196, 198
130	Traurno-triumfal'naya prelyudiya pamyati geroyev stalingradskoy bitvï [Funeral-triumphal prelude in memory of the heroes of the battle of Stalingrad], 1967	
131	Oktyabr' [October], sym. poem, 1967	
139	March of the Soviet Militia, military band, 1970	

(suites)

No.	Work	Pages
15a	Suite from The Nose, T, Bar, orch, 1927–8	
22a	Suite from The Age of Gold, 1930	206
27a	Suite from Bolt (Ballet Suite no.5), 1931	205
30a	Suite from Golden Mountains, 1931	183
32a	Suite from Hamlet, 1932	183
—	Suite for Jazz Orchestra no.1, 1934	183
—	Suite from The Tale of the Priest and his Worker, Blockhead, ?1935	183–4
50a	Suite for Jazz Orchestra no.2, 1938, lost	
—	Suite from 'Maxim' trilogy, with chorus, arr. L. Atovm'yan, pubd 1961	
64a	Suite from Zoya, with chorus, ?1944	
76a	Suite from Pirogov, arr. Atovm'yan, 1947	
78a	Suite from Michurin, with chorus, arr. Atovm'yan, 1948	
80a	Suite from Encounter at the Elbe, with vv, 1948	
—	Ballet Suite no.1, arr. Atovm'yan, 1949	
82a	Suite from The Fall of Berlin, with chorus, arr. Atovm'yan, 1949	
75a	Suite from The Young Guard, arr. Atovm'yan, 1951	
89a	Suite from The Unforgettable Year 1919, arr. Atovm'yan, 1951	
—	Ballet Suite no.2, arr. Atovm'yan, 1951	
—	Ballet Suite no.3, arr. Atovm'yan, 1952	
—	Ballet Suite no.4, arr. Atovm'yan, 1953	
97a	Suite from The Gadfly, arr. Atovm'yan, 1955	
99a	Suite from The First Echelon, with chorus, 1956	
85a	Suite from Belinsky, with chorus, arr. Atovm'yan, 1960	
111a	Suite from Five Days – Five Nights, arr. Atovm'yan, 1961	
114a	Suite from Katerina Izmaylova, S, orch, ?1963	
116a	Suite from Hamlet, arr. Atovm'yan, 1964	
120a	Suite from A Year is Like a Lifetime, ?1965	

205

CHORAL

No.	Work	Pages
—	Klyatva Narkomu [The oath to the people's commissar] [V. Sayanov], B, chorus, pf, 1941	
74	Poema o Rodine [Poem of the motherland], cantata, Mez, T, 2 Bar, B, chorus, orch, 1947	
81	Pesn' o lesakh [Song of the forests] [Ye. Dolmatovsky], oratorio, T, B, boys' chorus, chorus, orch, 1949	180, 190
88	Ten Poems (turn-of-the-century revolutionary poets), chorus, boys' chorus, unacc., 1951	
—	Ten Russian Folksong Arrangements, soloists, chorus, pf, 1951	

206

ORCHESTRATIONS

SELECTED WRITINGS

'K prem'ere "Nosa"' [On the occasion of the première of The Nose], Rabochiy i teatr (1929), no.24, p.12

'Pochemu "Nos"?' [Why The Nose?], Rabochiy i teatr (1930), no.3, p.11

'Deklaratsiya obyazannostey kompozitora' [Declaration of a composer's responsibilities], Rabochiy i teatr (1931), no.31, p.6

'Sovetskaya muzikal'naya kritika otstayot' [Soviet musical criticism is lagging], SovM (1933), no.3, p.120

'Tragediya-satira' [A tragedy-satire], Sovetskoye iskusstvo (16 Oct 1933); repr. in Dmitry Shostakovich, ed. L. Danilevich (Moscow, 1967), 13

'My opera "Lady Macbeth of Mtsensk"', MM, xii (1934–5), 23

'Moy tvorcheskiy put'' [My creative path], *Izvestiya* (3 April 1935), 3

'Autobiographie', *ReM*, no.170 (1936), 432

'Moi blizhayshiye raboti' [My next works], *Rabochiy i teatr* (1937), no.11, p.24

'Moy tvorcheskiy otvet' [My creative answer], *Vechernyaya Moskva* (25 Jan 1938), 3

'Moya sed'maya simfoniya' [My seventh symphony], *Vechernyaya Moskva* (8 Oct 1941); repr. in *Izvestiya* (13 Feb 1942), 3

'Sovetskaya muzïka v dni voynï' [Soviet music in the days of war], *Literatura i iskusstvo* (1 April 1944); repr. in *SovM* (1975), no.11, p.64

'Vospominaniya ob I. I. Sollertinskom' [Recollections of I. I. Sollertinsky], *Informatsionnïy byulleten' SK SSSR* (1944), no.5–6; repr. in *Muzïkal'nïy sovremennik*, i, ed. L. Danilevich (Moscow, 1973), 338

'Nasha rabota v godï Otechestvennoy voynï' [Our work during the years of the patriotic war], *Rabota kompozitorov i muzïkovedov Leningrada v godï Velikoy Otechestvennoy voynï* (Leningrad, 1946), 61

'Thoughts about Tchaikovsky', *Russian Symphony* (New York, 1947), 1

Speech at the gathering of composers and musicologists of the city of Moscow, *SovM* (1948), no.1, p.79

'Mï dolzhnï ob''edinit' nashi usiliya' [We should unite our efforts], *Vechernyaya Moskva* (29 March 1949); repr. in *Pravda* (30 March 1949), *Kul'tura i zhizn'* (31 March 1949), *Sovetskoye iskusstvo* (2 April 1949) [speech at New York Peace Congress]

'O podlinnoy i mnimoy programmnosti' [On genuine and imaginary programme music], *SovM* (1951), no.5, p.76

'Po puti narodnosti i realizma' [Along the road of national character and realism], *SovM* (1952), no.11, p. 6

'Pesni gneva i bor'bï' [Songs of rage and struggle], *SovM* (1953), no.6, p.33

'Radost' tvorcheskikh iskaniy' [The joy of creative quests], *SovM* (1954), no.1, p.40

'Otvet amerikanskomu muzïkal'nomu kritiku' [Answer to an American music critic], *SovM* (1956), no.3, p.142; see also *New York Times* (5 Jan 1956)

'O nekotorïkh nasushchnïkh voprosakh muzïkal'novo tvorchestva'

[On some vital questions of musical creativity], *Pravda* (17 June 1956); repr. in *Dmitry Shostakovich*, ed. L. Danilevich (Moscow, 1967), 16

'Dumï o proidennom puti' [Thoughts about the path traversed], *SovM* (1956), no.9, p.9

'Novoye o Mayakovskom' [Something new about Mayakovsky], *Literaturnaya gazeta* (9 Oct 1956); repr. in *Dmitry Shostakovich*, ed. L. Danilevich (Moscow, 1967), 25

'Po puti ukazannomu partiyey' [On the path shown by the party], *Sovetskaya kul'tura* (10 Sept 1957); repr. in *SovM* (1957), no.10, p.10

'Velikaya zabota partii o rastsvete sovetskoy muzïki' [The great concern of the party for the blossoming of Soviet music], *Pravda* (13 June 1958); repr. in *Sovetskaya kul'tura* (14 June 1958)

Znat' i lubit' muzïku. Beseda s molodyozh'yu [To know and love music: a conversation with youth] (Moscow, 1958)

'Bit' na visote velikikh zadach' [Being equal to great tasks], *SovM* (1959), no.1, p.7

'Shirokiye massï verni nastoyashchey muzïke' [The general public is faithful to real music], *Sovetskaya kul'tura* (14 Nov 1959); repr. in *SovM* (1959), no.11, p.6

Foreword to A. S. Rabinovich: *Izbrannïye stat'i i materialï* [Selected essays and materials] (Moscow, 1959)

Foreword to *I. O. Dunayevsky: Vïstupleniya, stat'i, pis'ma. Vospominaniya* [Speeches, articles, letters. Recollections], ed. E. Grosheva (Moscow, 1961), 9

'Nas vdokhnovlyayet partiya' [The party inspires us], *Muzïkal'naya zhizn'* (1962), no.2, p.1; repr. in *SovM* (1962), no.3, p.3

'Moya Alma Mater', *SovM* (1962), no.9, p.101

'Stranitsï vospominaniy' [Pages of recollections], *Leningradskaya konservatoriya v vospominaniyakh*, ed. G. Tigranov (Leningrad, 1962), 121

'Iz vospominaniy o Mayakovskom' [Recollections of Mayakovsky], *V. Mayakovskiy v vospominaniyakh sovremennikov* (Moscow, 1963), 315

'I. I. Sollertinsky', *I. Sollertinskiy: Istoricheskiye etyudï*, ed. M. Druskin (Leningrad, 2/1963), 3

Foreword to *Gustav Maler* [Mahler], ed. I. Barsova (Moscow, 1964, 2/1968)

213

Foreword to *B. Yavorskiy: Vospominaniya, stat'i, i pis'ma, t.1* [Reminiscences, essays and letters], ed. D. Shostakovich (Moscow, 1964, rev. 2/1972)

'Kak rozhdaetsya muzïka' [How music is born], *Literaturnaya gazeta* (21 Dec 1965); repr. in *Dmitry Shostakovich*, ed. L. Danilevich (Moscow, 1967), 35

'Avtobiografiya' [Autobiography], *SovM* (1966), no.9, p.24

The Power of Music (New York, 1968) [9 essays orig. pubd in *The Music Journal*, 1962–8]

'National'niye traditsii i zakonomernosti ikh razvitiya' [National traditions and the laws of their development], *SovM* (1971), no.12, p.34; Eng. trans. in *Composer*, no. 42 (1971–2), 1

'V 1928 gody ...' [In 1928], *Teatr* (1974), no.2, p.52

'Iz vospominaniy' [Recollections], *SovM* (1974), no.3, p.53

'Muzïka i vremya: zametki kompozitora' [Music and time: remarks of a composer], *Kommunist* (1975), no.7, p.38; repr. in *Muzïka i sovremennost'*, x (1976), 5

'Grand Slam', *Music and Musicians*, xxiv/1 (1975–6), 24

ed. G. Pribegina: *D. Shostakovich o vremeni i o sebe: 1926–1975* [Shostakovich about himself and his times] (Moscow, 1980; Eng. trans., 1981)

ed. C. Hellmundt and K. Meyer: *Erfahrungen: Aufsätze, Erinnerungen, Reden, Diskussionsbeiträge, Interviews, Briefe* (Leipzig, 1983)

Many articles in Eng. trans. in *The Current Digest of the Soviet Press*, *VOKS Bulletins*, *Information Bulletin of the Union of Soviet Composers*, *Music Section Bulletins of the Society for Cultural Relations with the USSR*

Several articles in Ger. trans. in *Musik und Gesellschaft*; for list and some articles, see Brockhaus (2/1963)

For list (inc.) of Russ. articles to 1964 see Sadovnikov (2/1965), 178

BIBLIOGRAPHY

CATALOGUES

E. Sadovnikov: *D. D. Shostakovich: notograficheskiy spravochnik* [Catalogue of works] (Moscow, 1961; enlarged, with bibliography, 2/1965)

M. Volodina: *Shostakovich: notograficheskiy spravochnik* (Moscow, 1976)

M. MacDonald: *Dmitri Shostakovich: a Complete Catalogue* (London, 1977)

D. C. Hulme: *Dmitri Shostakovich: Catalogue, Bibliography & Discography* (Muir of Ord, 1982)

COLLECTIONS OF ESSAYS

L. G. Berger, ed.: *Chertï stilya D. Shostakovicha* [Shostakovich's stylistic traits] (Moscow, 1962)

L. Danilevich, ed.: *Dmitry Shostakovich* (Moscow, 1967)

J. Breuer, ed: *In memoriam Dmitrij Sosztakovics* (Budapest, 1976)

Muzïkal'naya zhizn' (1976), no.17 [special issue]

G. Shneerson, ed.: *D. Shostakovich: stat'i i materialï* [Articles and materials] (Moscow, 1976)

SovM (1976), no.9; (1981), nos.9–10 [special issues]

C. Norris, ed.: *Shostakovich: the Man and his Music* (London, 1982)

LIFE AND WORKS

M. Grinberg: 'Dmitry Shostakovich' *Muzïka i revolyutsiya* (1927), no.11, p.16

R. Lee: 'Dmitri Szostakovitch; Young Russian Composer tells of Linking Politics with Creative Work', *New York Times* (20 Dec 1931)

N. Slonimsky: 'Dmitri Dmitrievitch Shostakovich', *MQ*, xxviii (1942), 415

G. Abraham: *Eight Soviet Composers* (London, 1943/R1976)

V. Seroff: *Dmitri Shostakovich: the Life and Background of a Soviet Composer* (New York, 1943/R1970)

M. Sahlberg-Vatchnadzé: *Chostakovitch* (Paris, 1945)

I. Martïnov: *Dmitry Shostakovich* (Moscow, 1946, 2/1956; Eng. trans., 1947/R1977)

D. Zhitomirsky: *Dmitry Shostakovich* (Moscow, 1947)

M. Koval': 'Tvorcheskiy put'' D. Shostakovicha' [Shostakovich's creative path], *SovM* (1948), no.2, p.47; no.3, p.31; no.4, p.8

A. Werth: *Musical Uproar in Moscow* (London, 1949/R1977)

A. Olkhovsky: *Music Under the Soviets: the Agony of an Art* (New York, 1955/R1975)

215

L. Danilevich: *D. Shostakovich* (Moscow, 1958)

B. Asaf'yev: 'Redkiy talant' [A rare talent], *SovM* (1959), no.1, p.19

D. Rabinovich: *Dmitri Shostakovich, Composer* (Moscow and London, 1959)

M. Sabinina: *Dmitri Shostakovich* (Moscow, 1959)

H. A. Brockhaus: *Dmitri Schostakowitsch* (Leipzig, 1962, abridged 2/1963) [2nd edn. incl. articles by Shostakovich in Ger. trans.]

I. Martïnov: *D. Shostakovich: ocherk zhizni i tvorchestva* [A study of his life and works] (Moscow, 1962)

R.-M. Hofmann: *Dmitri Chostakovitch: l'homme et son oeuvre* (Paris, 1963)

S. Khentova: *Shostakovich – pianist* (Leningrad, 1964)

L. Danilevich: *Nash sovremennik: tvorchestvo Shostakovicha* [Our contemporary: the work of Shostakovich] (Moscow, 1965)

V. Bogdanov-Berezovsky: 'Otrochestvo i yunost'' [Adolescence and youth], *SovM* (1966), no.9, p.26; repr. in *D. Shostakovich: stat'i i materialï*, ed. G. Shneerson (Moscow, 1976), 132

M. Jůzl: *Dmitrij Šostakovič* (Prague, 1966)

K. Laux: *Dmitri Schostakowitsch, Chronist seines Volkes* (Berlin, 1966)

N. Malko: *A Certain Art* (New York, 1966)

G. Orlov: *Dmitry Shostakovich* (Leningrad, 1966)

V. Vanslov: *Tvorchestvo Shostakovicha* [The work of Shostakovich] (Moscow, 1966)

G. Yudin: 'Za gran'yu proshlïkh let' [In bygone years], *Muzïkal' noye nasledstvo*, ii/1 (Moscow, 1966), 268

S. Lazarov: *Dmitry Shostakovich* (Sofia, 1967)

D. Zhitomirsky: 'Shekspir i Shostakovich' [Shakespeare and Shostakovich], *Dmitry Shostakovich*, ed. L. Danilevich (Moscow, 1967), 121

V. Del'son: 'Molodoy Shostakovich (o pianiste 20ïkh i 30ïkh gg.' [The young Shostakovich (as a pianist of the 1920s and 1930s)], *Voprosï muzïkal'no-ispolnitel'skovo iskusstva*, v (Moscow, 1969), 193

S. D. Krebs: *Soviet Composers and the Development of Soviet Music* (London and New York, 1970)

N. Kay: *Shostakovich* (London, 1971)

N. Slonimsky: *Music Since 1900* (New York, 4/1971)

B. Schwarz: *Music and Musical Life in Soviet Russia, 1917–70* (London, 1972; enlarged [*1917–81*], 2/1983)

R. S. Brown: 'An Interview with Shostakovich' *High Fidelity*, xxiii/10 (1973), 86

K. Meyer: *Szostakowicz* (Kraków, 1973; Ger. trans., 1980)

P. Buske: *Dmitri Schostakowitsch* (Berlin, 1975)

S. Khentova: *Molodïye godï Shostakovicha* [Shostakovich's youthful

years], i (Moscow, 1975); ii (Leningrad, 1980)

L. Mazel': 'Razdum'ya ob istoricheskom meste tvorchestva Shosta-kovicha' [Thoughts about the historical position of Shostakovich's work], *SovM* (1975), no.9, p.6; rev. in *Stat'i po teorii i analizu muzïki* (Moscow, 1982), 260

M. Barry: 'The Significance of Shostakovich', *Composer*, no.56 (1975–6), 11; no.57 (1976), 19

D. Oistrakh: 'Velikiy khudozhnik nashevo vremeni' [A great artist of our time], *D. Shostakovich: stat'i i materialï*, ed. G. Shneerson (Moscow, 1976), 23

G. Shneerson: 'Zhizn' muzïki Shostakovicha za rubezhom' [Shosta-kovich's music abroad], *D. Shostakovich: stat'i i materialï* (Moscow, 1976), 227

L. S. Tret'yakova: *Dmitry Shostakovich* (Moscow, 1976)

D. Tsïganov: 'Polveka vmeste' [A half century together], *SovM* (1976), no.9, p.29

Dmitry Shostakovich's Last Compositions (Moscow, c1976)

M. Kozlova: 'Vsegda dorozhu vashem mneniyem . . .' [I always value your opinion], *Vstrechi s proshlïm, sbornik materialov*, iii, ed. N. Volkova (Moscow, 1978), 253 [correspondence between Shos-takovich and Prokofiev]; Eng. trans. in 'Prokofiev's Correspond-ence with Stravinsky and Shostakovich', *Slavonic and Western Music: Essays for Gerald Abraham* (Ann Arbor and Oxford, 1985), 271

S. Khentova: *D. D. Shostakovich v godï Velikoy Otechestvennoy voynï* [Shostakovich in the years of World War II] (Leningrad, 1979)

——: *Shostakovich v Petrograde–Leningrade* (Leningrad, 1979, 2/1981)

M. Shaginyan: *O Shostakoviche* [On Shostakovich] (Moscow, 1979)

I. Sollertinsky: *Von Mozart bis Schostakowitsch* (Leipzig, 1979)

S. Volkov, ed.: *Testimony: the Memoirs of Dmitri Shostakovich* (London and New York, 1979)

L. Danilevich: *Dmitry Shostakovich: zhizn' i tvorchestvo* [Life and works] (Moscow, 1980)

L. E. Fay: 'Shostakovich Versus Volkov: Whose *Testimony*?', *Russian Review*, xxxix (1980), 484

L. Gakkel': 'Slovo Shostakovicha' [The words of Shostakovich], *SovM* (1980), no.3, p.14

D. Gojowy: *Neue sowjetische Musik der 20er Jahre* (Regensburg, 1980)

N. Luk'yanova: *Dmitry Dmitriyevich Shostakovich* (Moscow, 1980)

G. Norris: 'Bitter Memories: the Shostakovich Testimony', *MT*, cxxi (1980), 241

D. and L. Sollertinsky: *Pages from the Life of Dmitri Shostakovich* (New York, 1980)

A. Abramov: 'Moshch' i infantil'nost' geniya: k vïkhodu v svet memuarov Dmitriya Shostakovicha' [The power and infantilism of a genius: on the publication of Shostakovich's memoirs], *Vremiya i mï*, no.58 (1981), 155

A. Bush: 'Dmitry Dmitrievich Shostakovich', *Shostakovich: the Man and his Music*, ed. C. Norris (London, 1982), 219

S. Khentova: *D. D. Shostakovich: tridtsatiletiye 1945–1975* [The thirty years 1945–75] (Leningrad, 1982)

C. Norris: 'Shostakovich: politics and musical language', *Shostakovich: the Man and his Music* (London, 1982), 163

E. Roseberry: *Shostakovich: his Life and Times* (Tunbridge Wells and New York, 1982)

A. Shebalina, ed.: '. . . Eto bïl zamechatel'nïy drug: iz pisem D. D. Shostakovicha k V. Ya. Shebalinu' [He was a remarkable friend: from Shostakovich's letters to V. Shebalin], *SovM* (1982), no.7, p.75

B. Stevens: 'Shostakovich and the British Composer', *Shostakovich: the Man and his Music*, ed. C. Norris (London, 1982), 149

R. Stradling: 'Shostakovich and the Soviet System, 1925–1975', *Shostakovich: the Man and his Music*, ed. C. Norris (London, 1982), 189

F. Streller: *Dmitri Schostakowitsch* (Leipzig, 1982)

D. Gojowy: *Dimitri Schostakowitsch mit Selbstzeugnissen und Bilddokumenten* (Reinbek bei Hamburg, 1983)

D. Wang: 'Shostakovich: Music on the Brain?', *MT*, cxxiv (1983), 347

S. Khentova: *Podvig, voploshchenïy v muzïke* [A feat embodied in music] (Volgograd, 1984)

B. Schwarz: 'Shostakovich, Soviet Citizen and Anti-Stalinist', *Music and Civilization: Essays in Honor of Paul Henry Lang* (New York, 1984), 363

M. Shaginyan: 'Fifty Letters from Dmitri Shostakovich', *Soviet Literature* (1984), no.1, p.68

G. Vishnevskaya: *Galina: a Russian Story* (Eng. trans., San Diego, 1984)

STYLE

A. Dolzhansky: 'O ladovoy osnove sochineniy Shostakovicha' [On the harmonic foundation of Shostakovich's composition], *SovM* (1947), no.4, p.65; repr. in *Chertï stilya D. Shostakovicha*, ed. L. G. Berger (Moscow, 1962), 24

——: 'Iz nablyudeniy nad stilem Shostakovicha' [From observations on Shostakovich's style], *SovM* (1959), no.10, p.95; repr. in *Chertï stilya D. Shostakovicha*, ed. L. G. Berger (Moscow, 1962), 73

M. Ber: 'Orkestrovka melodicheskikh (soliruyushchikh) golosov v

Bibliography

proizvedeniyakh D. D. Shostakovicha' [Orchestration of melodic (solo) lines in Shostakovich's compositions], *Chertï stilya D. Shostakovicha*, ed. L. G. Berger (Moscow, 1962), 195

L. Berger: 'O vïrazitel'nosti muzïki Shostakovicha' [On the expressiveness of Shostakovich's music], *Chertï stilya D. Shostakovicha* (Moscow, 1962), 348

V. Bobrovsky: 'Pretvoreniye zhanra passakal'i v sonatno-simfonicheskikh tsiklakh D. Shostakovicha' [Reinterpretation of the genre passacaglia in the sonata–symphonic cycles of Shostakovich], *Muzïka i sovremennost'*, i (1962), 149

V. Kholopova: 'Neskol'ko nablyudeniy nad ritmikoy Shostakovicha (o mnogoobrazii tipov metroritmicheskoy organizatsii)' [Some observations on Shostakovich's rhythm (on the variety of types of metro-rhythmic organization)], *Chertï stilya D. Shostakovicha*, ed. L. G. Berger (Moscow, 1962), 283

L. Mazel': 'O stile Shostakovicha' [On Shostakovich's style], *Chertï stilya D. Shostakovicha*, ed. L. G. Berger (Moscow, 1962), 3; rev. in *Stat'i po teorii i analizu muzïki* (Moscow, 1982), 221

Vl. Protopopov: 'Voprosï muzïkal'noy formï v proizvedeniyakh D. Shostakovicha' [Questions of musical form in Shostakovich's compositions], *Chertï stilya D. Shostakovicha*, ed. L. G. Berger (Moscow, 1962), 87

V. Bobrovsky: 'O dvukh metodakh tematicheskovo razvitiya v simfoniyakh i kvartetakh Shostakovicha' [On two methods of thematic development in the symphonies and string quartets of Shostakovich], *Dmitry Shostakovich*, ed. L. Danilevich (Moscow, 1967), 359

E. Denisov: 'Ob orkestrovke D. Shostakovicha' [On Shostakovich's orchestration], *Dmitry Shostakovich*, ed. L. Danilevich (Moscow, 1967), 439

A. Dolzhansky: 'Aleksandriyskiy pentakhord v muzïke D. Shostakovicha' [The Alexandrian pentachord in the music of Shostakovich], *Dmitry Shostakovich*, ed. L. Danilevich (Moscow, 1967), 397

L. Mazel': 'Zametki o muzïkal'nom yazïke Shostakovicha' [Remarks on the musical language of Shostakovich], *Dmitry Shostakovich*, ed. L. Danilevich (Moscow, 1967), 303

K. Meyer: 'Z zagadnień tematyzmu w twórczości D. Szostakowicza' [On the problems of thematic material in Shostakovich's works], *Polsko–rosyjskie miscellanea muzyczne*, ed. Z. Lissa (Kraków, 1967), 265

V. Sereda: 'O ladovoy strukture muzïki Shostakovicha' [On the harmonic structure of Shostakovich's music], *Voprosï teorii muzïki*, i, ed. S. Skrebkov, (Moscow, 1968), 324

A. Bogdanova: 'Sochineniya D. Shostakovicha konservatorskikh let

219

(1919–1925)' [Shostakovich's compositions during his conservatory years], *Iz istorii russkoy i sovetskoy muzïki*, ed. A. Kandinsky (Moscow, 1971), 64

V. Kholopova: *Voprosï ritma v tvorchestve kompozitorov XX veka* [Questions of rhythm in the work of 20th-century composers], (Moscow, 1971), 100

A. Tsuker: 'Tema naroda u Shostakovicha i traditsii Musorgskovo' [The folk theme in Shostakovich and the traditions of Musorgsky], *Voprosï teorii i estetiki muzïki*, x (1971), 32

G. Grigor'yeva: 'Iz nablyudenniy nad rannim stilem D. Shostakovicha' [Some observations on the early style of Shostakovich], *Problemï muzïkal'noy nauki*, ii (Moscow, 1973), 133

V. Bobrovsky: 'O nekotorïkh chertakh stilya Shostakovicha shesti-desyatïkh godov' [On some features of Shostakovich's style in the 1960s], *Muzïka i sovremennost'*, viii (1974), 161; ix (1975), 39

G. Grigor'yeva: 'Osobennosti tematizma i formï v sochineniyakh Shostakovicha 60-kh godov' [Special features of thematicism and form in Shostakovich's compositions of the 1960s], *O muzïke: prob-lemï analiza*, compiled V. Bobrovsky and G. Golovinsky (Moscow, 1974), 246

Yu. Kholopov: 'Shostakovich', *Ocherki sovremennoy garmonii: issledovaniye* (Moscow, 1974), 224

M. Aranovsky: 'Zametki o tvorchestve' [Remarks on the works], *SovM* (1976), no.9, p.16

S. Belova: 'O melodizatsii formï i nekotorïkh chertakh melodi-cheskovo tematizma v instrumetal'nïkh proizvedeniya D. Shosta-kovicha' [On the melodic treatment of form and some features of melodic style in the instrumental works of Shostakovich], *Muzï-koznaniye*, viii–ix (1976), 57

D. Zhitomirsky: 'Iz razmïshleniy o stile Shostakovicha' [Reflections on Shostakovich's style], *SovM* (1976), no.9, p.55

L. Berezovchuk: 'Stileviye vzaimodeystviya v tvorchestve D. Shosta-kovicha kak sposob voploshcheniya konflikta' [Stylistic interac-tions in the work of Shostakovich as a means of the embodiment of conflict], *Voprosï teorii i estetiki muzïki*, xv (1977), 95

G. Kocharova: 'Osobennosti garmonicheskovo stilya D. D. Shosta-kovicha' [Peculiarities of Shostakovich's harmonic style], *SovM* (1977), no.9, p.112

V. Shirokova: 'O stilisticheskoy semantike instrumental'noy muzïke Shostakovicha' [On the stylistic semantics of Shostakovich's in-strumental music], *Analiz, Kontseptsii, Kritika*, ed. L. Dan'ko (Leningrad, 1977), 19

N. Tiftikidi: 'O prelomlenii v melodike Shostakovicha nekotorïkh intonatsionnïkh struktur russkoy protyazhnoy pesni' [On the in-

Bibliography

terpretation in Shostakovich's melodic writing of some intonational structures of Russian melismatic folksong], *Teoreticheskiye problemï muzïki XX veka*, ii, ed. Yu. Tyulin (Moscow, 1978), 5
E. Fedosova: *Diatonicheskiye ladï v tvorchestve D. Shostakovicha* [Diatonic modes in the work of Shostakovich] (Moscow, 1980)
E. Sokolova: 'Funktsional'naya sistema garmonii pozdnevo perioda tvorchestva D. Shostakovicha' [The functional system of harmony in works of Shostakovich's late period], *Problemï lada i garmonii: sbornik trudov*, lv (Moscow, 1981)
V. Zaderatsky: 'O melodiko-tematicheskikh strukturakh' [On melodic-thematic structures], *SovM* (1981), no.10, p.13
J. Braun: 'The Double Meaning of Jewish Elements in Dimitri Shostakovich's Music', *MQ*, lxxi (1985), 68

DRAMATIC WORKS

S. Gres: 'Ruchnaya bomba anarkhista' [An anarchist's hand-grenade], *Rabochiy i teatr* (1930), no.10, p.6 [on *The Nose*]
'*Nos*', *Opera v 3 deystviyakh, 10 kartinakh po N.-V. Gogolyu: Muzïka D. Shostakovicha* [The Nose: opera in 3 acts, 10 scenes after Gogol, music by Shostakovich] (Leningrad, 1930) [pamphlet; incl. articles by Shostakovich and N. Malkov, with lib of *The Nose*]
'*Nos*', *opera v 3-kh aktakh po N.-V. Gogolyu: 15-ye sochineniye D. Shostakovicha* [The Nose: opera in 3 acts after Gogol: Shostakovich's op.15] (Leningrad, 1930) [pamphlet; incl. articles by Shostakovich, I. Sollertinsky and Dmitriyev]
I. Sollertinsky: ' "Nos" – orudiye dal'noboynoye' [*The Nose* – a long-range gun], *Rabochiy i teatr* (1930), no.7, p.6
D. Zhitomirsky: ' "Nos" – opera D. Shostakovicha' [*The Nose* – an opera by D. Shostakovich], *Proletarskiy muzïkant* (1930), no.7–8, p.33
'*Bolt*'. *Balet v 3 deystviyakh* [Bolt: ballet in 3 acts] (Leningrad, 1931) [pamphlet; incl. article by I. Sollertinsky, with lib]
'*Zolotoy vek*'. *Balet v 3 deystviyakh* [The Age of Gold: ballet in 3 acts] (Leningrad, 1931) [pamphlet; incl. articles by Shostakovich, A. V. Gauk, V. Khodasevich and N. Malkov]
M. Sokol'sky: 'Opera i kompozitor' [Opera and composer], *Sovetskoye iskusstvo* (16 Oct 1932); repr. in *Musorgsky. Shostakovich: stat'i, retsenzii* [Articles and reviews] (Moscow, 1983), 85 [on *Lady Macbeth*]
A. Ostretsov: ' "Ledi Makbet Mtsenskovo uyezda": opera D. Shostakovicha', *SovM* (1933), no.6, p.9
B. Asaf'yev: 'O tvorchestve D. Shostakovicha i evo opera "Ledi Makbet Mtsenskovo uyezda" ' [On Shostakovich's works and his opera *Lady Macbeth*], '*Ledi Makbet Mtsenskovo uyezda*' (Len-

221

ingrad, 1934); repr. in *D. Shostakovich: stat'i i materialï*, ed. G. Shneerson (Moscow, 1976), 150

'*Katerina Izmaylova*' (Moscow, 1934) [pamphlet; articles by Shostakovich, V. I. Nemirovich-Danchenko and A. Ostretsov]

'*Ledi Makbet Mtsenskovo uyezda*' (Leningrad, 1934) [pamphlet; articles by Shostakovich, I. Sollertinsky, B. Asaf'yev and S. Samosud on *Lady Macbeth*]

I. Sollertinsky: 'Ledi Makbet Mtsenskovo Uyezda', *Rabochiy i teatr* (1934), no.4, p.2; repr. in *I. Sollertinsky: Kriticheskiye stat'i*, ed. M. Druskin (Leningrad, 1963), 73

'*Svetlïy ruchey*' (Leningrad, 1935) [pamphlet; articles by Shostakovich, M. Druskin and Yu. Slonimsky on *The Limpid Stream*]

'Baletnaya fal'sh' ' [Balletic falsity], *Pravda* (6 Feb 1936); repr. in *SovM* (1936), no.2, p.6 [on *The Limpid Stream*]

'Sumbur vmesto muzïki: ob opere "Ledi Makbet Mtsenskovo Uyezda" D. Shostakovicha' [Chaos instead of music: on Shostakovich's opera *Lady Macbeth*], *Pravda* (28 Jan 1936), 3; repr. in *SovM* (1936), no.2, p.4

B. Asaf'yev: 'Volnuyushchiye voprosï [Stirring questions], *SovM* (1936), no.5, p.24 [reply to 'Baletnaya fal'sh'' and 'Sumbur vmesto muzïki' above]

V. Bogdanov-Berezovsky: 'Operï Shostakovicha' [The operas of Shostakovich], *Sovetskaya opera* (Leningrad and Moscow, 1940), 111

M. Sabinina: 'Moskva, Cheryomushki', *SovM* (1959), no.4, p.41

A. Veprik: 'Tri orkestrovïye redaktsii pervoy kartinï prologa operï Musorgskovo "Boris Godunov" ' [Three orchestral editions of the first scene of the prologue of Musorgsky's opera *Boris Godunov*], *Ocherki po voprosam orkestrovïkh stiley* (Moscow, 1961, 2/1978), 75

K. Sakva: 'Novaya vstrecha s "Katerinoy Izmaylovoy" ' [A new encounter with *Katerina Izmaylova*], *SovM* (1963), no.3, p.57; Ger trans. in *Musik und Gesellschaft*, xiii (1963), 428

G. Grigor'yeva: 'Pervaya opera Shostakovicha "Nos" ' [Shostakovich's first opera – *The Nose*], *Muzïka i sovremennost'*, iii (1965), 68

N. Shumskaya: 'Traditsiya i novatorstvo v opere Shostakovicha "Katerina Izmaylova" ' [Tradition and innovation in Shostakovich's opera *Katerina Izmaylova*], *Muzïka i sovremennost'*, iii (1965), 104

G. Ordzhonikidze: 'Vesna tvorcheskoy zrelosti' [The spring of creative maturity], *SovM* (1966), no.9, p.38 [on *Katerina Izmaylova*]

M. Sabinina: 'Zametki ob opere "Katerina Izmaylova" ' [Remarks on *Katerina Izmaylova*], *Dmitry Shostakovich*, ed. L. Danilevich (Moscow, 1967), 132

Bibliography

E. Fradkina: 'O nekotorïkh intonatsionnïkh oborotakh v kinomuzïke Shostakovicha' [On some intonational trends in Shostakovich's film music], *Iz istorii muzïki XX veka: sbornik statey*, ed. M. Druskin (Moscow, 1971), 52

V. Gurevich: 'Shostakovich v rabote nad "Khovanshchina"' [Shostakovich at work on *Khovanshchina*], *Voprosï teorii i estetiki muzïki*, xi (1972), 84

L. Bubennikova: 'Meyerkhol'd i Shostakovich: iz istorii sozdaniya operï "Nos"' [Meyerhold and Shostakovich: the history of the creation of the opera *The Nose*], *SovM* (1973), no.3, p.43

A. Bretanitskaya: 'O muzïkal'naya dramaturgii operï "Nos"' [On the musical dramaturgy of the opera *The Nose*], *SovM* (1974), no.9, p.47

E. Fradkina: 'Muzïka k kinofil'mu "Gamlet" – programmnaya simfoniya Shostakovicha' [Music to the film *Hamlet:* Shostakovich's programme symphony], *Voprosï teorii i estetiki muzïki*, xiii (1974), 126

A. Bogdanova: 'Ranniye proizvedeniya Shostakovicha dlya dramaticheskovo teatra' [Shostakovich's early works for the theatre], *Iz proshlovo sovetskoy muzïkal'noy kul'turï*, ed. T. Livanova (Moscow, 1975), 7

L. Bubennikova: 'K probleme khudozhestvennovo vzaimodeystviya muzïkal'novo i dramaticheskovo teatrov' [On the problem of the artistic interaction of musical and dramatic theatre], *Problemï muzïkal'noy nauki*, iii (Moscow, 1975), 38 [on *The Nose*]

A. Bretanitskaya: 'Vtoroye rozhdeniye "Nosa"' [The second birth of *The Nose*], *Muzïka Rossii: muzïkal'noye tvorchestvo i muzïkal'naya zhizn' respublik Rossiyskoy Federatsii*, i, *1973–74*, ed. E. Grosheva (Moscow, 1976), 310

G. Fedorov: 'Vokrug i posle "Nosa"' [Around and after *The Nose*], *SovM* (1976), no.9, p.41

S. Nikelberg: 'Muzïka D. Shostakovicha k kinofil'mu "Gamlet"' [Shostakovich's music for the film *Hamlet*], *Iz istorii russkoy i sovetskoy muzïki*, iii (Moscow, 1978), 234

L. Rotbaum: 'V poiskakh stsenicheskovo resheniya "Katerinï Izmaylovoy"' [In search of scenic solutions for *Katerina Izmaylova*], *Muzïka Rossii: muzïkal'noye tvorchestvo i muzïkal'naya zhizn' respublik Rossiyskoy Federatsii*, ii, *1975–6*, ed. E. Grosheva (Moscow, 1978), 337

A. Bogdanova: *Operï i baletï Shostakovicha* [Shostakovich's operas and ballets] (Moscow, 1979)

——: 'Shostakovich – znakomïy i neznakomïy' [Shostakovich – familiar and unfamiliar], *Muzïkal'naya zhizn'* (1979), no.11, p.8 [on *The Gamblers*]

G. Norris: 'Shostakovich's *The Nose*', *MT*, cxx (1979), 393

R. Walker: 'Dmitri Shostakovich – The Film Music', *Music and Musicians*, xxviii/8 (1979–80), 34

L. E. Fay: 'Musorgsky and Shostakovich', *Musorgsky: In Memoriam, 1881–1981*, ed. M. H. Brown (Ann Arbor, 1982), 215

G. Norris: 'An Opera Restored: Rimsky-Korsakov, Shostakovich and the Khovansky Business', *MT*, cxxiii (1982), 672 [on Shostakovich's version of Musorgsky's *Khovanshchina*]

——: 'The Operas', *Shostakovich: the Man and his Music*, ed. C. Norris (London, 1982), 105

A. Bretanitskaya: *'Nos' D. D. Shostakovicha* [Shostakovich's *The Nose*] (Moscow, 1983)

R. S. Brown: 'The Three Faces of Lady Macbeth', *Russian and Soviet Music: Essays for Boris Schwarz* (Ann Arbor, 1984), 245

L. E. Fay: 'The Punch in Shostakovich's *Nose*', *Russian and Soviet Music: Essays for Boris Schwarz* (Ann Arbor, 1984), 229

ORCHESTRAL WORKS

N. Malkov: 'Simfoniya D. Shostakovicha' [Shostakovich's Symphony (no.1)], *Zhizn' iskusstva* (1925), no.22, p.14

D. Kabalevsky: 'Pyataya simfoniya Shostakovicha', *Sovetskoye iskusstvo* (29 Dec 1937) [on Sym. no.5]

A. Tol'stoy: 'Pyataya simfoniya Shostakovicha', *Izvestiya* (28 Dec 1937), 3 [on Sym. no.5]

M. Druskin: *Pervaya simfoniya Dm. Shostakovicha* (Leningrad, 1938) [on Sym. no.1]

G. Khubov: 'Pyataya simfoniya D. Shostakovicha', *SovM* (1938), no.3, p.14; rev. in *O muzïke i muzïkantakh: ocherki i stat'i* (Moscow, 1959), 224 [on Sym. no.5]

B. Asaf'yev: 'Vos'maya simfoniya Shostakovicha', *Moskovskaya filarmoniya* (Moscow, 1945); repr. in *Izbranniye trudï*, v, ed. T. N. Livanova and others (Moscow, 1957), 132 [on Sym. no.8]

A. Khachaturyan: 'Desyataya simfoniya D. Shostakovicha', *SovM* (1954), no.3, p.23 [on Sym. no.10]

B. Yarustovsky: 'Desyataya simfoniya D. Shostakovicha', *SovM* (1954), no.4, p.8 [on Sym. no.10]

'Znachitel'noye yavleniye sovetskoy muzïki (diskussiya o Desyatoy simfonii D. Shostakovicha)' [A significant occurrence in Soviet music (debate about Shostakovich's Tenth Symphony)], *SovM* (1954), no.6, p.119 [Composers' Union report]

A. Dolzhansky: 'O kompozitsii pervoy chasti Sed'moy simfonii' [On the composition of the first movement of Symphony no.7], *SovM* (1956), no.4, p.88; repr. in *Chertï stilya D. Shostakovicha*, ed. L. G. Berger (Moscow, 1962), 43

D. Oistrakh: 'Voploshcheniye bol'shovo zamïsla: o skripichnom kontserte Shostakovicha' [The realization of a great project; on

Bibliography

Shostakovich's (First) Violin Concerto], *SovM* (1956), no.7, p.3; Ger. trans. in *Sowjetwissenschaft, Kunst und Literatur*, iv (1956), 877

Yu. Kremlyov: 'O desyatoy simfonii D. Shostakovicha', *SovM* (1957), no.4, p.74 [on Sym. no.10]

A. Dolzhansky: 'Kratkiye zamechaniya ob Odinnadtsatoy simfonii D. Shostakovicha' [Brief remarks on Shostakovich's Symphony no.11], *SovM* (1958), no.3, p.29; repr. in *Chertï stilya D. Shostakovicha*, ed. L. G. Berger (Moscow, 1962), 61

L. Lebedinsky: 'Revolyutsionnïy fol'klor v Odinnadtsatoy simfonii D. Shostakovicha' [Revolutionary folklore in Shostakovich's Symphony no.11], *SovM* (1958), no.1, p.42

M. Sabinina: *Skripichnïy kontsert D. Shostakovicha* [Shostakovich's Violin Concerto (no.1)] (Moscow, 1958)

I. Nest'yev: 'Sto sed'moy opus' [Opus 107], *SovM* (1959), no.12, p.9; Ger. trans. in *Musik und Gesellschaft*, x (1960), 198 [on Vc Conc. no.1]

I. Postnikov: *Vtoroy fortep'yannïy kontsert Shostakovicha* (Moscow, 1959) [on Pf Conc. no.2]

V. Protopopov: 'O yedinstve tsikla v Odinnadtsatoy simfonii "1905 god" D. D. Shostakovicha' [On the cyclic unity in Shostakovich's Symphony no.11], *Soobshcheniya Instituta istorii iskusstv AN SSSR*, xv, ed. A. Alekseyev and others (Moscow, 1959), 23

T. Boganova: *Violonchel'nïy kontsert D. Shostakovicha* [Shostakovich's (First) Cello Concerto] (Moscow, 1960)

L. Lebedinsky: *Sed'maya i odinnadtsataya simfonii D. Shostakovicha* [The Seventh and Eleventh symphonies of Shostakovich] (Moscow, 1960)

L. Mazel': *Simfonii D. D. Shostakovicha* [Shostakovich's symphonies] (Moscow, 1960)

L. Berger: *Odinnadtsataya simfoniya D. D. Shostakovicha* (Moscow, 1961) [on Sym. no.11]

G. Orlov: *Simfonii Shostakovicha* (Moscow, 1961–2)

V. Frumkin: 'Osobennosti sonatnoy formï v simfoniyakh D. Shostakovicha' [Peculiarities of sonata form in the symphonies of Shostakovich], *Chertï stilya D. Shostakovicha*, ed. L. G. Berger (Moscow, 1962), 126

L. Rappoport: 'O nekotorïkh osobennostiyakh orkestrovki simfoniy D. Shostakovicha' [On some peculiarities of the orchestration of Shostakovich's symphonies], *Chertï stilya D. Shostakovicha*, ed. L. G. Berger (Moscow, 1962), 254

A. Ladïgina: 'Slushaya trinadtsatuyu simfoniyu . . .' [Listening to the Thirteenth Symphony], *Sovetskaya Belorussiya* (2 April 1963); repr. with Eng. trans. (Chicago, n.d.)

L. Mazel': 'O traktovke sonatnoy forme i tsikla v bol'shikh sim-

225

foniyakh D. Shostakovicha' [On the treatment of sonata and cyclic form in the great symphonies of Shostakovich], *Muzïko-teoreticheskiye problemï sovetskoy muzïki*, ed. S. Skrebkov (Moscow, 1963), 60

V. Bobrovsky: 'Programmnïy simfonism Shostakovicha' [Shostakovich's programmatic symphonic writing], *Muzïka i sovremennost'*, iii (1965)

M. Sabinina: *Simfonizm Shostakovicha* (Moscow, 1965)

A. Shnitke: 'Zametki ob orkestrovoy polifonii v Chetvyortoy simfonii D. D. Shostakovicha' [Remarks on the orchestral polyphony in Shostakovich's Fourth Symphony], *Muzïka i sovremennost'*, iv (1966), 127–61

T. Souster: 'Shostakovich at the Crossroads', *Tempo*, no.78 (1966), 2 [on Syms. nos. 4–5]

B. Yarustovsky: ' "Voyennïye" simfonii D. Shostakovicha' [Shostakovich's 'war' symphonies], *Simfonii o voyne i mire* (Moscow, 1966), 27–61

V. Bobrovsky: 'Programmnïy simfonism Shostakovicha, statya vtoraya (o trinadtsatoy simfonii)' [Shostakovich's programmatic symphonic writing, part 2 (on Symphony no.13], *Muzïka i sovremennost'*, v (1967)

T. Levaya: 'Devyataya simfoniya Shostakovicha', *Muzïka i sovremennost'*, v (1967), 3 [on Sym. no.9]

G. Ordzhonikidze: 'XIII simfoniya D. Shostakovicha', *Dmitry Shostakovich*, ed. L. Danilevich (Moscow, 1967), 188 [on Sym. no.13]

G. Orlov: 'V seredine puti: k 30-letiyu sozdaniya IV simfonii' [In the middle of the path: the 30th anniversary of the composition of Symphony no.4], *Dmitry Shostakovich*, ed. L. Danilevich (Moscow, 1967), 166

S. Shlifshteyn: ' "Kazn' Stepana Razina" Shostakovicha i traditsii Musorgskovo' [Shostakovich's *Execution of Stepan Razin* and the traditions of Musorgsky], *Dmitry Shostakovich*, ed. L. Danilevich (Moscow, 1967), 223

A. Shnitke: 'Nekotorïye osobennosti orkestrovovo golosovedeniya v simfonicheskikh proizvedeniyakh D. D. Shostakovicha' [Some peculiarities of orchestral part-writing in Shostakovich's symphonic works], *Dmitry Shostakovich*, ed. L. Danilevich (Moscow, 1967), 499–532

N. Kay: 'Shostakovich's Second Violin Concerto', *Tempo*, no.83 (1967–8), 21

P. Lawson: 'Shostakovich's Second Symphony', *Tempo*, no.91 (1969–70), 14

L. Danilevich: 'Chetïrnadtsataya' [The Fourteenth (Symphony)], *SovM* (1970), no.1, p.14

Bibliography

G. Reinäcker and V. Reisling: *Die 11. und 12. Sinfonie von Dmitri Schostakowitsch* (Berlin, 1970)

M. Sabinina: 'Zametki o 14-oy simfonii' [Notes on Symphony no.14], *SovM* (1970), no.9, p.22

L. Ginzburg: 'Violonchel'nïye kontsertï Shostakovicha' [Shostakovich's cello concertos], *Issledovaniya, stat'i, ocherki* (Moscow, 1971), 158

G. Orlov: 'Simfonizm Shostakovicha na perelome' [Shostakovich's symphonic writing at a turning point], *Voprosï teorii i estetiki muzïki*, x (1971), 3 [on the music written during the 1960s]

E. Fedosova: 'Diatonika kak osnova tematizma poemï D. D. Shostakovicha "Kazn' Stepana Razina" ' [Diatonicism as the basis of the thematic writing in Shostakovich's *The Execution of Stepan Razin*], *Problemï muzïkal'noy nauki*, i (Moscow, 1972), 138

N. Kay: 'Shostakovich's 15th Symphony', *Tempo*, no.100 (1972), 36

Yu. Korev: 'O pyatnadtsatoy simfonii D. Shostakovicha', *SovM* (1972), no.9, p.8 [on Sym. no.15]

H.-P. Müller: 'Die Fünfzehnte: Gedanken zur jüngsten Sinfonie von Dmitri Schostakowitsch', *Musik und Gesellschaft*, xxii (1972), 714

M. Aranovsky: 'Problema zhanra v vokal'no–instrumental'nïkh simfoniyakh D. Shostakovich' [The problem of genre in Shostakovich's vocal–instrumental symphonies], *Vosprosï teorii i estetiki muzïki*, xii (1973), 61

H. Lindlar: 'Spätstil? Zu Schostakowitschs Sinfonien 13–15', *SMz*, cxiii (1973), 340

V. Zaderatsky: 'Pro symfonizm Shostakovicha' [About Shostakovich's symphonic writing], *Suchasna muzyka*, i (Kiev, 1973), 60

M. H. Brown: 'The Soviet Russian Concepts of "Intonazia" and "Musical Imagery" ', *MQ*, lx (1974), 557 [on the 1st movt of Sym. no.7]

G. Ordzhonikidze: 'O chetïrnadtsatoy simfonii Dmitriya Shostakovicha i evo sochineniyakh kontsa 60-kh–nachala 70-kh godov' [On Symphony no.14 and works of the late 1960s and early 1970s], *Sotsialisticheskaya muzïkal'naya kul'tura: traditsii, problemï, perspektivï*, ed. G. Ordzhonikidze and Yu. El'sner (Moscow, 1974), 105

E. Makarov: 'Masterstvo orkestrovoy dramaturgii (opït analiza partiturï Pyatnadtsatoy simfonii D. Shostakovicha)' [Mastery of orchestral dramaturgy (an attempt at analysis of the score of Symphony no.15)], *Muzïka Rossii: muzïkal'noye tvorchestvo i muzïkal'naya zhizn' respublik Rossiyskoy Federatsii*, i, *1973–74*, ed. E. Grosheva (Moscow, 1976), 234

M. Sabinina: *Shostakovich – simfonist: dramaturgiya, estetika, stil'* [Shostakovich as symphonist: dramaturgy, aesthetics, style] (Moscow, 1976)

S. Slonimsky: 'Pobeda Stepana Razina' [Stepan Razin's victory], *D. Shostakovich: stat'i i materialï*, ed. G. Shneerson (Moscow, 1976), 211

M. Aranovsky: 'Pyatnadtsataya simfoniya D. Shostakovicha i nekotorïye voprosï muzïkal'noy semantiki' [Shostakovich's Fifteenth Symphony and some questions of musical semantics], *Voprosï teorii i estetiki muzïki*, xv (1977), 55

H. Ottaway: *Shostakovich Symphonies* (London, 1978)

S. Volkov: 'Dmitri Shostakovich and *Tea for Two*', *MQ*, lxiv (1978), 223

R. Blokker: *The Music of Dmitri Shostakovich: the Symphonies* (London, 1979)

Yu. Paysov: 'Pyatnadtsataya simfoniya D. D. Shostakovicha', *Muzïkal'nïy sovremennik*, iii (Moscow, 1979), 5 [on Sym. no.15]

A. Tsuker: 'Traditsii muzïkal'novo teatra Musorgskovo v simfonicheskom tvorchestve Shostakovicha' [The traditions of Musorgsky's musical theatre in the symphonic works of Shostakovich], *Muzïkal'nïy sovremennik*, iii (Moscow, 1979), 39

R. Dearling: 'The First Twelve Symphonies: Portrait of the Artist as Citizen–composer', *Shostakovich: the Man and his Music*, ed. C. Norris (London, 1982), 47

VOCAL WORKS

L. Lebedinsky: *Khorovïye poemï Shostakovicha* [Shostakovich's choral poems], (Moscow, 1957)

L. Polyakova: *Vokal'nïy tsikl D. Shostakovicha 'Iz Yevreyskoy narodnoy poezii'* [Shostakovich's vocal cycle From Jewish Folk Poetry] (Moscow, 1957)

Yu. Levashev: 'Desyat' poem dlya khora D. D. Shostakovicha' [Shostakovich's Ten Poems for chorus], *Ocherki po teoreticheskomu muzïkoznaniyu*, ed. Yu. Tyulin (Leningrad, 1959), 211 [on op.88]

V. Bobrovsky: *Pesni i khorï Shostakovicha* [The songs and choruses of Shostakovich] (Moscow, 1962)

E. Dobrïnina: ' "Vernost' ": Tsikl khorovïkh ballad Dmitriya Shostakovicha' [*Loyalty*: Shostakovich's cycle of choral ballads], *Muzïkal'naya zhizn'* (1971), no.7; repr. in *Lyubitelyam muzïki posvyashchaetsya* (Moscow, 1980), 7

E. Mnatsakanova: 'O tsikle Shostakovicha "Sem' romansov na stikhi Aleksandra Bloka" ' [On Shostakovich's cycle Seven Romances on Poems of Alexander Blok], *Muzïka i sovremennost'*, vii (1971), 69

T. Kurïsheva: 'Blokovskiy tsikl Shostakovich' [Shostakovich's Blok cycle], *Blok i muzïka* (Moscow and Leningrad, 1972)

E. Dobrïkin: 'Muzïkal'naya satira v vokal'nom tvorchestve D. Shostakovicha' [Musical satire in the vocal works of Shostakovich],

Bibliography

Problemï muzïkal'noy nauki, iii (Moscow, 1975), 17

T. Levaya: 'Tayna velikovo iskusstvo (O pozdnikh kamerno-vokal'nikh tsiklakh D. D. Shostakovich)' [The secret of great art (on the late chamber-vocal works of Shostakovich)], *Muzïka Rossi: muzïkal'noye tvorchestvo i muzïkal'noya zhizn' respublik Rossiyskoy Federatsii*, ii, *1975–6*, ed. E. Grosheva (Moscow, 1978), 291

V. Vasina-Grossman: 'Kamerno-vokal'noye tvorchestvo D. Shosta-kovicha [The chamber-vocal works of Shostakovich], *Sovetskaya muzïkal'naya kul'tura: istoriya, traditsii, sovremennost'*, ed. D. Daragan (Moscow, 1980), 15

——: 'Shostakovich', *Mastera sovetskovo romansa* (Moscow, 2/1980), 218

M. MacDonald: 'Words and Music in Late Shostakovich', *Shosta-kovich: the Man and his Music*, ed. C. Norris (London, 1982), 125

I. Brezhneva: 'Formirovaniye vokal'novo stilya Shostakovicha na primere rannikh sochineniy ('Basni Krïlova' i shest' romansov yaponskikh poetov)' [The formation of Shostakovich's vocal style on the example of early works (Two Fables of Krïlov and Six Romances on Texts of Japanese Poets)], *Problemï stilevovo obnovleniya v russkoy klassicheskoy i sovetskoy muzïke* (Moscow, 1983)

N. Ogarkova: 'Nekotorïye osobennosti vzaimodeystviya poezii i muzïki v pozdnikh kamerno-vokal'nïkh tsiklakh D. Shostakovich' [Some features of the interaction between poetry and music in Shostakovich's late chamber-vocal cycles], *Muzïkal'naya klassika i sovremennost': voprosï istorii i estetiki*, ed. A. Porfir'yeva (Len-ingrad, 1983), 25

J. Braun: 'Shostakovich's Song Cycle *From Jewish Folk Poetry*: Aspects of Style and Meaning', *Russian and Soviet Music: Essays for Boris Schwarz* (Ann Arbor, 1984), 259

CHAMBER MUSIC

M. Druskin: 'O fortepiannom tvorchestve Shostakovicha' [On Shostakovich's piano works], *SovM* (1935), no.11, p.52

I. Martïnov: 'Novïye kamernïye sochineniya Shostakovicha' [New chamber compositions by Shostakovich], *Sovetskaya muzïka: pyatïy sbornik statey* (1946), 21 [on Pf Trio no.2 and Str Qt no.2]

A. Nikolayev: 'Fortepiannaya muzïka D. D. Shostakovicha' [Shosta-kovich's piano music], *Voprosï muzïkoznaniya*, ii, ed. A. S. Ogole-vets (Moscow, 1956), 112

D. Rabinovich: 'Shestoy kvartet D. Shostakovicha', *SovM* (1957), no.3, p.14 [on Str Qt no.6]

Yu. Keldïsh: 'Avtobiograficheskiy kvartet' [An autobiographical

quartet], *SovM* (1960), no.12, p.19; Eng. trans. in *MT*, cii (1961), 226 [on Str Qt no.8]

A. Yusfin: *Shestoy kvartet Shostakovicha* (Moscow, 1960) [on Str Qt no.6]

V. Bobrovsky: *Kamernïye instrumental'nïye ansambli Shostakovicha* [Shostakovich's instrumental chamber music] (Moscow, 1961)

I. Beletsky: 'Fortep'yannïy kvintet D. Shostakovicha' [Shostakovich's piano quintet], *Chertï stilya D. Shostakovicha*, ed. L. G. Berger (Moscow, 1962), 309

C. Mason: 'Form in Shostakovich's Quartets' *MT*, ciii (1962), 531

L. Mazel': 'O fuge do mazhor Shostakovicha' [On Shostakovich's C major Fugue], *Chertï stilya D. Shostakovicha*, ed. L. G. Berger (Moscow, 1962), 332

A. Dolzhansky: *24 prelyudii i fugi D. Shostakovicha* (Leningrad, 1963, 2/1970)

——: *Kamernïye instrumental'nïye proizvedeniya D. Shostakovicha* [Shostakovich's instrumental chamber works] (Moscow, 1965)

J. M. Chominski: '24 Preludia i Fugi op.87 D. Szostakowicza', *Polsko-rosyjskie miscellanea muzyczne*, ed. Z. Lissa (Kraków, 1967), 287

M. Kotyńska: 'Kwartety smyczkowe Dymitra Szostakowicza jako wyraz postawy klasycyzujacej' [Shostakovich's string quartets as an expression of classical attitudes], *Muzyka*, xii/3 (1967), 36

E. Mnatsakanova: 'Nekotorïye nablyudeniya nad stilem sbornika "24 prelyudii i fugi" ' [Some observations on the style of the 24 Preludes and Fugues], *Dmitry Shostakovich*, ed. L. Danilevich (Moscow, 1967), 264

T. Nikolayeva: 'Ispolnyaya Shostakovicha' [Performing Shostakovich], *Dmitry Shostakovich*, ed. L. Danilevich (Moscow, 1967), 287

N. O'Loughlin: 'Shostakovich's String Quartets', *Tempo*, no.87 (1968), 9

E. Ovchinikov: 'Vtoraya fortepiannaya sonata Shostakovicha' [Shostakovich's Second Piano Sonata], *Voprosï teorii muziki*, i, ed. S. Skrebkov, (Moscow, 1968), 239

V. Zaderatsky: *Polifoniya v instrumental'nïkh proizvedeniyakh Shostakovicha* [Polyphony in the instrumental works of Shostakovich] (Moscow, 1969)

H. Keller: 'Shostakovich's Twelfth Quartet', *Tempo*, no.94 (1970), 6

E. Ochs: 'Die Streichquartette Dmitri Schostakowitschs', *OM*, iii/4 (1970), 109

V. Del'son: *Fortepiannoye tvorchestvo Shostakovicha* [The piano works of Shostakovich] (Moscow, 1971)

Bibliography

S. Slonimsky: 'O blagorodstve chelovecheskovo dukha' [On the nobility of the human spirit], *SovM* (1971), no.7, p.31 [on Str Qt no.13]

M. Tarakanov: 'Zametki o novom sochineniy' [Notes about a new composition], *SovM* (1971), no.7, p.33 [on Str Qt no.13]

V. Del'son: 'Interpretatsiya fortepiannïkh proizvedeniy Shostakovicha' [The interpretation of Shostakovich's piano works], *Muzïkal'noye ispolnitel'stvo: vos'moy sbornik statey* (Moscow, 1973), 57

N. O'Loughlin: 'Shostakovich's String Quartets', *MT*, cxv (1974), 744

B. Tishchenko: 'Razmïshleniya o 142-m i 143-m opusakh' [Reflections on opp.142 and 143], *SovM* (1974), no.9, p.40

C. Norris: 'The String Quartets of Shostakovich', *Music and Musicians*, xxiii/4 (1974–5), 26

A. Knayfel': 'I pravda kak zvezda v nochi otkrïlas'' [And the truth was revealed like a star in the night], *SovM* (1975), no.11, p.78 [on Str Qt no.15]

V. Bobrovsky: 'Instrumental'nïye ansambli Shostakovicha' [Shostakovich's instrumental chamber music], *D. Shostakovich: stat'i i materiali*, ed. G. Shneerson (Moscow, 1976), 193

N. Kuz'mina: 'O kvartetnom tvorchestve Shostakovicha' [On Shostakovich's string quartets], *Analiz, Kontseptsii, Kritika*, ed. L. Dan'ko (Leningrad, 1977), 5

L. Raaben: 'Obraznïy mir poslednikh kamerno-instrumental'nïkh sochineniy D. Shostakovicha' [The artistic universe of Shostakovich's last chamber-instrumental works], *Voprosï teorii i estetiki muzïki*, xv (1977), 44

C. Rowland and A. George: 'Interpreting the String Quartets', *Shostakovich: the Man and his Music*, ed. C. Norris (London, 1982), 13

R. Stevenson: 'The Piano Music', *Shostakovich: the Man and his Music*, ed. C. Norris (London, 1982), 81

N. Shantïr': 'Poslednoye slovo mastera' [The master's last word], *SovM* (1983), no.11, p.94 [on the Va Sonata]

Index

Index

Index

237

Index